Dancing Cultures

DANCE AND PERFORMANCE STUDIES

General Editors:

Helen Wulff, *Stockholm University* and **Jonathan Skinner**, *Queen's University, Belfast*

Advisory Board:

Alexandra Carter, Marion Kant, Tim Scholl

In all cultures, and across time, people have danced. Mesmerizing performers and spectators alike, dance creates spaces for meaningful expressions that are held back in daily life. Grounded in ethnography, this series explores dance and bodily movement in cultural contexts at the juncture of history, ritual and performance, including musical, in an interconnected world.

Volume 1

Dancing at the Crossroads: Memory and Mobility in Ireland
Helena Wulff

Volume 2

Embodied Communities: Dance Traditions and Change in Java
Felicia Hughes-Freeland

Volume 3

Turning the Tune: Traditional Music, Tourism and Social Change in an Irish Village
Adam Kaul

Volume 4

Dancing Cultures: Globalization, Tourism and Identity in the Anthropology of Dance
Edited by Hélène Neveu Kringelbach and Jonathan Skinner

Volume 5

Dance Circles: Movement, Morality and Self-Fashioning in Urban Senegal
Hélène Neveu Kringelbach

Volume 6

Learning Senegalese Sabar: Dancers and Embodiment in New York and Dakar
Eleni Bizas

Dancing Cultures

Globalization, Tourism and Identity in
the Anthropology of Dance

Edited by

Hélène Neveu Kringelbach and Jonathan Skinner

Published in 2012 by
Berghahn Books
www.berghahnbooks.com

© 2012, 2014 Hélène Neveu Kringelbach and Jonathan Skinner
First paperback edition published in 2014

All rights reserved. Except for the quotation of short passages
for the purposes of criticism and review, no part of this book
may be reproduced in any form or by any means, electronic or
mechanical, including photocopying, recording, or any information
storage and retrieval system now known or to be invented,
without written permission of the publisher.

Library of Congress Cataloging-in-Publication Data

Dancing cultures : globalization, tourism and identity in the anthropology of dance / edited by Hélène Neveu Kringelbach and Jonathan Skinner.
    p. cm. -- (Dance & performance studies ; v. 4)
  Includes bibliographical references and index.
  ISBN 978-0-85745-575-8 (hardback : alk. paper) – ISBN 978-1-78238-522-6 (paperback : alk. paper) – ISBN 978-0-85745-576-5 (ebook)
 1. Dance--Anthropological aspects. 2. Dance--Social aspects. 3. Tourism--Anthropological aspects.
 4. Tourism--Social aspects. I. Neveu Kringelbach, Hélène, 1969- II. Skinner, Jonathan, Ph. D.
  GV1588.6.D394 2012
  306.4'846--dc23

                                                                          2012013684

British Library Cataloguing in Publication Data

A catalogue record for this book is available from the British Library

Printed on acid-free paper

ISBN: 978-1-78238-522-6 paperback
ISBN: 978-0-85745-576-5 ebook

Contents

List of Figures   vii

Acknowledgements   viii

Introduction   The Movement of Dancing Cultures   1
Hélène Neveu Kringelbach and Jonathan Skinner

Part I: Dance and Globalization

1. Globalization and the Dance Import–Export Business: The Jive Story   29
   Jonathan Skinner

2. Ballet Culture and the Market: A Transnational Perspective   46
   Helena Wulff

3. 'We've Got This Rhythm in Our Blood': Dancing Identities in Southern Italy   60
   Karen Lüdtke

Part II: Tourism, Social Transformation and the Dance

4. Performance in Tourism: Transforming the Gaze and the Tourist Encounter at Híwus Feasthouse   77
   Linda Scarangella-McNenly

5. Movement on the Move: Performance and Dance Tourism in Southeast Asia   100
   Felicia Hughes-Freeland

6. Dance, Visibility and Representational Self-awareness in an Emberá Community in Panama   121
   Dimitrios Theodossopoulos

Part III: Dance, Identity and the Nation

7. Moving Shadows of Casamance: Performance and Regionalism in Senegal   143
   Hélène Neveu Kringelbach

8	*Ballet Folklórico Mexicano*: Choreographing National Identity in a Transnational Context *Olga Nájera-Ramírez*	161
9	Dance, Youth and Changing Gender Identities in Korea *Séverine Carrausse*	177
10	Preparation, Presentation and Power: Children's Performances in a Balinese Dance Studio *Jonathan McIntosh*	194

Epilogue Making Culture through Dance 211
  Caroline Potter

Notes on Contributors 219

Index 223

List of Figures

2.1	Gina Tse in Swan Lake with Royal Swedish Ballet	47
5.1	Guests participate in the Saravahn dance in Vientiane, Laos	105
5.2	Urban visitors participate in a rural *tayuban* in Java	107
5.3	Overseas visitors participate in tourist *tayuban* in Java	108
5.4	Locals join in at the Tayuban Festival in Java	109
7.1	Bakalama women dancers performing in Dakar, April 2003	149
7.2	Bakalama musicians performing in Dakar, April 2003	155
8.1	Grupo Folklórico de la Universidad de Guadalajara, circa 1965	163
8.2	Arce Manjares family performing in Guadalajara, circa 1960s	164
10.1	Happy applies make-up to Tomi's face prior to a *pentas*	203
10.2	Costume for the female welcome dance, *Tari Panyembrama*	206

Acknowledgements

The authors of this volume would like to thank the following for their support and encouragement of this volume. The European Association of Social Anthropologists gave us the initial prompt in the direction of Dancing Cultures in their 2004 annual conference in Vienna, where we convened a panel under the title, 'Meaning in Motion: Advancing the Anthropology of Dance'. The panel was the first step towards the constitution of a network of dance anthropologists who have met subsequently, shared and explored similar approaches to dance and culture and, ultimately, led to this volume. Andrée Grau was a discussant on the EASA panel, and her perceptive comments have substantially helped to shape the theme of the book and all of our discussions. We should also like to thank the anonymous reviewers at Berghahn Books for their constructive comments and support, and Barnaly Pande for her editing assistance.

Berghahn Books generously supports the study of dance and performance through their 'Dance and Performance Studies' book series. We are grateful to Berghahn and to the series editors for including this volume in the series. On the production side, we are also grateful to the staff at Berghahn, Ann Przyzycki especially, for their patience and encouragement towards the completion of this project.

Introduction

The Movement of Dancing Cultures

Hélène Neveu Kringelbach and Jonathan Skinner

> Nigerian nationality was for me and my generation an acquired taste – like cheese. Or better still, like *ballroom* dancing. Not dancing per se, for that came naturally; but this titillating version of slow-slow-quick-quick-slow performed in close body contact with a female against a strange, elusive beat. I found, however, that once I had overcome my initial awkwardness I could do it pretty well.
> —Chinua Achebe

Thus opens the Nigerian writer Chinua Achebe's reflections on life growing up in colonial Nigeria as a 'British-protected child' (Achebe 2010). Achebe acknowledges that he inhabits – and embodies – the 'middle ground' between colonialism and postcolonialism. Whilst he has fond nostalgia for his imperious school teachers, he craves for an independent, strong and free Nigeria, but also laments the failings and difficulties of a country in disarray. The above analogy sums up Achebe's postcolonial ambivalence. 'His' dancing comes naturally, driven by a drum beat, but he is also attracted to the colonial quickstep, a European import, acquired, refined and 'cultured'. Argentinean dance scholar Marta Savigliano writes about her identity and the tango dance with similar ambivalence: it is the 'locus of [her] identification … ever since [she] moved outside of her culture' (Savigliano 1995: 12). She recognizes that it is a stereotype of her culture but that she still needs it as her cultural prop. Yet as a woman in a male-dominated postcolonial South American world, it is a dance where she can find some space to 'decolonize' herself doubly:

> Tango is the main ingredient in my project of decolonization because I have no choice. It is the stereotype of the culture to which I belong. If I reject my stereotype I fall, caught in nowhere. Caught in endless explanations of what I am not and justifications of what I am. Caught in comparisons with the colonizer. By assuming the tango attitude and taking it seriously, I can work at expanding its meaning and power. My power, actively tango. Tango is my strategic language, a way of talking about, understanding, exercising decolonization. (Savigliano 1995: 16)

Such is the importance of dance in a person's life, strong identifications carried with them, in this case a dance borne out of rural displacement, 'a tense dance' (Savigliano 1995: 30) of embrace and healing in a time of separation and violence.

Dancing Cultures is a volume featuring and exploring dance as it relates to culture. As terms, 'dance' and 'culture' share a lack of concreteness: they are – they become – in their doing. Culture, a politically charged concept, is a creative process, one of integration as much as differentiation, and the boundaries between the two cannot be clear-cut. It is also an essential premise of this volume that there is a close relationship between dance and social change. Our contention is that dance does not simply 'reflect' what happens in society or serve a particular 'function', but that it is often as central to social life as music and other universal forms of expression. We would like to suggest, therefore, that anthropology has much to gain from giving due attention to dance in its multiple forms and social contexts. One of the objectives of this collection is indeed to demonstrate that a focus on dance has the potential to reveal domains of individual experience and social life that remain hidden from view in an exclusive focus on the verbal. Dance makes meaning, but in different ways from the verbal, since as Farnell reminds us, 'body movement [can] provide human beings with a resource for action in a semiotic modality that frequently elides spoken expression but is never separate from the nature, powers, and capacities of linguistically capable agents' (Farnell 1999: 343). Dance is often performed together with music, song, sometimes poetry or other oratorical performance, as in the West African traditions of praise singing. To reflect the entanglement of dance with other elements, it has become increasingly frequent to use the term 'performance', and several contributors in this volume do so deliberately. But there is also a conscious choice to retain the term 'dance' because bodily movement is our primary focus, and because many studies of performance in anthropology have emphasized music at the expense of a holistic approach to what bodies do (see Moore 1997; Wade 2000; Askew 2002; Ebron 2002; White 2008). Can dance, then, simply be equated with body movement?

The Nature of Dance

In the 1960s and 1970s, as the anthropology of dance was being established as a sub-discipline, the question of its object of study seemed urgent. There was heated debate on the nature of 'dance'. Most dance scholars agreed with Mauss (1973 [1935]) that dance movement and its evaluation varied cross-culturally, but there was disagreement as to whether the study of dance should be subsumed within that of music, whether dance necessarily possessed a purposefully aesthetic dimension, whether it had to be addressed to an audience to qualify as 'dance', or whether movement had to be recognized as 'dance' in a given cultural context to be worthy of study. Much of the debate is summed up in Hanna (1979a) and in the comments and reply that followed her theoretical review.

The debate has faded somewhat, and few scholars now attempt to come up with a universal definition, even though, as Wulff notes, 'dance anthropologists seem to converge on a consideration of bounded rhythmical movements that are performed during some kind of altered state of consciousness' (Wulff 2001: 3209). What this points to is that dance is usually experienced as set apart from ordinary movement. This is true whether people join in the dance or simply watch it, even though the two positions are often experienced in very different ways. James captures this conversation between everyday and performative movement when she writes that 'the performative and experiential aspects of the various formal genres of patterned movement, ritual, marching, and dancing are not just a spill-over from the "ordinary" *habitus*, but derive their power partly by speaking against, resonating ironically with, this very base' (James 2003: 78–79). In an earlier text she had pointed to a dialectical relationship between dance and non-dance, suggesting that this was 'because the world of non-dance is to a large extent a bodily world too: a world of work, of sexuality, a world of physical effort in battle, a world also of submission to the imposed disciplines of timing and spatial movement' (James 2000: 141).

Gell (1985) argued rather for the 'spill-over' perspective in his work on Umeda dance, suggesting that the difference between dance and everyday movement was simply one of style. For Gell, the movement style people adopt when dancing defines a context in which the rules differ from those of everyday life, while referring back to it in a symbolic way. Whether one finds resonance with one view or the other depends on the social context and the theoretical perspective of the researcher. To give another example, phenomenologist Sheets-Johnstone looks at dance as intimately connected to the human capacity to produce movement before anything else goes on: 'It forms the I that moves before the I that moves forms movement. It is the foundation of our conceptual life' (Sheets-Johnstone 1999: xxi). Or, as she states later on: 'In the beginning, after all, we do not *try* to move, *think* about movement possibilities, or put ourselves to *the task* of moving. We come straightaway moving into the world; we are precisely not *stillborn*' (Sheets-Johnstone 1999: 136, original emphasis). What we find useful, for the purposes of this volume, is the notion of a conversation between dance and non-dance movement. This notion informs the theme of 'dance and culture' running through this volume.

Even though anthropologists are no longer trying to define 'dance', we are still faced with the issue of naming the practices we write about in a way that the people involved will recognize. This is a challenge since dance may be a universal practice, but as a semantic category it is fairly Eurocentric. Gore (2001), for example, reminds us that many West African languages do not have a specific word for 'dance'. In Wolof, 'dance' is best translated as *fecc*, but beyond the professional scene this refers to popular dances and has a distinctly female connotation. In Spencer's (1985a) work on the Samburu of Kenya, dance is spoken of as 'play', while in Brazil, Lowell Lewis (1992) found that trying to understand *capoeira*, usually described by practitioners as *dança-luta* (dance-fight), led him to explore the categories of 'game', 'sport', 'play' and 'martial art'. Gore suggests that perhaps we should not try to isolate dance in culture, not only because this is the product of the 'deeply-ingrained Eurocentric habit of conceiving of art as compartmentalised and specialised practice', but also because this devalues performance in 'socially and ritually significant contexts' (Gore 2001: 33). Yet we must find ways of talking and writing about it without going back to the earlier anthropological blindness to the multiple practices that constitute dance. There is no single solution to the challenge of capturing dance in emic terms while not losing sight of its specific qualities, and most contributors in this volume follow Wulff's (1998) suggestion that we should search for dance, loosely defined as patterned rhythmical movements, while redefining our object of study every time.

From Dance as Exotica to the Anthropology of Dance

The study of dance in anthropology is almost as old as the discipline itself.[1] Inspired by Herbert Spencer's (1857) work on music and Durkheim's (1915) *Elementary Forms of Religious Life*, founding figures of anthropology such as Marrett (1909), Radcliffe-Brown (1922), Malinowski (1948) and Boas (1930) mostly looked at dance as a component of ritual. Dance was not acknowledged as a practice worthy of study in its own right. Marrett (1909) saw dance as a component of religious practice, but did not spend much time elaborating on its significance. Radcliffe-Brown (1922) dedicated a chapter of his Andaman monograph to music and dance, which he suggested generated a collective ecstatic state that worked to bind society together. In other words, the 'function' of dance, within the functionalist paradigm of the time, was to regulate the emotions and desires of individuals so as to make them conform to the interests of the group.

In what is probably the most detailed ethnography of dance in the first half of the twentieth century, in the very first issue of the journal *Africa* Evans-Pritchard (1928) used his work on the Zande funeral beer dance, the *gbere buda*, to launch a scathing attack on Radcliffe-Brown's functionalism. Evans-Pritchard argued that whereas there certainly were 'functional' dimensions in the *gbere buda* – such as the socialization of children or a space in which to 'canalise the forces of sex into socially harmless channels, and by doing so to assist the processes of selection and to protect the institutions of marriage and the family' (Evans-Pritchard 1928: 458) – dance events also exacerbated individualistic tendencies:

> Anyone who watched several beer dances would see quarrels and could not subscribe to the statement that the dance was always an activity of perfect concord in which individual vanity and passions were completely socialized by the constraining forces of the community. Radcliffe-Brown has not recognized the complexity of motives in the dance. (Evans-Pritchard 1928: 460)

For Evans-Pritchard, the totality of social structure was contained in community-wide events of this kind. In support of his argument he paid careful attention to the songs, organizational structure and spatial patterns of the *gbere buda* and, to a lesser degree, movement. In fact he did not provide much description of movement, but an often overlooked element of his study is his dozen or so snapshots of a single performance of the *gbere buda*.[2] Those photographs were taken at such close intervals that a whole section of the dance could be reconstituted by flipping through the shots in chronological order, in a manner reminiscent of Julie Taylor's *Paper Tangos* (Taylor 1998). Of course, in the paradigm of the time, a single event was taken to stand for a long-standing practice, and Evans-Pritchard did not have sources at his disposal to account for historical changes in the *gbere buda*.

The study of dance did not expand much in anthropology until the 1960s, with the notable exception of Mitchell's *Kalela Dance*, a study of urban ethnicity on the Zambian Copperbelt (Mitchell 1956). Now regarded as a classic Marxist work coming out of the Manchester School, the study tried to make sense of the contrast between the songs, which spoke of ethnic differentiation in the languages of the region, and the distinctively smart, European dress of the participants. There was little description of movement and other elements in the *kalela*. The mind–body dichotomy inherited from the Platonic-Cartesian tradition, as well as a long-standing bias towards the verbal as a key to human thought, are often cited by dance scholars as the main factors behind this relative neglect. Ironically, it was partly the recognition by social linguists in the 1960s that 'body language' constituted an integral part of language that paved the way for a booming interest in the body in the social sciences. Hanna (1979b) also pointed to the bourgeois Puritan ethics in which she argued many European scholars were raised. In this view, dance was a useless form of entertainment that would distract people from serious work and life as good Christians.

In her comprehensive review article on moving bodies, Farnell (1999) added that anthropologists interested in the body had long feared accusations of biological reductionism, and therefore shied away from it. Drawing on Ardener's (1989) idea that anthropologists' awareness of events depends on the 'modes of registration and specification' available to them, Farnell also argued that anthropologists were often blind to body movements because they lacked the tools to register, record and analyse them. Indeed, dance scholars have often pointed out that watching and writing about dance was best done by people who possessed a form of 'skilled vision' attuned to rhythmic movement. Thus Wulff (1998) noted how her informants, in this case ballet dancers, could tell that she had been a dancer from the way that she was watching them. What this vision may consist of is now being explored by interdisciplinary projects reaching far beyond the confines of anthropology (e.g., Brown, Martinez and Parsons 2006). In the meantime, our collective experience as anthropologists of dance suggests that it is the integrated outcome of focused attention, observation of multiple performances in a given context over time, and to some degree experiencing movement through one's own body.

It is hardly a coincidence, then, that it was only when dancers became anthropologists in their own right that dance took on new life as a topic of study in anthropology. One of the under-acknowledged pioneers was African American dancer Katherine Dunham, who studied anthropology at the University of Chicago in the 1930s. Dunham carried out ethnographic fieldwork throughout the Caribbean from 1936 onwards, spending years in Haiti in particular, and incorporated movement she had learned there into her choreography (Kolcio 2010). Dance, she thought, was the ultimate form of embodied ethnography. Later,

Gertrude Kurath (1960), a student of Franz Boas, sought to bring mainstream anthropological research methods into the study of dance. From the 1970s onwards, new generations of anthropologist-dancers began to criticize earlier approaches for not paying sufficient attention to the practice itself, and for describing dance 'in terms of adaptive responses either to the social, the psychological, or the physical environment' rather than as a social phenomenon in itself (Farnell 1999: 350).

In very broad strokes, the anthropological study of dance since the 1970s has developed in four interconnected, partially overlapping directions: the American-British anthropology of dance that came out of ethnomusicology and dance studies, and which some proponents refer to as ethnochoreology or dance ethnology; the continental European folklorist school; the semasiology school derived from structural linguistics; and the study of dance within wider anthropological themes. Most anthropologists of dance have been influenced by several approaches simultaneously.

The first of these directions really took off in the United States with the creation of the Congress for Research on Dance (CORD) in 1965, whose first publications appeared in 1969 (Grau and Wierre-Gore 2005), and the Society of Dance History Scholars (SDHS) in 1978.[3] The founders were dancer-scholars from various disciplines, and some of them like Kurath, Judith L. Hanna, Anya Peterson Royce and Joann Kealiinohomoku, were also anthropologists. While trained in European classical ballet, they all did research in dance in other parts of the world and tried to push the emerging field of dance studies in North America to regard all dance forms as equally worthy of study. One of Kealiinohomoku's (1983) early papers, originally published in 1970 and in which she argued that classical ballet was not an artistic apotheosis but rather a form of 'ethnic dance' among others, is considered to be a landmark in this respect.

Because of its origins in Boasian anthropology, an early concern of this school was to record 'Native American' dances before they disappeared completely. The anthropology of dance in Northern America is now shared between dance studies and anthropology departments and, although the salvation perspective has been largely abandoned, the study of 'Native American' or creolized performance in America remains important, as exemplified by Scarangella-McNenly's and Nájera-Ramírez's chapters in this volume. In dance studies, which combine scholarly training with dance practice, a bias towards European and American theatrical genres often remains but classical ballet no longer dominates and, since the late 1980s, a plethora of studies of modern, postmodern and contemporary dance have been published (Foster 1986, 1996; Novack 1990; Franko 1995, 2002; Morris 1996; Desmond 1997; Burt 1998, 2006; Grau and Jordan 2000). The University of California, Riverside, is central to this trend and was the first to offer a doctoral programme in dance studies in the United States. In the past three decades US-trained dance scholars have increasingly integrated anthropological approaches (see Foster 2009).

Recent work in dance studies has also integrated philosophical approaches to movement and power (Martin 1998; Lepecki 2004, 2006), and indeed there has been a growing concern with the politics of movement in relation to issues of race

(Albright 1997; DeFrantz 2002, 2004; Foulkes 2002; Gottschild 2003; Chatterjea 2004; Manning 2004), gender (Burt 1995; Albright 1997; Banes 1998) and ability (Albright 1997). In the neighbouring field of dance criticism, until recently few individuals straddled the boundaries between practice, scholarship and critical writing on dance. Sally Banes, who worked with cross-disciplinary performance companies in Chicago in the 1970s and later wrote extensively on experimental dance in New York, is a prolific exception (Banes 1983, 1994, 2003).[4] Importantly, American dance anthropology has begun to turn its gaze on the world beyond North America (e.g., Shay 2002; Hahn 2007; O'Shea 2007; Sloat 2010). Foster charts this development well in the introduction to the *Worlding Dance* edited volume (Foster 2009).

There was a British movement related to the American one, but with differences in emphasis and contexts of research. In Britain, ethnomusicologist John Blacking's work on the Venda of Southern Africa (e.g., Blacking 1970, 1971, 1985) was a turning point: he worked alongside American colleagues to bring the anthropological study of dance to the same level as that of music (Blacking and Kealiinohomoku 1979). Blacking was not a dancer himself, but some of his students were, most notably Andrée Grau, who has greatly contributed to the development of the discipline in the UK. Georgiana Gore, a dancer trained by Ronald Frankenberg in the anthropology of the body, has helped to establish the anthropology of dance in France.

The second direction has its roots in studies of folklore in continental Europe, particularly in Eastern Europe, Germany and France. Although much discredited in dance scholarship since the 1970s,[5] Curt Sachs' (1937) ambitious classification of the world's dances was a foundational text. Sachs was working within the *Kulturkreis* diffusionist ideas that dominated Germanic anthropology at the time, and reproduced the unfortunate assumption that the dances of 'primitive' people reflected the primitiveness of their culture. His emphasis was on European folklore, however, and there is a degree of continuity between his work and that of later continental scholars working on French, Hungarian and other Eastern European folklore such as Martin and Pesovár (1961), Jean-Marie Guilcher (1963) and Roderyk Lange (1975). This approach has been mainly concerned with the classification and description of the formal characteristics of dance, often with a tendency to neglect their historical and political context. This is due in large part to the regionalist agenda contained in such research (in the French case) and to the political framework within which East European scholars were forced to work throughout the cold war.

The third direction has equally placed the emphasis on the formal characteristics of movement, but from the perspective of linguistic analysis. In the 1970s, anthropologists of dance began to draw on sociolinguistics, semiotics, Hall's (1968) 'proxemics' on the dynamic use of space in human thought, and Birdwhistell's (1970) 'kinesics' to analyse dance as a form of language or non-verbal communication. Drawing on her fieldwork with the Ubakala Igbo in Nigeria, Judith Hanna (1979b) used communication theory to suggest that the holistic aspect of dance, as well as its capacity to encapsulate multiple meanings, accounted for its potential to supplement and even transcend verbal language. Others, like Adrienne Kaeppler (1971, 1985, 1993), Drid Williams (1976a, 1976b, 1982, 2004) and Brenda Farnell (1994, 1995), drew on Saussurian linguistics, semiotics, Rudolf Laban's movement theory and feminist theory. These analyses focused on the capacity of human movement to produce metaphors and other categories of meaning in a way comparable to, but different from verbal language. In this approach, the meaning of movement can be accessed through long-term fieldwork and appropriate recording methods (movement notation and video) followed by structural analysis.

Though the linguistic approach was not taken up widely within the discipline, in large part for methodological reasons, it remains influential if not always explicitly acknowledged. Most importantly, it helped to generate new conceptual and analytical tools for the anthropological study of dance. It was probably the most sophisticated in challenging the Eurocentric division between dance and non-dance movement or verbal and non-verbal domains of action, and Williams's Saussurian 'semasiology' (see Williams 1982) was important in challenging the view that movement necessarily stood for something else. Though not a movement specialist per se, Jackson (1983) acknowledged this problem but offered a different perspective when revisiting his earlier fieldwork on initiation rituals among the Kuranko of Sierra Leone. Confessing that his earlier obsession with decoding the 'meaning' of dance and other bodily practices had yielded very little, he called for anthropologists to treat such practices as phenomena in themselves, not necessarily reducible to something else:

> The meaning of body praxis is not always reducible to cognitive and semantic operations: body movements often make sense without being intentional in the linguistic sense, as communicating, codifying, symbolising, signifying thoughts or things that lie outside or anterior to speech. Thus an understanding of a body movement does not invariably depend on an elucidation of what the movement 'stands for'. (Jackson 1983: 329)

The fourth direction is more diffuse, and could best be described as a trend rather than a school or a movement. Since the late 1980s, the study of dance has slowly made its way into the various fields of mainstream anthropology, from social anthropology to medical anthropology, material culture studies, and even cognitive and evolutionary anthropology. Social anthropologists with an interest in dance, some of them dancers themselves, have not identified exclusively with the anthropology of dance, and have also looked at dance in the light of current topics such as gender and sexuality (Cowan 1990; Thomas 1993; Washabaugh 1998), ethnicity, identity and nationalism (Daniel 1995; Mendoza 2000; Castaldi 2006; Wulff 2007), migration and identity (James 1999), transnationalism (Wulff 1998), postcolonialism (Ness 1992; Savigliano 1995) and the changing place of the arts in society (Hughes-Freeland 1997, 2008). Studies of dance have also been shaped by regional writing traditions in anthropology (see Fardon 1990). Studies of masquerade in West Africa, for example, often emphasize how this type of performance relates to intergenerational politics (de Jong 1999, 2007; Argenti 2007; Pratten 2008), whereas a number of recent ethnographies of dance in East Africa have been concerned with questions of conflict, displacement and memory (James 2000, 2007).

Taken together, the contributors in this volume draw on all four directions. However, there are important differences in background, and whereas some identify themselves as anthropologists of dance, others would rather be described as social or cultural anthropologists who happen to do research on dance alongside other aspects of the societies they study. Whereas some set out to study dance out of personal interest and long-standing practice, others were drawn to it as they found that people spent a great deal of time dancing.

This volume is different, then, from works such as Helen Thomas's *Dance in the City* which expressly only 'locates dance within the spectrum of urban life in late modernity' (Thomas 1997: x), and features dances such as the jitterbug, stripping, aerobics, ballroom and rave. The present volume is more diverse and wider-ranging geographically. It is also different from Desmond's (1997) collection, *Meaning in Motion*, which draws on cultural studies and feminist theory, and focuses almost exclusively on theatrical dance practices. As anthropologists, we are interested in tracing the flows and movements of dance, its social significance as well as its carriers such as migrants and tourists. Our unity here is in our desire to recognize creativity and agency in the dance. This collection also follows on from Paul Spencer's edited collection *Society and the Dance* (Spencer 1985b). Spencer's volume showcases an excellent range of anthropological analyses of dance performed in societies from the Venda of South Africa and the Lugbara of Uganda to Tonga and the Highlands of Papua New Guinea. Each contribution in Spencer's volume addresses theoretical approaches to the anthropology of dance, be it dance as safety valve, as vehicle of social control, or as ritual drama. As Spencer writes: 'society creates the dance, and it is to society that we must turn to understand it' (Spencer 1985b: 38). But there is also a focus on 'traditional' dance forms and on small-scale societies; our volume, by contrast, emphasizes the interconnectivity of styles, the movement of people on a wider scale, and the role of nation-states in shaping dance practices.

Dance and 'Culture'

In the 1920s and 1930s, the American Culture and Personality School and the German *Kulturkreis* ideology both assumed a straightforward, unproblematic relationship between dance and culture (Youngerman 1974). The continuity with these early approaches is evident in the massive Choreometrics project (Lomax 1968) begun in the late 1960s to collate examples of dance across cultures. Underpinning this project is the (Maussian) idea that physical activity (stance, movement style, gesture) is a component of culture. In traditional societies, this connection was suggested to be very much apparent: a fish-cutting action in Eskimo movement patterns could be seen to be translated similarly into Eskimo dance (Polhemus 1993: 9).

Although these approaches have been much criticized since then, the idea that there is a straightforward relationship between dance and culture remains implicit in many studies of dance. This is problematic, however, and is all too often predicated on an older anthropological notion of 'world cultures' as bounded and homogeneous entities. Even though anthropologists of the colonial period often had more sophisticated ideas about the heterogeneity and changing nature of 'culture' than is often acknowledged (Brumann 1999; Hannerz 1999), this view was one of the cardinal sins anthropology has been accused of ever since Writing Culture (Clifford and Marcus 1986) and the concomitant postmodern turn. Brumann summed up the problem in an article which sparked strong reactions from both defenders of the concept of culture, to which Brumann himself belongs, and those who argued that it had become too charged to be salvaged: 'The major concern of the sceptical discourse on culture is that the concept suggests boundedness, homogeneity, coherence, stability, and structure whereas social reality is characterized by variability, inconsistencies, conflict, change, and individual agency' (Brumann 1999: S1). Does it follow that we should simply abandon the search for dance in culture, or dance and culture? On the contrary, we want to suggest that the concept of culture may help us to explore the aesthetic dimensions of social life, not least because the very people whose lives we try to understand have appropriated it to a variety of ends. One of the inadvertent successes of anthropology is that its most cherished concepts have taken on a life of their own far beyond academic circles.

We also wanted to invite contributors to reflect on the validity and usefulness of 'culture' in its various modalities. When adults spend hours trying to force specific movement styles into the bodies of children, it is about more than creating perfection for a single show, as the seriousness of Balinese children's dance training in McIntosh's chapter attests. Following Hannerz, we propose retaining the 'core understanding of culture as consisting of meanings and practices acquired (in varied ways) in social life' (Hannerz 1999: S19), while also challenging the notions of boundedness, homogeneity and fixity that are always too ready to creep into our analyses because they make it easier to construct a coherent narrative. In other words, we would like to explore 'culture' as it relates to dance, albeit without overemphasizing its significance in determining what people do. As the chapters in this volume seek to demonstrate, dance can be used by anthropologists to understand and comment upon culture.

Our thinking on the relationship between dance and culture is informed by a number of anthropological studies which have explored this theme, sometimes implicitly. In her groundbreaking work on contact improvisation, Cynthia Novack (1990) showed how this practice, which developed in the United States in the 1960s and 1970s, made a conscious attempt to infuse movement with a free-flowing, non-gendered, egalitarian ethos. Modern dance had already emerged in the first half of the twentieth century as a reaction against the classical ballet tradition, but the Californian students who experimented with 'contact' in the 1960s sought to go further in breaking down the boundaries between male and female, choreographer and dancer, and performer and audience. The improvisational quality of the practice, in which movement was generated by the constant flow of energy, and by chance variations at the points of contact between two bodies, also challenged the utilitarian idea that individuals could be in total control of their actions at all times. Practices of this kind not only reflected, but also helped to shape radical transformations in white, urban, liberal American culture over two decades by giving young, middle-class urbanites committed to egalitarian ideals a space in which to try them out on their own bodies. Novack interpreted the decline of contact practice in the 1980s as an effect of cultural changes in America during which egalitarian ideals receded to the background, and the experimental quality of movement in contact practice came to be seen as messy, in need of technique and control.

Ness's (1992) landmark study of *sinulog* dancing in Cebu City, in the Philippines, also explored the dance and culture theme, but here culture was understood as the outcome of a localized urban history. Looking at three forms of the *sinulog* (a Christian ritual, a dance drama and a 'cultural' exhibition dance), Ness examines the ways in which significant aspects of Cebuano culture, such as impermanence, fluidity and the importance of using space in an optimal way in a crowded city, were embodied in the various versions of the dance. She also considered how social inequalities and postcolonial history left their mark on the bodies of *sinulog* performers in ways that were left unspoken.

The suggestion of culture embodied or sedimented in the moving body is apparent in other dance analyses. Barbara Browning (1995) subtitles her study of samba, 'resistance in motion', describing the dance as a form that narrates a history of cultural contact between Africans, Europeans, and indigenous Brazilians. Samba dancers themselves speak about the practice as a way of articulating their cultural identity, just as second-generation Puerto Ricans in the United States claim to be dancing salsa to 'reconnect' with their culture (Skinner 2007a). The obligatory fake tan – the 'brownface' look as McMains (2006: 109–70) refers to it – in dancesport Latin dances is the theatrical representation of Latinness for a transnational, predominantly white competitive culture. This 'darkening' of the body through dance can be contrasted by the 'whitening' complaint that Brazilian *capoeira* is becoming detached from its authentic, ethnic and folkloric roots (Downey 2005: 169–85), a black art becoming a white sport (Frigerio 1989).

Hughes-Freeland refers to a similar embodiment of social life when she says that 'dance is a refraction of social life, not simply a reflection' (Hughes-Freeland 2008: 108). The Javanese court dances in her study are a highly disciplined practice, a high art with a system of etiquette that refracts normal social practice.[6] They are used as a form of ceremonial body diplomacy to maintain relations between people and are more than just a means of cultural expression. Javanese court dances are held to belong to the nation; they are a feature of national identity taught to the young and staged for tourists (see Hughes-Freeland, this volume; see also McIntosh, this volume). But their meaning is not fixed, and neither is the social life they form part of; they are open to the subjective interpretation of audiences and dancers alike. Here culture is fluid because it is located in the changing interaction, over time, between performers and audiences or patrons. The codification, training and rehearsal practices that come across in all the contributions in this volume also remind us that dance cannot exist outside socially constructed conventions of movement. Dance movement is always created within a schema of aesthetics and agreed codes of gender expression (Hanna 1988; Desmond 2001).

A concern that is central to many of these studies is that of the location of individual agency in social change. Mauss (1973) perceived in the 1930s that every bodily activity, from that requiring years of training to the seemingly natural, such as walking and running, was shaped by people's social environment. Bourdieu (1977) built further on Mauss's ideas and developed the notions of 'habitus' and 'hexis' to explain the 'role of habitual bodily and spatial practices in social action' (Farnell 1999: 347). But Bourdieu did not have the specific qualities of dance in mind. Dance movement carries aesthetic dimensions, a projection of energy and an intended communication between performers and audience that gives it a specific potential to transform human experience in multiple ways. It is in this sense that dance is a powerful form of social action; it is part of the social fabric and not simply a reflection of it. Paraphrasing Shakespeare in *Hamlet*, the contributors in this volume agree that 'the dance is the thing'.

This is also suggested by Schieffelin whose work on ritual performance in Papua New Guinea remains highly influential. For him, the Aristotelian divide between a 'world of spectator which is real and a world conjured up by performers which is not' or has a 'virtual or imaginary' reality (Schieffelin 1998: 200), prevents us from grasping the relationship between performance and the 'social construction of reality'. In the Kaluli *Gisaro* ceremony, the performers sang with nostalgia about the landscape their audience was emotionally attached to (Schieffelin 1976). People would be so moved by the performance that they would often end up attacking the dancers and burning them on the shoulders with torches. It is not that the Kaluli are unable to conceive of the performance as a virtual world, Schieffelin argues; it is rather that they take it as a provocation. We would agree with Schieffelin in suggesting that in many cases the fusion of realities in the experience of the participants may well explain how performance accomplishes something unique.

Globalizing Dance Practices

'Participation in competitive ballroom dancing involves dancers in transnational systems of aesthetics, social networks and cultural codes that work through both body and mind', Jonathan Marion (2008: 1) writes. For Marion, culture is produced through activity, in this case by ballroom dancing. An activity, then, is also a site of culture for Marion (2008: 1). He continues, by suggesting that ballroom dancers are 'practically' – quite literally – a 'tribe' of dancers with a collective identity, the shared experience of a translocal ballroom culture of practice and competition which exists side-by-side with members' own national culture (Marion 2008: 25–28). The same might be said of tango, salsa and jive dancers sharing their interest or, more widely, of any social group with a shared practice to which people commit much of their lives. This culture-as-practice thesis rests upon 'the institutionalisation of action' (Marion 2008: 25). Frederik (2005) criticized this thesis in an exchange with Marion (2005a, 2005b) in *Anthropology News*. There, Marion described his translocal field sites, the very similar competition spaces around the Western world where professional dancers come together to compete. Sharing the ballroom standard, Marion describes these dancers as a self-defining, self-affiliating 'community' (Marion 2005a: 18). Frederik (2005) disputes the possibility of such a clear-cut division between the practice studio where dancers train and the competition space where Marion interviews dancers who have competed. He argues rather for a continuation, a flow between the local and the translocal as competitors relocate their activities. Community is more than the theatrical presentation of dance choreography at competition. As Skinner (2007b) argues, developing Frederik's point, the anthropologist should follow that translocation from studio to competition site, and share the journey and its meaning for those involved rather than just interview competitors about their performances. Culture does not just manifest itself in competition practice; it is there in the minds and bodies of the dancers but cannot be so easily delineated, or else all practices from ablutions to driving would lead to all sorts of cultures. Wulff (1998: 146) writes of a 'touring culture' in her study of transnational ballet, but it is a culture with a small 'c', one reactivated as each tour starts afresh. Caroline Picart (2006: 21) details 'studio culture' differing from one part of the city to the next, and studio etiquette – detailed training and common practices – differing more broadly from the 'street' styles and practices found in the social dance night clubs where swing, jive and salsa predominate. She characterizes it as Old World versus New World (Picart 2006: 15). Furthermore, Marion's culture of practice denies a sense of internalization, interpretation or imagination (cf. Anderson 1991) held within the dancer, or alternatively the feeling of belonging that might not be apparent in the competitors, or might be faked like the excessive representations of sexuality and heteronormativity in the routines. The meaning of the dance is not straightforward and is very often independent from the dancer, as the philosopher Suzanne Langer (1953) points out; so too, perhaps, the relationship between dance and culture.

One of the themes addressed in this volume is that of how dance practices move and become globalized as a result of the mobility of those who perform them. Inevitably, those practices become transformed in the process, as evident in the chapters by Skinner, Hughes-Freeland, Neveu Kringelbach and Nájera-Ramírez. In the literature, Pietrobruno (2006) looks at urban salsa as a transnational dance that has moved all over the globe since the 1980s. It has migrated through the dancers; it 'travels to new locations through the bodies, minds, and memories of its dancers' (Pietrobruno 2006: 2), shifting between cultural heritage and leisure commodity. Pietrobruno uses salsa to explicate urban life for South and Central American migrants in Montreal who identify with the dance. She also describes the historical habitus of the dance which – for all its transnational movements – continues to retain physical elements from its past, such as the European partner dance format, Cuban rumba foot isolations or Afro-Cuban bent knees and empowering *contra* body motion. The salsa dance is following the well trodden path of the other Latin dances[7] and their appropriation into ballroom and dancesport. They are all examples of globalization: '[D]ance culture based in lived realities ... channeled into the capitalist economy, rendered more restrictive, codified at the level of movement vernacular, and refigured in terms of American and British culture' (Pietrobruno

2006: 26). Competition in dance, and its commoditization in a world of flow, migration and diffusion has, we argue, not resulted in a divorce between dance and culture. Rather, both 'carry' each other.

Dance, Nation, Identities

The capacity of dance to encapsulate a multiplicity of messages, and to remain open to interpretation, means that it lends itself particularly well to embodying identities in the making. Dance is not fixed outside the bodies of performers and is therefore malleable enough to be manipulated according to context, ideology, and purpose. As Reed puts it, 'dance is a powerful tool in shaping nationalist ideology and in the creation of national subjects, often more so than are political rhetoric or intellectual debates' (Reed 1998: 511).

Daniel's (1995) study is an illuminating example that speaks to this theme. She explains that rumba was promoted as the national dance in post-revolutionary Cuba because it had been associated with the Afro-Cuban working class since the nineteenth century. Rumba was therefore a more appropriate means for representing socialist ideology than ballet,[8] *son* and other popular dance forms. But the authorities were not entirely successful in spreading rumba to all segments of society, a reminder that the ways in which people appropriate dance practices can never be completely controlled from above, an aspect that comes across in different ways in the chapters by Lüdtke, Neveu Kringelbach, Nájera-Ramírez and Carrausse. This is also the point made by Askew (2002) in her study of nation building and musical performance in Tanzania. Askew points out that nation building only happens when nationalist ideologies are reappropriated 'from below' and that musical performance (which in this case includes dance) has been central as a vehicle for Tanzanians to explore and imagine what their postcolonial nation was made of.

Alongside these examples, studies of dance and politics have multiplied since the early 1990s, as Reed (1998) identified more than a decade ago. In addition to exploring the ways in which dance practices can be co-opted to promote or contest political agendas, a number of studies have begun to pay due attention to the role of various institutions, bureaucracies and funding agencies in shaping dance. In her study of Irish dance, Wulff (2003, 2007), for example, discusses the multiple ways in which promoting and controlling dance – along with the Irish language – have been an integral part of the Irish national project since the late nineteenth century. In fact dance has been more successful than language in many ways because it helped to maintain a sense of Irishness among the diaspora in Great Britain, North America, Australia and New Zealand. Wulff also links the nationalistic aspect to other important issues in the redefinition of contemporary Irish identity, showing, for example, how dance becomes again and again entangled with religion and moral politics, as well as debates about authenticity, tradition and modernity in national culture. The lack of hip use in the dance style points to long-standing histories of Christian puritanism. It might even be possible to moot a postcolonial Irish moving body, Wulff (2003: 190) suggests.

Indeed the darker moments of national histories often leave their marks on dance practices. Looking at tango in Argentina, Taylor (1998: 71) shows how the dance became the trope for a culture of terror deep-seated within the country. For Taylor, tango was her research gatekeeper: '[w]hat the tango says about Argentina, the nation that created it, illuminates aspects of Argentine behaviour that have long puzzled outsiders' (Taylor 1998: 1). Dance has also become a productive avenue for looking at the self-fashioning of national gendered bodies, as in Archetti's (1999) work on how various constructions of masculinity in Argentina are played out through dance (tango) and sport (polo and football). This is a useful reminder that national identities always intersect with other identities shaped by gender, generation, race and class. Nowhere is this as evident as in performance.

The Chapters

The contributions to this volume engage with dance through the following themes: dance and globalization; tourism, social transformation and dance; and dance, identity and nation. These themes are considered in sections. The first, especially, engages with the movement, spread and commoditization of dance, be it the diffusion of jive as part of processes of American urbanization, the commercial transnational touring of national ballet companies, or the commoditization of a danced healing ritual in southern Italy. The second theme links chapters exploring the impact of tourism upon local indigenous dance and identity in Java, Panama and Native American Canada. The chapters in the third section consider the relationship between dance, nation and identity, with studies of national and migrants' dance groups, and children and young citizens growing up in nations where dance retains a political status. Taken together, the chapters in this collection examine the many dimensions and locations of *Dancing Cultures*.

More specifically, Jonathan Skinner opens the volume with a chapter about dance style transitions: how dances diffuse, mutate and feed into each other and how dancers co-opt and create moves. The examples here are primarily the American jive story as it developed out of the swing era when urban migration, racial tension and new technologies of musical production and reproduction were coming into play. The dance became an alternate public sphere for new urban arrivals – the rural disembedded but not disembodied – who used their bodies as currency, a dance community in the dance hall or in the block party. This dance is an illustration of globalization theory, the Americanization of a dance turned global and eventually franchised and marketed as a retro modern jive (ceroc) to appeal to the imaginative nostalgia of more contemporary generations seeking to connect and reconnect with others as well as themselves. Other social dances such as salsa and tango follow similar storylines, hybrid dance imports and exports turned to by new cosmopolitans in a globalized world.

Helena Wulff continues the theme of globalization and dance with an ethnographic analysis of transnational ballet and its funding. There is an uneasy duet danced here between high art dance and the less aesthetic commercial marketing and financing of its practice. Wulff looks at the similarities in ballet culture between old ballet centres such as Paris and London, and how they contrast with the more brash and aggressive marketing and patronage found in New York at the American Ballet Theatre. Despite the heterogeneity of ballet marketing, often now with a populist slant to it, Wulff found that dancers and business were highly aware of their company-space and its relationship with other ballet centres, thus suggesting that globalization and transnationality do not necessarily imply deterritorialization or the loss of identity. Dancers, more so than company marketing specialists, wrestled with what they perceived as the extreme opposites of the cultural capital of their dancing and the market capitalization of their product (more recently sold as tickets, merchandise, memoirs and even souvenirs, such as Nureyev's costumes and jewellery). Corporate sponsors such as tobacco companies buy into ballet to legitimate their ill-gained economic capital with cultural capital: 'capital laundering' in the world's capitals. There is both heterogeneity and homogeneity in the transnational cultural processes in these ballet company worlds, Wulff concludes.

'We were bitten by the beat, if not by spiders, and we used it to counter the disconnect of our stressed-out, over-burdened, spirit-starved modern lives ... We used this music to dance together, to try to heal ourselves, to drive away negative emotions, to invoke the spirits of our ancestors, offer support for each other ... to temporarily break away from our everyday stresses'. This is the commentary made by an Italian-American *pizzica* enthusiast who learnt *pizzica* in New York City. It is relayed in Karen Lüdtke's chapter on tarantism, a dance cult from Salento, Southern Italy, associated from medieval times with the tarantula spider, and *pizzica*, the traditional music of the region and a symbol of local identity. With a resurgence in the 1990s, both local music and dance are now a tourist attraction. Not only that, tarantism and *pizzica* have been adopted as modern identity-framing activities as well as commercial interest practices: in a modern Europe of cosmopolitan citizens, these revamped 'old traditions' allow Salentines to negotiate different levels of regional, national and continental identity, to retain a niche in an increasingly porous wall. A political tool, a fun practice, a financial asset, a tourist ad: *pizzica* is no longer just a source of healing and spirituality. It has changed significantly and grown in its importance as well as its meaning. In large part this is a response to the forces of globalization: cultural commoditization but still with a strong local bite to it.

Tourism has become the main driver of social transformation in the second section in this volume as Scarangella-McNenly, Hughes-Freeland and Theodossopoulos attest. In examples from different parts of the world, the nature of performance and the politics of cultural meaning are unpacked. Linda Scarangella-McNenly looks at traditional song and dance in cultural tourism amongst Coastal Salish, a First Nation people of British Columbia. Though their Híwus feasthouse is open to the tourists' gaze, Scarangella-McNenly contends that the Salish 'open' ceremonies are not just staged versions of authenticity. The tourists are, in fact, witnesses of 'tourism as ceremony', as she describes it. The Salish are not just Foucauldian disciplined natives (see also McIntosh, this volume) staging authentic exotic performances in public spaces. They play an active role in the production, expression and experience of 'the Native' under tourist scrutiny, with Bear, Eagle and Mountain Lion dances owned by specific performers just as much as their costumes. Ownership, however, comes with genealogical and spiritual relationships with the community and the place, the dances embodying the performers' relationships with their ancestors and exemplifying their local rights and privileges. The tourist 'cultural revivals' taking place at the Híwus feast house are thus just as much for the locals as well as the visitors. They become complex public spaces of cultural interaction that challenge modernist static and essentializing views of culture and authenticity, dance as authentic in terms of verisimilitude and genuineness, originality and the production of meaning. In his now classic analysis of tourism amongst the Maasai in Kenya, Edward Bruner (2005: 47) describes the tourists' view of the dancing and hosting given to them as a form of 'experience theatre', a space where host and guest meet and interact, an imaginary space constructed with 'realism' if not authenticity. Scarangella-McNenly draws on Bruner in her analysis of the Híwus feasthouse performances.

In the following chapter, Hughes-Freeland makes broader use of Bruner to make sense of dance events and culture in tourism-dependent environments in Southeast Asia. Hughes-Freeland's focus is upon dance culture as the pattern of relationships between performers, audiences and students of dance. These relationships change gradually, or are transformed dramatically by the tourist encounter or the loss of a patron. Hughes-Freeland explores the degrees of participation and interaction in dance tours to Laos and Indonesia, staged dance events, and dance lessons for visitors and students. Her approach is transactional in that she is interested in the relationships around the dance rather than in its commoditization and market value. Increasingly, cultural tours include workshops for tourists to participate in. Should the tourist stay longer and study the dance, then they change category from tourist to student or scholar. The art of cosmopolitanism in this context is to be able to negotiate shifts along these continuums, as the Salentines in Lüdtke's chapter have learned: Didik Nini Thowok is a Javanese choreographer able to move between the dance school where he teaches, parts of the island where he learns local traditions, and embassy evenings overseas where he performs.

The final chapter in this section, by Theodossopoulos, celebrates 'indigenous tourism' amongst the Embera of Parara Puru in Chagres National Park, Panama. The Embera both dance for and with the tourists visiting them: local animal dances, and rumba and cumbia dances adopted and made local. The former are often animal imitations, not far removed from some those studied in the Choreometrics Project: a dance representing the everyday natural environment of the Embera, with the dance leader representing a flower stamen with fellow dancers as petals; a line of dancers imitating the moving body of a snake; a dancer imitating a hummingbird drinking from a flower. These dance occasions are explained by the Embera as a working and reworking of their culture, a strengthening and consolidation of their cultural traditions for themselves as well as their tourist visitors. Furthermore, Theodossopoulos addresses the politics of Embera cultural representation and the typically inappropriate and unfounded exoticization of indigenous groups. This

Western aesthetic creeps into academic notions of (in)authenticity in dance as well as tourist expectations. Theodossopoulos's suggestion is that it is more productive to concentrate upon the cultural distance between the tourist and the performer rather than to fall into essentialist debates about 'dancing culture' as authentic or inauthentic representations of the people concerned.

The third and final section in this volume is concerned with the ways in which dance shapes and is shaped by national, regional and youth identities. In the four chapters by Neveu Kringelbach, Nájera-Ramírez, Carrausse and McIntosh, the agency of states and institutions (national theatres, universities, schools) is central in shaping moving bodies, but these bodies in turn appropriate performance to pursue their own agendas.

In the first chapter in this section, looking at the appropriation of a national dance culture 'from below' in Senegal, Neveu Kringelbach charts the genesis of the 'neo-traditional' genre of performance fostered by colonial school theatre, and developed further after Independence by the Senegalese National Ballet and its offshoots. Designed to create the illusion of a unified nation, the genre was a cornerstone of the nation-building project while also projecting the image of Senegal's first President, Léopold Sédar Senghor, as a powerful leader and a patron of the arts. While the fortunes of the National Ballet declined with Senegal's economy, neo-traditional performance was successfully appropriated by various groups who had been marginalized in the new nation, particularly the Jola of Casamance. Neveu Kringelbach shows how numerous Casamançais dance troupes were established by migrant associations in Dakar in the 1960s and 1970s, and how their staging of Casamançais 'traditions' contributed to the articulation of a regional culturalist discourse. As the younger generations of Casamançais performers came of age, however, these troupes introduced changes designed to enlarge the repertoire of identities they were able to speak to, from regional to national and even transnational.

In the second chapter in this section, Nájera-Ramírez looks at *ballet folklórico* as another example of the choreography of a new national culture that became successfully appropriated by people at the margins. *Folklórico* dance was developed shortly after the Mexican Revolution of 1910 from the merging of classical ballet and regional folk dance as a way of showcasing the cultural diversity of the nation while simultaneously legitimizing its unity. By the 1930s, the Mexican state sponsored efforts to collect folk dances from throughout Mexico, and to integrate them into the school curriculum. The Ballet Folklórico de Mexico, founded by Amalia Hernández in 1952, was instrumental in codifying the genre. But it was in the United States that the genre truly blossomed in the late 1960s and 1970s, Nájera-Ramírez suggests, because it became associated with the Chicano civil rights movement. This was important in maintaining a sense of common identity across the Mexico–US border. Even more importantly, *folklórico* groups in the United States now used their performances as a way of displaying the richness of Mexican heritage, thereby using a fairly recent dancing culture as a tool to instil discipline and pride into the bodies of younger Chicanos.

In the third chapter of the section, Carrausse's study of university student dance societies in South Korea, continues with the theme of dance, youth and transnationalism, even though here the transnational dimension is imagined rather than real. Carrausse begins this two-part chapter with a description of 'traditional' Korean mask dances and their material culture, all shaped by the successive influences of Buddhism, Confucianism and shamanism. The first part brings to the fore the aesthetics contained in these dances, such as the importance of creating a feeling of suspension and the texture of flowing energy. These aesthetics also place value on maintaining a physical distance between male and female bodies, and the magnificent costumes are designed to ensure that skin-to-skin contact never occurs. While these dances are still practised by many young Koreans, in the second part of the chapter Carrausse shows how, in recent years, a growing number of students in Seoul have become aficionados of simple, modern choreographed forms and global dance styles such as salsa and jive. For Carrausse, these dances do not embody a disaffection with Korean culture; rather, they enable youths under considerable social pressure regarding educational achievement to experience the collective fun, freedom from constraints and veiled eroticism of dancing in a socially acceptable space.

In the fourth chapter of the section and final piece in the book, McIntosh looks at the dance training of children in a village studio (*sanggar tari*) in Bali. At the *sanggar*, children learn Balinese dances, of course, but as McIntosh suggests, drawing on Foucault's work, much more is going on within the process of choreographic transmission. The lengthy preparation process leading up to a performance involves adult teachers forcing a specific movement style into the children's bodies, dressing them in incredibly elaborate costumes and applying flamboyant make-up. During this process, McIntosh shows how the children are doing more than becoming highly competent dancers: they also internalize the power of the older over the younger, and socially appropriate ways of being male and female. Balinese notions of good citizenship become almost literally 'bent' into their bodies. The younger children are less competent dancers than the older ones, but their young selves also seem to have more of a capacity to 'resist' the culture of the dance. In a strong sense, then, dance in rural Bali 'makes' persons.

It is our hope that this collection will further illuminate the significance of dance practices in social life and spark fresh debates across the fields of anthropology and dance studies.

Notes

1. For comprehensive reviews of anthropological approaches to dance, see also Kaeppler (1978), Hanna (1979a), Spencer (1985b), Reed (1998), Wulff (2001), Williams (2004) and Grau and Wierre-Gore (2005). Royce's (1977) book is both a review and a discussion of the various theoretical approaches used in the anthropology of dance until the 1970s. It was republished with a new introduction twenty-five years later (Royce 2002).
2. Evans-Pritchard's extraordinary collection of photographs has been made available on-line thanks to an AHRC-funded digitalizing project led by Christopher Morton at the Pitt Rivers Museum: http://southernsudan.prm.ox.ac.uk/index.php. Also see Morton (2009).

3. See Kolcio (2010) for a comprehensive review of the role of the six most important dance associations in the development of dance studies in American academia: CORD and SDHS, but also the American Dance Guild (formed 1956), the American Dance Therapy Association (1966), the American College Dance Festival Association (1973) and the Dance Critics Association (1974).
4. Also see Banes, Harris, Acocella and Garafola (2007) for informed commentaries on Banes's work and a compilation of her writings as a dance critic.
5. See especially Youngerman (1974) and Castaldi (2006) for a critique of Sachs's text.
6. Dance can also relate to the abnormal, to the extremes in society, or even to the divine, such as in trance dancing, which is associated more explicitly with the deities and their possession of the dancer in vodou dancing found in Haiti and West Africa (Friedson 2005), and implicitly in the clubbing scene (Jackson 2004).
7. Chasteen (2004) refers to these dances as transgressive national rhythms of Latin America with 'African roots', effectively a deep history of protest residing in the body.
8. Ballet was also promoted in Cuba, but to a lesser degree than rumba. In Cuba, ballet was introduced through the Russian school and did not, therefore, carry the same associations with bourgeois entertainment as it did in Europe.

References

Achebe, C. 2010. 'The Elephant that Flew', *Guardian*, 23 January, p.18.

Albright, A.C. 1997. *Choreographing Difference: The Body and Identity in Contemporary Dance*. Middletown, CT: Wesleyan University Press.

Anderson, B. 1991. *Imagined Communities: Reflections on the Origin and Spread of Nationalism*, rev. edn. New York: Verso.

Archetti, E. 1999. *Masculinities: Football, Polo and the Tango in Argentina*. Oxford: Berg.

Ardener, E. 1989[1973]. 'Some Outstanding Problems in the Analysis of Events', in *The Voice of Prophecy and Other Essays*, ed. M. Chapman. Oxford: Blackwell, pp.86–104.

Argenti, N. 2007. *The Intestines of the State: Youth, Violence, and Belated Histories in the Cameroon Grassfields*. Chicago: University of Chicago Press.

Askew, K. 2002. *Performing the Nation: Swahili Music and Cultural Politics in Tanzania*. Chicago: University of Chicago Press.

Banes, S. 1983. *Democracy's Body: Judson Dance Theater, 1962–1964*. Ann Arbor, MI: UMI Research Press.

────── 1994. *Writing Dancing in the Age of Postmodernism*. Middletown, CT: Wesleyan University Press.

────── 1998. *Dancing Women: Female Bodies on Stage*. London: Routledge.

────── (ed.). 2003. *Reinventing Dance in the 1960s: Everything Was Possible*. Madison: University of Wisconsin Press.

Banes, S., A. Harris, J.R. Acocella and L. Garafola. 2007. *Before, Between, and Beyond: Three Decades of Dance Writing*. Madison: University of Wisconsin Press.

Birdwhistell, R.L. 1970. *Kinesics in Context: Essays on Body Motion Communication*. Philadelphia: University of Pennsylvania Press.

Blacking, J. 1970. 'Tonal Organization in the Music of Two Venda Initiation Schools', *Ethnomusicology* 14(1): 1–56.

────── 1971. 'Deep and Surface Structures in Venda Music', *Yearbook of the International Folk Music Council* 3: 91–108.

———— 1985. 'The Context of Venda Possession Music: Reflections on the Effectiveness of Symbols', *Yearbook for Traditional Music* 17: 64–87.
Blacking, J., and J. Kealiinohomoku (eds). 1979. *The Performing Arts: Music and Dance*. The Hague: Mouton.
Boas, F. 1930. *The Religion of the Kwakiutl Indians*. New York: Columbia University Press.
Bourdieu, P. 1977. *Outline of a Theory of Practice*. Cambridge: Cambridge University Press.
Brown, S., M. Martinez and L. Parsons. 2006. 'The Neural Basis of Human Dance', *Cerebral Cortex* 16: 1157–67.
Browning, B. 1995. *Samba: Resistance in Motion*. Bloomington: Indiana University Press.
Brumann, C. 1999. 'Writing for Culture: Why a Successful Concept Should Not Be Discarded', *Current Anthropology* 40: S1–S27.
Bruner, E. 2005. *Culture on Tour: Ethnographies of Travel*. Chicago: University of Chicago Press.
Burt, R. 1995. *The Male Dancer: Bodies, Spectacle, Sexualities*. London: Routledge.
———— 1998. *Alien Bodies: Representations of Modernity, 'Race' and Nation in Early Modern Dance*. London: Routledge.
———— 2006. *Judson Dance Theater: Performative Traces*. London: Routledge
Castaldi, F. 2006. *Choreographies of African Identities: Negritude, Dance, and the National Ballet of Senegal*. Urbana: University of Illinois Press.
Chasteen, J. 2004. *National Rhythms, African Roots: The Deep History of Latin American Popular Dance*. Albuquerque: University of New Mexico Press.
Chatterjea, A. 2004. *Butting Out: Reading Resistive Choreographies through Works by Jawole Willa Jo Zollar and Chandralekha*. Middletown, CT: Wesleyan University Press.
Clifford, J., and G. Marcus (eds). 1986. *Writing Culture: The Poetics and Politics of Ethnography*. Berkeley: University of California Press.
Cowan, J. 1990. *Dance and the Body Politic in Northern Greece*. Princeton, NJ: Princeton University Press.
Daniel, Y. 1995. *Rumba: Dance and Social Change in Contemporary Cuba*. Bloomington: Indiana University Press.
DeFrantz, T. 2004. *Dancing Revelations: Alvin Ailey's Embodiment of African American Culture*. Oxford: Oxford University Press.
———— (ed.). 2002. *Dancing Many Drums: Excavations in African American Dance*. Madison: University of Wisconsin Press.
De Jong, F. 1999. 'Trajectories of a Mask Performance: The Case of the Senegalese "Kumpo"', *Cahiers d'Etudes Africaines* 53: 49–71.
———— 2007. *Masquerades of Modernity: Power and Secrecy in Casamance, Senegal*. Edinburgh: Edinburgh University Press.
Desmond, J. (ed.). 1997. *Meaning in Motion: New Cultural Studies of Dance*. Durham, NC: Duke University Press.
———— (ed.). 2001. *Dancing Desires: Choreographing Sexualities On and Off the Stage*. Madison: University of Wisconsin Press.
Downey, G. 2005. *Learning Capoeira: Lessons in Cunning from an Afro-Brazilian Art*. Oxford: Oxford University Press.
Durkheim, E. 1915[1912]. *The Elementary Forms of Religious Life*, trans. J.W. Swain. London: Allen and Unwin.
Ebron, P. 2002. *Performing Africa*. Princeton, NJ: Princeton University Press.
Evans-Pritchard, E.E. 1928. 'The Dance', *Africa* 1: 446–62.

Fardon, R. (ed.). 1990. *Localizing Strategies: Regional Traditions of Ethnographic Writing*. Edinburgh: Scottish Academic Press.

Farnell, B. 1994. 'Ethno-graphics and the Moving Body', *Man* 29(4): 929–74.

——— 1995. *Do You See What I Mean? Plains Indian Sign Talk and the Embodiment of Action*. Austin: University of Texas Press.

——— 1999. 'Moving Bodies, Acting Selves', *Annual Review of Anthropology* 28: 341–73.

Foster, S. 1986. *Reading Dancing: Bodies and Subjects in Contemporary American Dance*. Berkeley: University of California Press.

——— 1996. *Corporealities: Dancing, Knowledge, Culture, and Power*. London: Routledge.

——— (ed.). 2009. *Worlding Dance: Studies in International Performance*. London: Palgrave Macmillan.

Foulkes, J. 2002. *Modern Bodies: Dance and American Modernism from Martha Graham to Alvin Ailey*. Chapel Hill, NC: University of North Carolina Press

Franko, M. 1995. *Dancing Modernism/Performing Politics*. Bloomington: Indiana University Press.

——— 2002. *The Work of Dance: Labor, Movement and Identity in the 1930s*. Middletown, CT: Wesleyan University Press.

Frederik, L. 2005. 'Competition Ballroom Dancing: The Native's Point of View', *Anthropology News*, December, pp.19–20.

Friedson, S. 2005. 'Where Divine Horsemen Ride: Trance Dancing in West Africa', in A. Hobart and B. Kapferer (eds), *Aesthetics in Performance: Formations of Symbolic Construction and Experience*. Oxford: Berghahn, pp.109–28.

Frigerio, A. 1989. 'Capoeira: De arte negra a esporte branco', *Revista Brasileira de Ciências Socias* 4(10): 85–98.

Gell, A. 1985. 'Style and Meaning in Umeda Dance', in P. Spencer (ed.), *Society and the Dance*. Cambridge: Cambridge University Press, pp.183–205.

Gore, G. 2001. 'Present Texts, Past Voices: The Formation of Contemporary Representations of West African Dances', *Yearbook for Traditional Music* 33: 29–36.

Gottschild, B.D. 2003. *The Black Dancing Body: A Geography from Coon to Cool*. New York: Palgrave McMillan.

Grau, A., and S. Jordan. 2000. *Europe Dancing: Perspectives on Theatre, Dance and Cultural Identity*. London: Routledge.

Grau, A., and G. Wierre-Gore. 2005. 'Introduction générale', in A. Grau and G. Wierre-Gore (eds), *Anthropologie de la Danse: Genèse et Construction d'une Discipline*. Paris: Centre National de la Danse, pp.7–27.

Guilcher, J.-M. 1963. *La Tradition Populaire de Danse en Basse-Bretagne*. Paris: Mouton.

Hahn, T. 2007. *Sensational Knowledge: Embodying Culture Through Japanese Dance*. Middletown: Wesleyan University Press.

Hall, E. 1968. 'Proxemics', *Current Anthropology* 9(2/3): 83–108.

Hanna, J. 1979a. 'Movements Toward Understanding Humans through the Anthropological Study of Dance', *Current Anthropology* 20(2): 313–39.

——— 1979b. *To Dance is Human: A Theory of Non-verbal Communication*. Chicago: University of Chicago Press.

——— 1988. *Dance, Sex and Gender: Signs of Identity, Dominance, Defiance, and Desire*. Chicago: University of Chicago Press.

Hannerz, U. 1999. 'Comment' on C. Brumann, 'Writing for Culture: Why a Successful Concept Should Not Be Discarded', *Current Anthropology* 40: S18-S19.

Hughes–Freeland, F. 1997. 'Art and Politics: From Javanese Court Dance to Indonesian Art', *Journal of the Royal Anthropological Institute* 3(3): 473–95.
_____ 2008. *Embodied Communities: Dance Traditions and Change in Java*. Oxford: Berghahn.
Jackson, M. 1983. 'Knowledge of the Body', *Man* 18: 327–45.
Jackson, P. 2004. *Inside Clubbing: Sensual Experiments in the Art of Being Human*. Oxford: Berg.
James, D. 1999. *Songs of the Women Migrants*. Edinburgh: Edinburgh University Press.
James, W. 2000. 'Reforming the Circle: Fragments of the Social History of a Vernacular African Dance Form', *Journal of African Cultural Studies* 13(1): 140–52.
_____ 2003. *The Ceremonial Animal: A New Portrait of Anthropology*. Oxford: Oxford University Press.
_____ 2007. *War and Survival in Sudan's Frontierlands: Voices from the Blue Nile*. Oxford: Oxford University Press.
Kaeppler, A. 1971. 'Aesthetics of Tongan Dance', *Ethnomusicology* 15(2): 175–85.
_____ 1978. 'Dance in Anthropological Perspective', *Annual Review of Anthropology* 7: 31–49.
_____ 1985. 'Structured Movement Systems in Tonga', in P. Spencer (ed.), *Society and the Dance*. Cambridge: Cambridge University Press, pp.92–118.
_____ 1993. *Poetry in Motion: Studies in Tongan Dance*. Nukualofa, Tonga: Vava.
Kealiinohomoku, J. 1983[1970]. 'An Anthropologist Looks at Ballet as a Form of Ethnic Dance', in R. Copeland and M. Cohen (eds), *What is Dance? Readings in Theory and Criticism*. New York: Oxford University Press, pp.533–49.
Kolcio, K.P. 2010. *Movable Pillars: Organizing Dance 1956–1978*. Middletown, CT: Wesleyan University Press.
Kurath, G. 1960. 'Panorama of Dance Ethnology', *Current Anthropology* 1(3): 233–54.
Lange, R. (ed.). 1975. *The Nature of Dance: An Anthropological Perspective*. London: McDonald and Evans.
Langer, S. 1953. *Feeling and Form: A Theory of Art Developed from Philosophy in a New Key*. New York: Scribner.
Lepecki, A. 2006. *Exhausting Dance: Performance and the Politics of Movement*. London: Routledge.
_____ (ed.). 2004. *Of the Presence of the Body: Essays on Dance and Performance Theory*. Middletown, CT: Wesleyan University Press.
Lewis, J. 1992. *Ring of Liberation*. Chicago: University of Chicago Press.
Lomax, A. 1968. *Folk Song Style and Structure*. Washington: American Association for the Advancement of Science.
McMains, J. 2006. *Glamour Addiction: Inside the American Ballroom Dance Industry*. Middletown, CT: Weslyan University Press.
Malinowski, B. 1948[1925]. *Magic, Science and Religion, and Other Essays*. New York: Doubleday.
Manning, S. 2004. *Modern Dance, Negro Dance: Race in Motion*. Minneapolis: University of Minnesota Press.
Marion, J. 2005a. '"Where" is "There"? Towards a Translocal Anthropology', *Anthropology News*, May, pp.18–19.
_____ 2005b. 'Why "Ballroom" is Bigger than the Studio Floor', *Anthropology News*, December, p.20.
_____ 2008. *Ballroom: Culture and Costume in Competitive Dance*. Oxford: Berg.

Marrett, R. 1909. *The Threshold of Religion*. London: Methuen.
Martin, G., and E. Pesovár. 1961. 'A Structural Analysis of the Hungarian Folk Dance: A Methodological Sketch', *Acta Ethnographica* 10(1–2): 1–40.
Martin, R. 1998. *Critical Moves: Dance Studies in Theory and Politics*. Durham, NC: Duke University Press.
Mauss, M. 1973[1935]. 'Techniques of the Body', *Economy and Society* 2(1): 70–88.
Mendoza, Z. 2000. *Shaping Society through Dance: Mestizo Ritual Performance in the Peruvian Andes*. Chicago: University of Chicago Press.
Mitchell, J. 1956. *The Kalela Dance: Aspects of Social Relationships among Urban Africans in Northern Rhodesia*. Manchester: Manchester University Press.
Moore, R. 1997. *Nationalizing Blackness: Afrocubanismo and Artistic Revolution in Havana 1920–1940*. Pittsburgh, PA: University of Pittsburgh Press.
Morris, G. (ed.). 1996. *Moving Words: Re-writing Dance*. London: Routledge.
Morton, C. 2009. 'The Initiation of Kamanga: Visuality and Textuality in Evans-Pritchard's Zande Ethnography', in C. Morton and E. Edwards (eds), *Photography, Anthropology and History: Expanding the Frame*. Farnham: Ashgate Publishing, pp.119–42.
Ness, S.A. 1992. *Body, Movement, and Culture: Kinesthetic and Visual Symbolism in a Philippine Community*. Philadelphia: University of Pennsylvania Press.
Novack, C. 1990. *Sharing the Dance: Contact Improvisation and American Culture*. Madison: University of Wisconsin Press.
O'Shea, J. 2007. *At Home in the World: Bharata Natyam on the Global Stage*. Middletown, CT: Wesleyan University Press.
Picart, C. 2006. *From Ballroom to Dancesport: Aesthetics, Athletics and Body Culture*. New York: State University of New York Press.
Pietrobruno, S. 2006. *Salsa and Its Transnational Moves*. Oxford: Lexington Books.
Polhemus, T. 1993. 'Dance, Gender and Culture', in H. Thomas (ed.), *Dance, Gender and Culture*. London: Macmillan, pp.3–16.
Pratten, D. 2008. 'Masking Youth: Transformation and Transgression in Annang Performance', *African Arts* 41(4): 44–59.
Radcliffe-Brown, A. 1922. *The Andaman Islanders*. Cambridge: Cambridge University Press.
Reed, S. 1998. 'The Politics and Poetics of Dance', *Annual Review of Anthropology* 27: 503–32.
Royce, A.P. 1977. *The Anthropology of Dance*. Bloomington: Indiana University Press.
—— 2002. *The Anthropology of Dance*, 2nd edn. Alton: Dance Books.
Sachs, C. 1937[1934]. *World History of the Dance*. New York: Norton.
Savigliano, M. 1995. *Tango and the Political Economy of Passion*. Boulder, CO: Westview.
Schieffelin, E. 1976. *The Sorrow of the Lonely and the Burning of the Dancers*. New York: St Martin's Press.
—— 1998. 'Problematizing Performance', in F. Hughes–Freeland (ed.), *Ritual, Performance, Media*. London: Routledge, pp.194–207.
Shay, A. 2002. *Choreographic Politics: State Folk Dance Companies, Representations and Power*. Middletown, CT: Wesleyan University Press.
Sheets-Johnstone, M. 1999. *The Primacy of Movement*. Amsterdam: John Benjamins Publishing.
Skinner, J. 2007a. 'The Salsa Class: A Complexity of Globalization, Cosmopolitans and Emotions', *Identities* 14(4): 485–506.
—— 2007b. 'Leading Questions' *Anthropology News* 48(2): 17–18.

Sloat, S. 2010. *Making Caribbean Dance: Continuity and Creativity in Island Cultures.* Gainesville: University Press of Florida.

Spencer, H. 1857. *Essays: Scientific, Political and Speculative.* London: Williams and Norgate.

Spencer, P. 1985a. 'Dance as Antithesis in the Samburu Discourse', in P. Spencer (ed.), *Society and the Dance.* Cambridge: Cambridge University Press, pp.140–64.

_____ (ed.). 1985b. *Society and the Dance: The Social Anthropology of Process and Performance.* Cambridge: Cambridge University Press.

Taylor, J. 1998. *Paper Tangos.* Durham, NC: Duke University Press.

Thomas, H. (ed.). 1993. *Dance, Gender and Culture.* Basingstoke: Macmillan.

_____ (ed.) 1997. *Dance in the City.* New York: St Martin's Press.

Wade, P. 2000. *Music, Race, and Nation: Música Tropical in Colombia.* Chicago: University of Chicago Press.

Washabaugh, W. (ed.). 1998. *The Passion of Music and Dance: Body, Gender and Sexuality.* Oxford: Berg.

White, B. 2008. *Rumba Rules: The Politics of Dance Music in Mobutu's Zaire.* Durham, NC: Duke University Press.

Williams, D. 1976a. 'Deep Structures of the Dance, Part 1: Constituent Syntagmatic Analysis', *Journal of Human Movement Studies* 2(3): 123–44.

_____ 1976b. 'Deep Structures of the Dance, Part 2: The Conceptual Space of the Dance', *Journal of Human Movement Studies* 2(3): 155–71.

_____ 1982. 'Semasiology', D. Parkin (ed.), *Semantic Anthropology.* London: Academic Press, pp.161–82.

_____ 2004. *Anthropology and the Dance: Ten Lectures*, 2nd edn. Urbana: University of Illinois Press.

Wulff, H. 1998. *Ballet across Borders: Career and Culture in the World of Dancers.* Oxford: Berg.

_____ 2001. 'Anthropology of Dance', in N. Smelser and P. Bates (eds), *International Encyclopedia of the Social and Behavioral Sciences.* Oxford: Pergamon, pp.3209–12.

_____ 2003. 'The Irish Body in Motion: Moral Politics, National Identity and Dance', in N. Dyck and E. Archetti (eds), *Sport, Dance and Embodied Identities.* Oxford: Berg, pp.179–96.

_____ 2007. *Dancing at the Cross Roads: Memory and Mobility in Ireland.* Oxford: Berghahn.

Youngerman, S. 1974. 'Curt Sachs and His Heritage: A Critical Review of *World History Of the Dance* with a Survey of Recent Studies that Perpetuate His Ideas', *Congress On Reseearch in Dance News* 6(2): 6–19.

PART I

Dance and Globalization

Chapter 1

Globalization and the Dance Import–Export Business: The Jive Story

Jonathan Skinner

> All the jive is gone!
> All the jive is gone!
> What an awful fix, can't get my kicks,
> 'Cause all the jive is gone!
> —Andy Kirk and the Twelve Clouds of Joy, 'All the Jive is Gone' (1936)

'Are You Hep to the Jive?'

Jive is a living history. It is a language and a movement – both bodily and counter-cultural – which spans the centuries and crosses the continents, and takes us from the Middle Passage to the D-Day landings, from swing and Lindy hop 'joints a jumpin'' in Harlem, New York, to zoot-suit retro swing revivals in Herrang, Sweden. In his history of jive, Bill Milkowski refers to jive as a language, 'like cussing ... a language of emotion: a means of describing how one is affected by certain experiences or situations' (Milkowski 2001: 20). Like soul and hiphop, jive can be a slang of inclusion, a cockney ebonics, an idiolect marking out a group, fraternal and black – 'African-American bohemianism' (Saul 2003: 7) in this case. It is a term said to have been invented in the 1920s by the Chicago-based musician Louis Armstrong, and popularized in the 1930s by Cab Calloway, the 'Professor of Jive'. 'Are You Hep to the Jive' (1940) is – besides 'Minnie the Moocher' (1931) and 'Take the "A" Train' (1941) – one of Calloway's signature numbers, one which asks the listener if they are up to date, 'hip with' the jive, the dance as well as the latest trends and fashions.[1] 'Jive' was also a codeword for marijuana on the streets and in the lyrics of many big-band anthems. Calloway published his own *Hepster's Dictionary* (Calloway 1944) that defined jive as Harlemese speech for 'stuff', as in 'did you bring the jive', or as blarney as in 'He can jive his way into any hep cat's heart'. Postwar, jive lost this meaning and 'hep' fell out of favour as a popular term.

Jive became a term of derision, slang for someone talking nonsense ('You're just jiving with me'), cajoling, jarring ('What you say don't jive with what I saw') or misleading another, an insult even ('You jive-ass motherfucker'). Jive did, however, remain as a term referring to a dance style, a variation on the jitterbug, a swing dance with roots in Lindy hop, 'syncopated raw emotion' in the words of William White (cited in Erenberg 1998: 37).

This chapter is about the hybrid history of this jive dance, a tale of dance imports and dance exports which covers its transformation from 1940s African-American swing expression to 1990s British ceroc franchise. This story concentrates upon the dancers and their creative take up of the dance, its adoption and adaptation, and its connection with social and technological change in the twentieth century. As such, jive has been associated – variously – with resistance, moral corruption and depraved identities, sensual and sexy swing counter-culture, and modern sassy high-impact entertainment organization. In all of its guises and through all its transformations, jive – mid twentieth-century 'traditional' and late twentieth-century 'modern' – has played upon and played with people's emotions, affections and imaginations. Incorporated into this social study of jive is also an apologue on emotion, one that shows how emotional cultural forms are commercially appropriated. Implicit in this account of jive is the thesis that identity and the emotions are not obviated by the globalization of dance styles – the commoditization of a dance. Rather, modern-day dance organizations featuring swing – and salsa – 'dance imports, serve a key social purpose as an emotional outlet in an increasingly indifferent society.

Jive Origins: Personal and Emotional, Global and Historical

> We also learned about what had happened to Swing through the rest of the country. The dance had been transformed, and in different ways, depending on local conditions. The Carolinas had a languid, slowed-down version that had become known as the Shag. St. Louis had a fast version – the Imperial Style, they called it – that retained certain features of the old Charleston. Texas had two styles called the Push and the Whip. California was home to a version called the West Coast Swing. Not only were these different stylistically from each other and from the Lindy (or Savoy Style Swing, as some began to call it), but outside of New York, Swing clubs tended to emphasize competitions, while we tended to view our dances as social events. (Crease 1996: 259)

Jive has historical tentacles in a number of dance styles, foremost among them the jitterbug and other swing dances. In order to understand jive – the dance as opposed to the codeword-like language – whether from traditional jitterbug and swing, modern Ceroc and *le roc*, or ballroom jive (rock-step and chassis-to-the-side), it is thus important to situate it in the matrix of dance styles and the historical context of its inception in the swing era before exploring its own global diffusion. Let me take you, then, to prewar North America during the Great Depression when crooners and balladeers were the popular musicians, when Cab Calloway and Louis Armstrong and Benny Goodman were making their breakthrough, making a living playing to segregated audiences, earning white dollars from their gigs that they were unable to spend in the segregated diners and cafés outside their music venues.

According to Lewis Erenberg (1998: 3–6) in his cultural history of big-band jazz, *Swingin' the Dream*, the swing era was ushered in at the end of the Prohibition years (1919 to 1933) by Benny Goodman and his racially integrated orchestra – of 'Sing, Sing, Sing' (1937) fame – with their cross-country tour of the US.[2] In early 1935 they left New York on the brink of failure, struggling to get bookings in competition with the sweet singers who had toppled the jazz era and were then in vogue. In a ballroom in Michigan they played to an audience of barely thirty people, mostly musicians. At the Elitch Gardens near Denver the audience demanded that they play waltzes, and when Goodman and his orchestra declined they demanded their money back. They had their break, however, on the last night of their tour at the Los Angeles Palomar Ballroom on 21 August 1935: after opening with some conventional melodies 'trumpeter Bunny Berigan yelled "let's cut this shit", and Goodman decided that if they were going to fail, the band would go down swinging' (Erenberg 1998: 4). The evening was an outstanding success with the dancers mobbing the band during and after the numbers they played. And so, after a staggered return to New York via Chicago, the Goodman players returned as the triumphant 'Kings of Swing', playing to sell-out audiences for the rest of the swing era until disbanding in 1948 when that era gave way to bebop and the up-tempo jazzy melodies and improvisations of Charlie Parker and Dizzie Gillespie.

Sandwiched between jazz phases, the 'golden age' of swing (1935 to 1948) is associated with the rise of the ballroom and the decline of the nightclub; it was a time when music swept up the youthful masses: white Anglo-Saxon Protestants (WASPs), African-Americans and immigrants alike, one new pluralist democracy of dancers. This is not to idealize the past. The swing era was also a time of commercialism, mass music and exploitation: for Jones (1963), swing shifted from verb to noun to become a commodity to be bought and sold and manipulated by whites. Jive was to follow a similar commercial route as we shall see later on. The swing dance floors and band areas were generally segregated as a rule and, during this golden age there were great musical and dance struggles between black and white bands: the former with looser inflections and style than the latter, with band leader Paul Whiteman attempting to 'civilize' African-American music and Duke Ellington trying to claim European technique for black jazz (Erenberg 1998: xii); and, ostensibly, black and white dance styles as West African body movements competed with European steps, improvisational body movement from the hips with repetitive footwork and dance sequences (Batchelor 1997: 16–17).

The result was a blend as dancers brought to the musicians their muscle memories, their dance training, and what they saw around them and what had been brought to the dance floor in the past: ragtime (an array of 'trotting' dances dating from about 1890 to 1914 from the post-emancipation 'cakewalk' to the animal dances such as the 'turkey trot', all possibly arising as African-American parodies of white social dances; see Cook 1998: 136); the Charleston of the first two decades of the twentieth century (an eight-count dance with oppositional limb movements, shoulder shimmies and hip twists, a dance with African rhythms and Ashanti tribal movements which spawned the Lindy); and its successor the 'black bottom' dance, which was described and epitomized in Perry Bradford's 1919 dance song 'The Original Black Bottom Dance', an offbeat solo challenge dance thought to be a precursor to modern tap dancing:

> Hop down front and then you doodle [slide] back,
> Mooch to your left and then you mooch to your right,
> Hands on your hips and do the mess around,
> Break a leg [wobble] until you're near the ground,
> Now that's the old black bottom dance.
>
> Now listen folks, open your ears,
> This rhythm you will hear –
> Charleston was on the afterbeat –
> Old black bottom'll make you shake your feet,
> Believe me it's a wow.
> Now learn this dance somehow,
> Started in Georgia and it went to France,
> It's got everybody in a trance
> It's a wing, that old black bottom dance.[3]

Batchelor (1997: 59) notes that this dance from the American South migrated from New Orleans and Nashville, and was perhaps named after Nashville's river-front section, the Black Bottom, or after the black soils and mud of either the Suwannee river or the Mississippi delta.

These dances diffuse and mutate, interbreeding with each other. The Lindy hop, for example, is very much a dance derived by mutation (Batchelor 1997: 86–87). It is a mix of the Texas Tommy (a kick and a hop three times on each foot followed by a slide and then a breakaway where partners separated and could do what they wanted before returning together) with the 'collegiate' (similar to the Charleston) and the 'breakaway' (when partners break from a close and closed hold). Shorty George Snowden (of 'Shorty George' dance-step fame, a kind of bent-kneed ice-skating impression) is said to have defined the Lindy hop dance as a reaction to the dancing and celebrations around him in honour of Charles Lindbergh's non-stop flight from New York to Paris, a feat of great courage and good fortune, flying with a cracked fuel tank, a bag of sandwiches and with a periscope through the floor of the plane for navigation – 'Lindy' resorted to hailing trawlers to ask them the way! Shorty came up with an abbreviation of newspaper headlines, and trombonist TeRoy Williams's music 'The Lindbergh Hop'. Whether the Lindy hop has these beginnings – or is from Lindy Lou, the sobriquet for a coloured girl – it is a dance which is now associated with the

Savoy Ballroom in New York where it was initially banned before it was tolerated, accepted and then promoted and celebrated.

The Lindy hop was a dance that evolved with the music into a 4/4 rhythm as dancers and musicians challenged and fed off each other, before it turned into six- or eight-count Lindy. Through Evette Jensen, the jazz dancer Norma Miller gives a personal account of how the dancing looked then:

> The Lindy Hop started in Harlem with black dancers; when white bands became part of the Swing Era, white kids tended to follow bands like Benny Goodman's. It was about this time that the dance got faster and wilder. When the King of Swing, as they called Goodman, played at the Paramount Theater in New York in 1938, the audience went wild and danced in the aisles. Goodman supposedly said that they looked like a bunch of Jitterbugs, and the name stuck. The promoters picked up the term and started hyping the new dance, the Jitterbug. To the rest of us, it looked like the Lindy Hop. (Miller and Jensen 1996: 248)

At the time, more than one million African-Americans had moved to the great urban industrial cities such as New York and Chicago. These dances became their outlets as they socialized and relaxed at 'rent parties' and 'house shouts' or at the ballroom. Dances such as the Texas Tommy and the jitterbug blurred in contests, crossing and recrossing, mixing and remixing, as the dance communities self-perpetuated themselves through competitions, shows, block parties and ballroom socials. This migratory shift in population and the changing entertainment patterns at the start of the twentieth century are identified by Katrina Hazzard-Gordon as a move in the '"jook" continuum' (Hazzard-Gordon 1990: x–xi), from African-American working class bar-cum-diner-cum-dance venue to that of the 'commercial urban complex' of public (membership) clubs, city dance halls and ballrooms. This shift in location is expressed and described in the change in black music from blues and jazz to swing. It is an example of urbanization and globalization at the dawn of an era of new mass-market and new media technologies of production and reproduction, a time when the proscribed and punished black body began to turn into a new black aesthetic – 'from coon to cool' (Gottschild 2003).

Globalization and Dance Imports and Exports

> [A]s was the case with swing music, styles of playing and dancing change as these forms were appropriated by white practitioners and finessed to a white aesthetic standard. This meant that the grounded, from-the-hips, smooth style of dancing ... became a bouncy, upright, jerky style taught at white dancing schools such as those run by Arthur Murray. (Gottschild 2000: 74)

Dance diffused through the medium of musicians and dancers. Both performed a bricolage in public, drawing from their repertoires, their tool kits, to impress audiences. According to Batchelor, the dances evolved, diffused and blended from Africa to the New World of the Caribbean and the USA, spilling out of the 'communication hubs for land, water and rail travel' (Batchelor 1997: 15). Lindy steps are considered to have been seen amongst the Ejor of Sierra Leone and Hausa girls in Nigeria, Charleston steps amongst the Igbo of West Africa and in Shango on Trinidad. In the USA, these dances spread from centres such as New Orleans, travelling up the rivers on the river boats; from Chicago along the railroads; from New York via post-industrial advertising, and capitalist Mecca for clubs (the Cotton Club), dance halls (the Savoy Ballroom) and music labels (Decca); and from Hollywood, Los Angeles, the capital of the film industry and the centre of commercial broadcasting. Between New York and Los Angeles lay Kansas City and Denver, important stopovers for bands touring the east or west coasts. Other tours, Batchelor (1997: 29) identifies, were circuits of the Theatre Owners Booking Association (TOBA) which numbered some eighty theatres in 1929 with bands rotating through the South and Midwest – Chicago, Kansas City, Oklahoma City, Dallas, New Orleans, Atlanta, Durham. There was also a smaller 'Round the World' circuit for the more successful bands that rotated around New York (Harlem), Philadelphia, Baltimore and Washington. The idea behind these diffusion circuits was to maintain a steady stream of quality shows for the lowest possible price.

These bands and dancers – such as the Whitman Sisters vaudeville act with bands and dancers in toe, and the Cab Calloway Band which travelled by train (with their own carriages) – plied the new urban centres, playing to the new immigrants, the displaced and landless, the diasporic, and the successful and wealthy new capitalist elite. The dancing swinging world developed as an 'alternate public sphere' (Gilroy 1987) for the new urban arrivals who could practice an old illiterate technology, using their bodies as currency, treading and retreading their diasporas, first from Africa and second from plantation to city. The success and growth of the swing era is thus one which rides upon the rural exodus and the then new twentieth-century transport technologies and media innovations: the bands travelled by road and rail, a reversal south along some of the old 'structured travel circuits' (Clifford 1994: 309) of the underground slave escape routes; the dance was named after a famous transatlantic pilot; the music was broadcast by radio and sold on recordings. Swing, in turning from noun to verb to noun was harnessed by and harnesser of the features of advanced capitalism (cf. Anderson 1994), the birth of a mass media in particular. The 'spontaneous union' of the dancing jivers, swingers and jitterbugs, the testing and crossing of class and racial barriers, the 'feeling inside of togetherness not achieved in any other activity' (Erenberg 1998: 52), all came from these new swing dances which had been ushered in by Benny Goodman and his band. And we must remember that Goodman's success only came about in California, at the end of many months of travelling, and after a few shows on NBC's *Let's Dance* radio programme which had cued in the fans' musical tastes before Goodman's tipping-point evening with them.

Above, I have presented a history of the evolution and diffusion of swing. I have shown how it has been tied to certain regions and places: West Africa, the West Indies, New Orleans, Los Angeles, Chicago, New York and Harlem. These places are all diaspora signifiers for African-Americans. They are all places that appeal to the imagination, the nostalgia, the resentment and indignation of the oppressed and persecuted. Taking a lead from postmodernist Fredric Jameson's essay on 'nostalgia for the present' (Jameson 1989), Arjun Appadurai describes the power of the imagination, referring to it as a new 'social fact', 'the imagination as a social practice' (Appadurai 1990: 5, emphasis removed). He writes that: '[t]he past is now not a land to return to in a simple politics of memory. It has become a synchronic warehouse of cultural scenarios, a kind of temporal central casting' (Appadurai 1990: 4). This past as a place is fashioned and refashioned, styled and restyled from the advantage of the present. The present-day attraction of the music and dancing lie in escapism (similar to the escapisms of the past), invoking and immersing oneself in a rose-tinted 'happy' environment (frequently twenty-first century dancers speak about being born in the wrong age, preferring to live in their version of another). Appadurai suggests that there is a new role for the imagination in our social life, collective aspirations improving upon Durkheimian collective representations mediated through the media. True enough, we might live in an age of 'reflexive modernization' (Giddens 1991), a period characterized by 'the intensive practice of identity' (Friedman 1990: 312), repractised and honed, but there is no external social fact dictating that pace (see the Introduction to this volume). Furthermore, we should, as Gupta and Ferguson (1992) warn us, take care not to assume an easy isomorphism of space, place and culture, or dance patterns: we should – in this history of swing and the sub-shoot jive – be wary and guarded as to 'the process whereby a space achieves a distinctive *identity* as a place' (Gupta and Ferguson 1992: 8, original emphasis). For them, it is a 'convenient fiction' to map culture onto a place and people. We should shy away from these old-fashioned attempts that depict clearly delineated pathways and lines in what is essentially a blurred land of bewilderment, simulacra, doubling and redoubling (Gupta and Ferguson 1992: 10). This history is one of mobile people using their minds as well as their dancing bodies to construct a new and powerful lived world, homeland and body-land, all in a world on the move. This explains why swing dancers in London, Los Angeles, Edinburgh, New York, Herrang and Auckland dress in versions of period costume. The grid for such 'zoot-suit mapping' is complex, partial and multiple, to connect with Gupta and Ferguson's (1992) conclusions.[4]

Anthropologists Hannerz and Appadurai echo this stance in their approaches to the interplay between the global and the local. Both globalization theorists celebrate the local in a global world, the 'glocal'. Appadurai suggests that cultural forms in our modern world are 'fundamentally fractal', that interactions are more 'disjunctive flows' (Appadurai 1990: 20), complex, overlapping and chaotic than stable flows, movements and transfers. These disjunctures are further complicated – 'refracted' in Appadurai's (1990: 9) terminology – by powerful mediascapes and ideoscapes: 'image-centred, narrative-based accounts of strips of reality' imagined and internalized (Appadurai 1990: 9). We can add to this approach Hannerz's (1991) contention that all acts are made meaningful in social life by actors communicating and making new meanings: this extends through and with the new technologies and social practices of the twentieth century, 'creolized' (Hannerz 1987) rather than homogenized. Hannerz's treatment of culture is interpretative, midway between culture as trait (Wallerstein 1990) and culture contained in the individual's diverse world-views (Rapport 1993), and so should be accepted 'lightly'. Hannerz's global cultural economy has space only for the local, for the Nigerian entrepreneur, the bank clerk and the doctor, each with their degrees of involvement in the world system. Likewise, judicious use of Appadurai and his 'scapes' is necessary due to their lack of scope for the individual actor: 'images of agency are increasingly distortions of a world of merchandising so subtle that the consumer is consistently helped to believe that he or she is an actor, where in fact he or she is at best a chooser' (Appadurai 1990: 16). Both dance and globalization theory benefit from a degree of adoption and adaptation.

*****

> Dances in the jooks included the Charleston, the shimmy, the snake hips, the funky butt, the twist, the slow drag, the buzzard lope, the black bottom, the itch, the fish tail, and the grind. Most of these trace back to Africa and can be observed there today (as well as in African and African-American communities around the world). For example Scratching is part of West African ceremonial dance to the god Legba, 'guardian of the crossroads.' Melville Herskovits observed a dance of the Winti people in Suriname in which dancers tug at their clothing as though scratching. This gesture became a standard routine known as the 'itch' in black American social dancing; in tap dancing it was accompanied by eccentric footwork. By the late 1940s the itch had been incorporated into the breakaway of the lindy hop. It turned up again as an embellishment in the rhythm and blues dances of the 1950s. I observed it performed by Bill T. Jones and Arnie Zane. And so we have an African dance that re-emerged in the Southern jooks and from there into the contemporary setting and eventually onto the modern dance stage. (Hazzard-Gordon 1990: 83–84)

*****

The history of dance is one balanced between the diffusion of the dance and the influence of the dancer. Rather than abandon the historical accounts of jive by Batchelor and Erenberg, and the testimonies and imaginations of Norma Miller (Miller and Jensen 1996) and Maya Angelou (1974), we should add to the history of American social swing dance a concern for consciousness, audience emotions and individual struggles, as well as the vested financial and publishing-house interests behind the production and reproduction of the written accounts. This is because the swing era was ushered in by individuals, by chance and good fortune, by changes in technology and the production and dissemination of music, as well as the receptive audience who first cursed and then cheered the dance and music.

In terms of globalization theory, the history of swing (including jive) is an account of the Americanization of dance taking place in the key globalization period between the 1880s and 1925, when global cultures were emerging (Robertson 1990: 19). It is a tale of mobility, creolization and disjuncture. The dance fashion spread chaotically across the US and then further afield – just like the waltz which swept across Europe, spread by performance and word of mouth by ambassadors returning home from the post-Napoleonic Empire 1815 Congress of Vienna. It is almost as though the popularity of these dances comes as a response to the difficulties of war, depression and postwar struggle. Between 1911 and 1918, ragtime emerged in a similar popular vernacular 'black' fashion, though it was subsequently popularized by the 'white' Castles couple who first starred in Paris before touring throughout the US promoting their version of an immigrant working-class dance. The Castles, however, played in opera houses in an attempt to turn the dance into a modern, upmarket 'healthy' dance, dance as a 'beautifier', a dance to cure one of nervous troubles, such as neurasthenia (Castle and Castle 1914). Ragtime has been described as a white dance of grace and posture, but 'passionless' and with controlled, synthesized emotions (Crook 1998). There are parallels here with the designs of Harry Fox and his supposedly more dignified and flowing foxtrot steps which were created at the same time in opposition to the impressionistic and unskilled animal dances (the turkey trot, the grizzly bear, the bunny hug) which some considered had been turning dance halls into farm yards (see Theodossopoulos, this volume). Finally, the Lindy was further popularized at the 1939 New York World Fair which featured the world famous Whitey's Lindy Hoppers dance troupe (as well as *Swingin' the Dream*, Shakespeare's *A Midsummer-Night's Dream* set in jazzy New Orleans and starring Louis Armstrong as Bottom, a play that inspired Erenberg's work).

Modern salsa went through similar dance diffusion, imported and exported by diaspora (dancers, teachers and musicians) and by mediascape (radio and then television, tape, CD, DVD and now internet). In a more recent example of dance diffusion, Wieschiolek (2003: 120) explores the spread of salsa from New York in the 1960s and 1970s, describing it as a concept, a musical and dance mix of Cuban *son* (Spanish and African core harmonic and rhythmic elements with congas, bongos, maracas and clave sticks) and Puerto Rican *bomba*[5] with Americanized styles of rumba and mambo, interpretive boogaloo music and dance from New York in the 1950s and 1960s (Latin music with Afro-American jazz and soul). A blend of ingredients, salsa is named after the Spanish for sauce. It was cooked up amongst the Latin population of New York that was 80 per cent Puerto Rican in the 1960s. Wieschiolek (2003: 121) studies the spread of this sauce around the globe. Her case study of salsa in Hamburg is an example of a dance and music import, an example of internationalization, in my mind, rather than globalization because there is variety to the salsa; it is not a homogeneous style of dance or music.

> Today *salsa* has become internationalized to such an extent that it can no longer be associated with any one country or city. In Cuba, Miami, Colombia and West Africa new trends and styles developed in addition to the ones of the previous centres in New York and Puerto Rico. The boundaries between musical styles are even more blurred than in the early days of *salsa*. For the convenience of record shops and review pages all kinds of Latin dance music are included under the term *salsa*; not only its Cuban ancestors *son*, *guaracha*, *boogaloo*, and *mambo*, but Puerto Rican *plena* and *bomba*, and even the very different Dominican *merengues* and Colombian *cumbias* and *vallenatos*, as well. (Wieschiolek 2003: 121)

The social scientist Robertson (1990) gives us another distinction between internationalization and globalization. For him, the former refers to 'inter nation-state exchanges' (cf. Featherstone 1990: 6), whereas the latter, globalization, relates to a Giddens-inspired 'concrete structuration of the world as a whole' (Robertson 1990: 20, emphasis removed), to a process of global compression, to how the world became increasingly complex and intense, and to how the world is produced and reproduced – as though this occurs autonomously to the individual agent. This new global ecumene is also often given the following characteristics: it is centred in the West, a largely American conception of the world, 'enormously absorptive', and involving 'franchising' with contracting out and the purposeful creation of 'small independent local economies which are linked into multinational production' (Hall 1991: 28, 23; see below). I would suggest that these processes and features of globalization are visible but, after Clifford, Hannerz and Appadurai, they can be interpreted differently – locally, chaotically and with agency and creativity.

My argument here is for an exciting, innovative and creative mixing, matching, adopting, adapting diffusion of dance, its import and export tailor-made for consumer or not. Its history is one of complex and chaotic interplay between global and local. Robert Thompson gives us an evocative example of this diffusion: 'One of the mambo-inspired dances of the 1940s was "the commandos". It emerged ca. 1943 as a danced response to the allied commando raid on Dieppe on the coast of then-Nazi-occupied France. Dancers tapped out "V" for victory in Morse code, performing the commando mambo' (Thompson (2002: 337). In addition to this, Hazzard-Gordon (1990: 158) gives us an account of postwar leisure and entertainment opportunities in the cramped urban ghettoes of Cleveland, Ohio. The areas were swelled by a phase of in-migration of African-Americans from the South who brought with them the practice of 'spontaneous competitive dancing', dance contests to settle disputes and demonstrate dance competence and ability ('breakouts' as forerunners to break-dancing contests): block dances that temporarily expanded the living space of the neighbourhood.

Dance steps – and dances – spread through such local performance opportunities, an example of the possibility of globalization from below, 'nontotalizing' and not reliant upon 'hegemonizing technologies and communications' (Clifford 1994: 327, after Brecher, Brown and Cutler 1993). These are all examples of the angular fluidity of dance development.

Modern Jive

> When trumpeter Jimmy Maxwell joined Benny Goodman in 1939, he had to memorise the 210 scores in the book in only two weeks. 'I never really knew how I did it, because I don't have a good memory.' Later Maxwell realized that it was from watching girls dance. 'I would look at the next phrase and look out at a girl and she'd look up at you and then you'd keep waiting for her to come around again.' (Batchelor 1997: 43)

Sometimes it is the musician who is following the dancer. According to Batchelor (1997: 43), the Lindy can be danced to a six- or an eight-beat count whereas traditional jive is danced to the simpler six count. Batchelor is describing the traditional jive that came out of swing. He is not describing the late twentieth-century modern jive phenomenon presently reaching out from the UK: a dance that 'crosses over bars of music' (Keeble 2003a) and so can be danced to most types of music with a strong beat; a dance, then, that is not identified with any particular music; a dance contentious for its lack of footwork; a dance that its critics argue is not a dance at all. Like salsa, one might now describe jive as a concept and a dance with many variations. In Britain since the 1980s, a basic jive has been propounded by a dance franchise called Ceroc, and a dance federation called Le Roc French Jive Federation, both of which are examples of dance diffusion, import–export, globalization and a dance-historical and popular-culture imagination held by the dancers themselves.

Every night of the week, dotted across the United Kingdom but centred about London, the Midlands and Edinburgh, Ceroc is danced by old and young dancers. In 2010, there were over 345,000 dancers attending Ceroc nights at over 100 locations. There are annual Ceroc national championships bringing in international dancers from as far afield as Australia and New Zealand. This 'dance import' has now been turned into a franchise and 'dance export' with venues being tested or opening in France, Ireland and the US. The popular history and myth of this dance is that it is derived from the French *le roc*, a simplification of the jitterbug that the liberating GIs 'left behind' at the end of the Second World War. In the 1960s and 1970s the jitterbug-jive continued as a jive to disco beats in France whilst, elsewhere, new generations of dancers started twisting and disco dancing separated from other dancers. Christine Keeble was one of the pioneering jive dancers in the UK and has written a widely accepted, if brief, account of its origins in the UK:

> When the French learned jitterbug from GI's [*sic*] of the American liberating army, they were given no formal dance tuition and learned by imitation.

> The six beat and eight beat footwork patterns and swing outs were lost and footwork consisted of a simple stepping in and out. The French style was more upright, very tight and featured the characteristic 'gear-stick' action (the elbow of the man's holding arm tight to his chest). Moves or figures crossed over bars of music and intricate new ways of turning the girl developed. This style was well suited to the sounds of the eighties and nineties. (Keeble 2003b)

Sonny Watson's personal history of dance gives a very different account of the development of jive. His is an American perspective, removed from British rivalries but one nevertheless caught up in American dance debates. His lengthy, multi-voiced account suggests that the form of jive found in Europe is not American. It is, in fact, a European styling of what is thought to be American:

> The Jive Dance was first popular in the 1940s. The Jive was originally the European's (*U.K.*) version of the American Jitterbug and/or East Coast Swing during WWII (*who keeps trying to re-sell us something we already have*) ... Most Europeans do what they call the 'American Jive' a name that came briefly from WWII when the Jitterbug was called Jitterbug-Jive. When the war ended, the term Jitterbug-Jive ended as well in the States. The Europeans however kept using the name Jive, which supposedly is their version of what is done here in the States.
>
> Modern Jive or 'French Jive' in the UK was introduced in the 1980's [*sic*] to make it easier to teach people to do swing in the clubs. The dance is taught with no footwork, just walking the patterns which can be many. The names of modern Jive usually come from the club or association that taught the version being done and usually leads into a more structured form of swing dance as time goes on. It is similar to what people do here in the States before they learn a structured form of swing which we call just 'winging it', which has no form, lead or follow skills etc., although in the Modern Jive it is taught with patterns, lead and follow, timing rather than just the 'winging it' above so there is some structure to it more than one might think. The music is similar to the West Coast Swing format of dancing to all styles of music rather than just one specific genre/era with their dances or socials being called Freestyles ... Jive is an empty, fake, weak form of swing dance when compared to the others!!! ... nuff said! (Watson 1999, original emphasis)

Watson's passionate presumption is that the jive dance can be located and placed according to nation and national and nostalgic sentiment, and that the dance is diluted as it is diffused. For Watson, the authentic jive is 'hep', real, authentic, pure, lively and skilled, whereas the modern/French jive is inauthentic, simple and a poor but popular relation. Watson's critique is more against the quality and popularity of the dance than against its globalization. This is dance 'de-evolution' for a mass market.

The corporate history of the development of the dance differs from both the accounts above in that it is an account of one man's invention: James Cronin witnessed the dance at debutantes' balls in France, simplified it and brought it back to the UK where it was so popular that by 1991 he had turned 'ceroc', an abbreviation of *c'est le roc* ('this is rock 'n' roll'), into a successful business franchise, Ceroc Enterprises Ltd, one which listed moves and qualified dance teachers in-house (and which used to ban rival dance teachers from their venues when they started out). Apparently, it was in 1987 that Cronin and ceroc cabaret dancer and music-industry lawyer Sylvia Coleman developed their winning business partnership for the franchise. This partnership established the franchise around London. They had their own teacher-training course to ensure quality and consistency in ceroc dancing and training whilst Le Roc Federation expanded as a loose grouping of enthusiastic jive dancers and teachers. Le Roc-ers disliked the 'dance as business' direction Cronin was taking – as well as the rule-bound, 'straitjacketed' structure of this new dance. During this period of consolidation and split, Cronin's dance colleague Nicky Haslam took ceroc to Australia. In 1991, Haslam emigrated and set up the Ceroc Dance Company in Sydney with Mark Harding. They subsequently split their dance empires into Ceroc and Modern Jive Dance Company, and Ceroc Australia. Further to this, Angelique Meyer had previously successfully exported the ceroc model to her native New Zealand in 1988, eventually forming Ceroc New Zealand in 1990. Ceroc 'down under' are all variants on Cronin's ceroc by those originally involved in establishing the dance in London, though they are each autonomous businesses. With their regulations and legal structures, these leisure and entertainment practices are examples of globalization from above as the same model is rolled out in different places around the world. At the same time as these developments down under, Frenchman Franck Pauly opened the first ceroc franchise in Scotland. More recently, in 2003, Cronin sold his financial stake in Ceroc and passed the business side on to Mike Ellard, one of the longest serving ceroc teachers, a sale which many ceroc-ers resent because it highlighted the unemotional 'business' side lying behind their dancing passions.

Ceroc now advertises itself as a 'fusion of jive and salsa'.[6] And yet it is also sometimes still referred to as a 'French hybrid of jive and rock 'n' roll' (Walker 2000) to reflect its roots. It is a dance with approximately twenty basic jive moves, and several hundred current intermediate and advanced moves that are taught from an ever-changing 'ceroc moves' handbook of accepted, current and legitimate moves which have all been vetted and approved by the teachers and franchise owners. Sometimes ceroc is referred to as 'modern French jive' so that it is not confused with ballroom jive (an exaggerated knee action from a side-to-side chassis and back-step replace) that has its own jitterbug background. The Cronin ceroc 'springing' style is different from the continental *'Roc-ing'* which is very upright in posture, closed, tight and with a 'gear-stick' looking hold. This makes it appear to be slightly different from the more individualistic 'dip-drop-seducer' styles that can be found in the Antipodes where there are strong influences of 'dirty dancing' and lambada, the latter a dance with hip rolls and weight shifts between touching bodies (cf. Keeble 2003b).

Ceroc's success thus far has been its versatility and flexibility as a dance style that fits with so much dance music, and its ability as a franchise to position and reposition itself in the market so that it can now become more salsa influenced and so benefit from recent public fascination with the Latin exotic. From a French import, it has been turned into a British export, more global than absorptive as it pushes its style and concept. It is also individualistic (one man's corporation appealing to an increasingly mobile and leisure-oriented population of singletons), nationalistic (British, Australian, New Zealander), nostalgic (identified, romantically, with the Second World War Anglo-American swing era), and geared to the mass market (few foot patterns or body postures, catering especially for the dance novice). Whilst these criteria have resulted in a ceroc success story, ceroc is not without its critics: Watson (1999) refers to it as a fake dance; informants of mine have criticized it as 'the McDonalds of dance' (Skinner 2003); many non-ceroc dancers ridicule it as a non-dance; and many more have vilified Cronin for copyrighting and profiteering from a dance – ironically, as the ceroc figurehead, Cronin has often been attacked by his own ceroc dancers.

Global Dance and the Imagination

Lacking emotional input, not needing many skills, and not belonging to any particular place, people or music, ceroc has nevertheless confounded its critics to become a most popular dance form in the UK. Whereas Keeble (2003a) makes the point that ceroc, *le roc* and cosmopolitan jive clubs came up with a new dance, distinctive and with hundreds of new moves, Cronin is adamant – and careful to note – that he did not invent a new dance.[7] Instead, he draws attention to the structure of the evenings, to the beginner and intermediate tuition periods, to the freestyle before and after them, and to the notion of 'taxi dancers' whose task is to chaperone male and female novice dancers through their steps. With this formula, Cronin was reviving a traditional dance-hall practice from the 1920s and 1930s pre-swing era when taxi-dance hostesses worked the dance floor, using their body as a resource (Cressey 1968; see also Erenberg 1998: 24). Cronin refined and packaged this taxi-dancing concept for a modern and politically correct market, choosing attractive dancers and encouraging them to promote a veneer of warmth for paying customers. This is the continuation of an 'emotional labour' (Hochschild 1983) practice, harnessing the desires and sometimes lurid imaginations of the customer, turning their fantasies into commodities. In the entertainment world this is practically unavoidable, yet it has its critics when taken too far, such as when the young and attractive dance instructor uses the clients' emotions and loneliness to coerce elderly widows and middle-aged single male dance students to attend dance workshops and to sign up for expensive courses such as those at Arthur Murray studios or ceroc weekend workshops ('cerocshops').

Ceroc is a modern-day franchise taking a leaf out of the Arthur Murray dance business, a franchise that has been in existence since 1912 when it was established by a New York-based German who had started off as a student of the Castles, the ragtime dance couple. When enrolled on a business course at Georgia Tech, Murray first gained national attention by successfully teaching over one thousand children, and second by organizing a musical radio broadcast for his dance students in the vicinity (the first ever radio broadcast of live music). Murray went on to establish his Arthur Murray dance franchise on the back of a thriving and novel mail-order strategy: learn to dance by post – one foot at a time! In this enterprise, Murray was clearly harnessing the technological developments of his age. In 1950, with the arrival of television, Murray kept the post going, but switched from the radio to present the highly successful *Arthur Murray Dance Party* on CBS television. It was Murray's mail-order strategy that was eventually reworked by Cronin: Ceroc Enterprises Ltd structure their franchises around buying, selling and operating within postcode areas. The postcode franchisee has the guarantee that no other ceroc competition will take place in their purchased 'space'. Another similarity between the franchises lies in the nature of their internal controls and activities: both Arthur Murray and ceroc dance franchises regulate their dancers and instructors with specific teaching procedures and manuals, their own in-house events, competitions and judges, and they both take moves from other dances and give them their own 'call' names (steps from the popular shag and Suzie Q were given Murray names such as 'peel the apple', 'cut that apple', and popular jitterbug turning moves were given new names such as 'the yoyo' and 'the wurlitzer' by ceroc teachers).

In terms of globalization theory, the Arthur Murray and various ceroc franchises are modern attempts to capitalize – quite literally – upon the dance enthusiast by absorbing competitors' dance styles and organizations; by promoting the universal and homogeneous as opposed to the particular and heterogeneous; and by appealing to new cosmopolitan citizens who, lacking the stability of transgenerational knowledge and organic relations passed down by family associations and ties, turn to a mobile, decontextualized knowledge where they can develop their own sense of competence and expertise, feeling at home and comfortable in themselves and their body movements and regional migrations, happy and at ease – 'coherent' to use Hannerz's (1990: 249) turn of phrase. In a restless and runaway modern world of movement, migration and 'reflexive modernization' (Beck, Giddens and Lash 1994; see also Giddens 1991), erratic global flows, disjuncture and the wish and desire – 'proto-narratives' (Appadurai 1996) – for possible lives, it is still satisfying to see the dance diffusing, the story of jive connecting and disconnecting with swing, global (in ceroc) but not homogeneous (with its rivals), competitive and absorptive but ever creative, and forever imaginative.

Notes

1. See C. Calloway, 'Are You Hep to the Jive'. New York: Sony/Columbia Records, 1994[1940].
2. See B. Goodman, 'Sing, Sing, Sing', New York: Bluebird RCA, 1987[1937].
3. Lyrics from P. Bradford, 'The Original Black Bottom Dance', New York: Okeh, 1926.
4. See also Gilroy's tracking of counter-culture sounds of modernity on vinyl which span the Black Atlantic (Gilroy 1993).

5. *Bomba* is a style in which African and European instruments such as the congas, the guitar and brass are played and sung to European melodies and harmonies with African call and response, an African challenge dance mixed with French court dance.
6. See www.ceroc.com, retrieved 20 April 2011.
7. Interview with James Cronin, 2003.

References

Anderson, B. 1994. 'Exodus', *Critical Inquiry* 2: 314–27.
Angelou, M. 1974. *Singing and Swinging and Getting Merry Like Christmas*. New York: Random House.
Appadurai, A. 1990. 'Disjuncture and Difference in the Global Cultural Economy', *Public Culture* 2(2): 1–23.
―――― 1996. *Modernity at Large: Cultural Dimensions of Globalization*. Minneapolis: University of Minnesota Press.
Batchelor, C. 1997. *This Thing Called Swing: A Study of Swing Music and the Lindy Hop, the Original Swing Dance*. London: Original Lindy Hop Collection.
Beck, U., A. Giddens and S. Lash (eds). 1994. *Reflexive Modernisation: Politics, Tradition and Aesthetics in the Modern Social Order*. Cambridge: Polity Press.
Bradford, P. 1926. *The Original Black Bottom Dance*. New York: Okeh.
Brecher, J., J. Brown and J. Cutler (eds). 1993. *Global Visions: Beyond the New World Order*. Boston: South End Press.
Calloway, C. 1944. *Hepster's Dictionary*. New York: Self-published.
Castle, I., and V. Castle. 1914. *Modern Dancing*. New York: Harper and Row.
Clifford, J. 1994. 'Diasporas', *Cultural Anthropology* 9(3): 302–38.
Cook, S. 1998. 'Passionless Dancing and Passionate Reform: Respectability, Modernism, and the Social Dancing of Irene and Vernon Castle', in W. Washabaugh (ed.), *The Passion of Music and Dance*. Oxford: Berg, pp.133–50.
Crease, R. 1996. 'The Future of the Lindy and the New York Swing Dance Society: An Epilogue', in N. Miller and E. Jensen (eds), *Swingin' at the Savoy: The Memoir of a Jazz Dancer*. Philadelphia: Temple University Press, pp.255–61.
Cressey, P. 1968[1932]. *The Taxi-Dance Hall: A Sociological Study in Commercialized Recreation and City Life*. New York: Greenwood Press.
Erenberg, L. 1998. *Swingin' the Dream: Big Band Jazz and the Rebirth of American Culture*. Chicago: University of Chicago Press.
Featherstone, M. 1990. 'Global Culture: An Introduction', in M. Featherstone (ed.), *Global Culture: Nationalism, Globalization and Modernity*. London: Sage, pp.1–14.
Friedman, J. 1990. 'Being in the World: Localization and Globalization', *Theory, Culture and Society* 7(2): 311–28.
Giddens, A. 1991. *Modernity and Self-identity: Self and Society in Late Modernity*. Cambridge: Polity Press.
Gilroy, P. 1987. *There Ain't No Black in the Union Jack: The Cultural Politics of Race and Nation*. London: Hutchinson.
―――― 1993. *The Black Atlantic: Modernity and Double Consciousness*. Cambridge, MA: Harvard University Press.
Gottschild, B. 2000. *Waltzing in the Dark: African American Vaudeville and Race Politics in the Swing Era*. New York: St Martin's Press.
―――― 2003. *The Black Dancing Body: A Geography from Coon to Cool*. New York: Palgrave Macmillan.

Gupta, A., and J. Ferguson. 1992. 'Beyond "Culture": Space, Identity, and the Politics of Difference', *Cultural Anthropology* 7(1): 6–23.
Hall, S. 1991. 'The Local and the Global: Globalization and Ethnicity', in A. King (ed.), *Culture, Globalization and the World System: Contemporary Conditions for the Representation of Identity*. London: Macmillan, pp.19–40.
Hannerz, U. 1987. 'The World in Creolization'. *Africa* 57(4): 546–59.
⎯⎯⎯ 1990. 'Cosmopolitans and Locals in World Culture', in M. Featherstone (ed.), *Global Culture: Nationalism, Globalization and Modernity*. London: Sage, pp.237–51.
⎯⎯⎯ 1991. 'Scenarios for Peripheral Cultures', in A. King (ed.), *Culture, Globalization and the World System: Contemporary Conditions for the Representation of Identity*. London: Macmillan, pp.107–28.
Hazzard-Gordon, K. 1990. *Jookin': The Rise of Social Dance Formations in African-American Culture*. Philadelphia: Temple University Press.
Hochschild, A. 1983. *The Managed Heart: The Commercialisation of Human Feeling*. Berkeley: University of California Press.
Jameson, F. 1989. 'Nostalgia for the Present'. *South Atlantic Quarterly* 88(2): 517–37.
Jones, L. 1963. *Blues People: Negro Music in White America*. New York: William Morrow & Company.
Keeble, C. 2003a. 'How to Jive/LeRoc/French Jive: Ceroc & LeRoc'. Retrieved 11 September 2009 from: http://www.howtojive.com/intro-ceroc-leroc.htm.
⎯⎯⎯ 2003b. 'How to Jive/LeRoc/French Jive: Spotlight on Ceroc'. Retrieved 11 September 2009 from: http://www.howtojive.com/spotlight-ceroc.htm.
Kirk, A. 1936. 'All the Jive is Gone'. New York: Decca Records
Milkowski, B. 2001. *Swing It! An Annotated History of Jive*. New York: Billboard Books.
Rapport, N. 1993. *Diverse World-views in an English Village*. Edinburgh: Edinburgh University Press.
Robertson, R. 1990. 'Mapping the Global Conditions: Globalization as the Central Concept', in M. Featherstone (ed.), *Global Culture: Nationalism, Globalization and Modernity*. London: Sage, pp.15–30.
Saul, S. 2003. *Freedom Is, Freedom Ain't: Jazz and the Making of the Sixties*. Cambridge, MA: Harvard University Press.
Skinner, J. 2003. 'At the Busk and After Dusk: Ceroc and the Construction of Dance Times and Places', *Focaal* 42: 117–27.
Thompson, R. 2002. 'Teaching the People to Triumph over Time: Notes from the World of Mambo', in S. Sloat (ed.), *Caribbean Dance from Abakuá to Zouk: How Movement Shapes Identity*. Gainesville: University Press of Florida, pp.336–44.
Walker, V. 2000. 'Why So Many Fitness Fanatics Have Decided to Take to the Dance Floor', *The Times*, 19 August. Retrieved 15 May 2000 from: http://www.cerocnet.co.uk/medias.htm.
Wallerstein, I. 1990. 'Culture as the Ideological Battleground of the Modern World System', in M. Featherstone (ed.), *Global Culture: Nationalism, Globalization and Modernity*. London: Sage, pp.31–55.
Watson, S. 1999. 'The Jive'. Retrieved 12 September 2009 from: http://www.streetswing.com/histmain/z3jive.htm.
Wieschiolek, H. 2003. '"Ladies, Just Follow His Lead!": Salsa, Gender and Identity', in E. Archetti and N. Dyck (eds), *Sport, Dance and Embodied Identities*. Oxford: Berg, pp.115–38.

Chapter 2

Ballet Culture and the Market: A Transnational Perspective

Helena Wulff

In the ballet world, the market tends to be regarded with ambivalence. Ballet people are disturbed by the belief that the market wants to buy other 'commodities' than they are prepared to sell – i.e. unforgettable experiences of ballet art. For the audience, on the other hand, the milieu of gilded opera foyers and the opportunity to rub shoulders with famous people in the intermission may be what matters. This chapter discusses the market in the ballet world by applying a transnational perspective which uncovers both homogenizing and heterogenizing cultural processes produced by similarities in work practices and differences in funding systems. One centre and periphery structure in the ballet world follows transnational economic domination patterns through American corporate sponsoring, but there is also a separate structure of old and new ballet centres, which negates much rhetoric about globalization, especially in terms of American domination.[1]

The Emergence of the Transnational Ballet World: Politics, Mentors, Patrons

Ballet came about in the fourteenth century as an Italian Renaissance pastime that noble families supported with their increasing affluence (Wulff 1998, 2008).[2] These families took part in a pre-classical dance which combined peasant folk dancing and court processions. In the sixteenth century, the Florentine Catherine de Medici married the French Crown Prince Henry. Because of Medici's interest in lavish entertainment, and her position at the court in Paris, she invited and supported Italian musicians and dance teachers, among them Balthasar de Beaujoyeux, who created what has come to be regarded as the first ballet production, *Ballet Comique de la Reine*. But it was Louis XIV, an ardent ballet lover and dancer, who began a professionalization of ballet by organizing training academies and commercial theatres. The eighteenth century saw ballet companies in other European countries as well. Yet it was in Paris during the Romantic period that classical ballet gained

Figure 2.1 Gina Tse in Swan Lake with Royal Swedish Ballet.

the particular form of etherealness by which it is still characterized. This happened when the Swedish-Italian Marie Taglioni danced *La Sylphide* on pointe in 1832 to great acclaim, dressed in a delicate bell-shaped tutu. Taglioni had a Danish partner, August Bournonville, who was to develop a ballet style in Copenhagen. During the same period, in St Petersburg the French dancer Marius Petipa choreographed classics such as *Sleeping Beauty*, *Swan Lake* (in collaboration with Lev Ivanov) and some of *The Nutcracker*.

At the beginning of the twentieth century Russian culture did not attract any particular interest in Europe, but French art and lifestyle were greatly admired in Russia. When France and Russia became political allies against Germany, artistic exchange between the two countries was encouraged and funded by both governments. It was during this time that Sergei Diaghilev set up the Ballets Russes, which gave annual seasons in Paris and went on tour, mostly to London and New York. Because of the revolution in 1917, Diaghilev never went back to Russia. George Balanchine, who worked as a choreographer with Ballets Russes, was approached by Lincoln Kirstein, an American writer from a wealthy family, about establishing the School of American Ballet in New York, which they did together, as well as the New York City Ballet in the 1940s. By then the American Ballet Theatre had already been operating in New York for about a decade. One of the Ballets Russes dancers, Anglo-Irish Ninette de Valois, was to found a national ballet company in Britain, which became the Royal Ballet in London in the 1950s. Thereby the five old ballet centres – Paris, Copenhagen, St Petersburg, New York and London – were born. They all acquired transnational reputations based on their different schools, which have been conceptualized in terms of 'national ballet styles' seemingly expressing the essence of national characters, as it were. There are thus the 'chic' French, the 'cute' Danish, the 'dramatic' Russian, the 'athletic' American and the 'reserved' British ballet styles. There was also an Italian ballet style which emerged out of Milan, but it has never been identified as a national ballet style, possibly because Italy was not really united as a nation.

World politics, financial patrons and impressarios such as Diaghilev and Kirstein, who were driven by a passion for ballet, and artistic mentors who tend to be forceful individuals and choreographers, have thus built and structured ballet since its inception. Many of the influential figures in the ballet world have been foreigners working outside their country of origin, sometimes in political exile. These circumstances seem to have released a creative energy which they probably would not have had the opportunity to cultivate in their native countries. This also applies to those contemporary choreographers who have come to establish new centres for ballet and dance. There are thus, for example, Americans John Neumeier in Hamburg and William Forsythe in Frankfurt-am-Main, the Czech Jiri Kylián in the Hague, as well as French Maurice Béjart who worked in Brussels and Lausanne.

The historical association of ballet with court life and the upper classes is still being nurtured in the world of national classical ballet, where the companies have patrons and trustees, often royals who have a true interest in ballet. There are also ballet societies and friendship circles with a base in the upper classes that have been important for building audiences, and still often contribute financial support as well.

Market, Ballet and Distrust

Dancers are hardly unique among artists for regarding the market with unease and distrust. In art worlds, the market is often regarded as a threat to genuine artistic quality since artists who are aiming towards acquiring a reputation feel that they have to make accommodations to the market, which they would rather not do. Bensman (1983: 27) traces 'the familiar devils of economics' in the arts back to the Church, the aristocracy, the dynastic and national states and their religious, political and national ambitions. The development of the performing arts in the nineteenth century can be attributed both to mass audiences and patrons, states and municipalities. During the latter half of the twentieth century, the performing arts have become dependent on the welfare state; however, as Bensman (1983) points out, this may produce crises if such support is discontinued. Bourdieu (1993) notes that with the emergence of an art market, artists did get rid of the demands of patrons but found themselves having to negotiate with commercial interests. Ballet art versus the market was a common topic of conversation in the ballet world during my fieldwork, usually in terms of an opposition: ballet against market.

A part of dancers' distrust of the market included their own marketing and press departments. The dancers more often than not criticized the marketing of their company for being inefficient. At one point in my research in Stockholm, the dancers asked the head of the marketing department at the Opera House to come to a meeting and explain why she did not market them more. She then defended herself by saying that 'ballet doesn't need any marketing. It sells itself'. This obviously angered the dancers who then formed their own press group aiming to give advice to the marketing department about how to market ballet. But the tension remained. The marketing lady confessed to me in private that 'ballet is difficult to sell', referring to the shortage of money and staff and that only a fraction of all the press releases that are sent out are ever published.

The dancers wanted to open up the company and backstage to the world outside the theatre, invite a wider audience, broadcast trailers of upcoming performances on television, sell cheap tickets at hotels, and perform in schools. Most of the companies in my study had done part or all of this at some point. In order to reach new audiences, it also happened that marketing departments initated events in which dancers performed in shopping malls, department stores, on cruises as well as outdoors on open-air stages in parks in the summer. During my fieldwork, the Royal Ballet and Covent Garden got a lot of bad press. This was before the renovation of the Royal Opera House had begun, and the battles over power and funding were intense, as was the criticism of Covent Garden as 'elitist'. As a way of trying to mellow the criticism, a BBC team was allowed to make a backstage television documentary, *The House*, which revealed mismanagement and animosities between people in key positions at the Opera House. Such embarrassing revelations did, however, increase ticket sales, or so I was told by one of the ballet producers.

Although dancers have a basic distrust of marketing, they understand that it is unavoidable. But they do need to to be prepared, especially when media are involved. This is not always the case, such as one grey January morning when a television crew, with their huge bags and bulky equipment, stumbled into a class at the American Ballet Theatre. If the dancers had been informed in advance they would have had the time to practice and perhaps applied some make-up, and some of them would probably even have stayed away since they were out of shape after the Christmas holiday. Now they were moaning quietly trying not to show their discomfort with the strong spots and the camera men zooming in on one dancer at a time who struggled to look good.

One important explanation as to why dancers have a problem with marketing is that it is more often than not done through the media, which rarely conveys pictures, video or text about ballet or ballet culture in ways that dancers recognize: 'Watching themselves on video, dancers note that the dancing does not look from the outside like it feels from the inside while doing it' (Wulff 1998: 9). They rarely think that they are at their best in pictures or on film. Indeed, dancers frequently pointed out to me that something gets lost in mediated ballet – even though photography, film, video, text and the internet featuring dance may be imaginative and interesting pieces of art in themselves, they cannot represent or create the vibrating closeness, including a certain amount of unpredictability, of a live performance. So much can happen in a live performance: not only can things go wrong and mistakes be made, but dancers can also be inspired by the presence of a receptive audience. Unimaginable ballet art might be born on stage.

The marketing department at the American Ballet Theatre claims to be the first company in the ballet world to have been doing 'aggressive marketing'. This included both illustrated newspaper articles and advertisements, posters on town, features on television and radio at the beginning of a new season or a tour and gimmicks like famous dancers dancing on paint on a canvas which was then sold as a piece of art. On a tour to Chicago, dancers performed a section from *Swan Lake* at 8 a.m. at the zoo with real swans in the background which was filmed and broadcast on local television. The alleged 'agressiveness' of the marketing at the American Ballet Theatre was to a great extent a product of the competition and conflict that exists between itself and the other major New York company, the New York City Ballet. This tension runs especially high once a year in the spring when the American Ballet Theatre has its eight-week 'Met Season' at the Metropolitan Opera House next door to the State Theatre of the New York City Ballet at the Lincoln Center. There was, however, a certain regret at the marketing department of the American Ballet Theatre over the good times during the 1970s. This was during the height of the 'dance boom' and even people who did not have a special interest in dance or ballet went to ballet performances. New York was called 'the Mecca of dance' attracting dance and ballet people from all over the world. Some of these people, such as Mikhail Baryshnikov, came from the Soviet Union and defected, which meant a huge media coverage and thereby publicity for ballet. This also happened, although to a lesser extent, in Paris and London. The most famous ballet defector to Paris was undoubtedly Rudolf Nureyev who became a permanent guest artist with the Royal Ballet and eventually artistic director of the Paris Opéra Ballet.

It was Nureyev who discovered Sylvie Guillem when she was a young corps de ballet dancer, gave her the opportunity to do solo parts and made her a star aged nineteen. A principal guest artist with the Royal Ballet for many years, Sylvie Guillem has certainly established a name for herself, quite independently of the companies she has worked with. She is a good example of individual marketing by contrast with the marketing of the whole company: the two often have different and conflicting agendas. In a widespread advertisement for Rolex watches, Guillem did her celebrated routine of raising her leg straight up, almost above her head, illustrating 'six o'clock'. Famous dancers have agents who arrange guest performances for them, often abroad, given that they are skilled enough at negotiating about time off from their company schedule. Agents also look for openings in other companies for dancers which can be used in negotiations for higher salaries or more performances in the company a dancer is in. This primarily applies to those who have transnational fame, some of whom develop quite sophisticated marketing strategies by nurturing the media (including critics) through free tickets, invitations to dress rehearsals, parties, even weddings and other more private functions. Some dancers would not mind launching themselves on a kind of celebrity 'cool' glitterati market, but they prefer to keep a low profile because they do not feel particularly comfortable at rock concerts or fashion shows. They may also be reluctant to announce that they are gay, which is a status which is likely to be revealed were they to join the glitterati circuit.

One ethnographic instance of the conflict between marketing the whole company versus an individual dancer venturing out on his or her own took place one day at lunchtime in the green room at Covent Garden. Russian Irek Mukhamedov, a former Bolshoi dancer who had been launched as Rudolf Nureyev's heir in the West by the Royal Ballet marketing department (although he had not actually come close to Nureyev's extraordinary success), was urging his colleagues to buy the biography of him by Jeffery Taylor (1994). 'You can buy a signed copy for only £19 at the box office!' he was informing us all. The other dancers, who were having their sandwiches and snacks, said nothing. No one seemed to be planning to buy his book.

There are slightly different markets for ballet dancers depending on whether they have an intellectual inclination, such as Sylvie Guillem and Deborah Bull, or glamour capital such as Darcey Bussell, all acclaimed ballerinas with the Royal Ballet in the 1990s. Sylvie Guillem, for example, arranged her own video, titled *Evidentia*, which was originally made for television. In this video she introduces five new dance pieces, some of them by major contemporary choreographers, by dancing a short section of alternative choreography and talking about life and dance. Both Deborah Bull (1999) and Darcey Bussell (1998) have published autobiographies, although the one by Bussell is said to be 'with Judith Mackrell', a London dance critic. Bussell's book is a rather conventional ballet autobiography about the ups and downs of a prominent ballet career, including an account of when she had a wax model made of her at Madame Tussauds and her subsequent shock when she learnt that the model (herself, in a sense) would only be kept if her career continued to be successful. If not, it would be melted down! Bull's autobiography is a more outspoken diary of one of the recent turbulent years at Covent Garden. She did read some extracts of it for BBC Radio 4. One unusual PR gimmick which she describes in her book was when she was dancing at a press launch of a new Rolls Royce model: after she had finished her seven-minute surprise performance, the backdrop fell down uncovering the new car! Bull has established a reputation not only as a writer on dance discussing funding politics, fitness and diet schemes, but also as a speaker on dance at 'lecture demonstrations' in schools and at conferences where dancers perform a short section and then they or someone else explain the dancing verbally, at lectures for general audiences, and on television in ballet documentaries. Since Bull is a 'talking dancer' she has been a member of arts organizations, such as the board of the South Bank Centre in London and the Arts Council of England.

Otherwise the marketing of ballet companies is predictably done according to casting. Dancers the management want to promote or keep on top, for example, get to do leading roles and are then offered to journalists for interviews for advance features in the press (daily newspapers, dance magazines) and on chat shows on television and radio. It is likely that, as with the marketing done by famous individual dancers outside their company, focusing on one dancer at a time and personal biography is more efficient in attracting a new audience to ballet than when companies are presented as a collective but more anonymous entity. One way to cultivate a sense of community in ballet companies is to post positive reviews and feature articles about the company on noticeboards backstage, but not articles that are about only one dancer.

When Darcey Bussell appeared in a headshot with what looked like a diamond in her mouth in the glossy magazine the *Tatler*, she was doing it primarily in her capacity of a celebrity promoting herself; promoting ballet in general and her company was a secondary objective. It is not unusual that dancers, both men and women, do modelling, but often they do it anonymously. Occasionally, dancers are asked to take part in regular advertisements promoting all kind of products from mineral water to credit cards, airlines and sportswear, often displaying a characteristic ballet step which most people cannot perform, or just jumping upwards like Swedish dancer Anneli Alhanko did in an advertisement saying 'milk makes your legs strong'. In the 1970s, Anneli Alhanko and her partner Per Arthur Segerström had their picture on a Swedish stamp, since Alhanko in particular was hailed as an outstanding ballerina. To some extent Alhanko's recognition should be seen in the context of the new awareness of ballet and dance which the dance boom in London and New York had created at the time.

Besides ballet performances, there are a number of smaller commodities or cultural artefacts that circulate in the ballet marketplace and contribute to 'selling' ballet in general, a particular company, a certain tour or a star dancer. These include commercial videos, CD recordings, books, postcards, tee-shirts, cups, umbrellas, posters, even jewellery and other souvenirs that are for sale at box offices, stalls in theatres, and at ballet wear and book shops. They also display point shoes, an object of great fetishism in the ballet world, worn and signed by famous dancers (Wulff 1998, 2002). There are ballet and dance cd-roms, such as William Forsythe's *Improvisation Technologies or Self Meant to Govern*, an 'installation' from 1994 which is both an art work and an introduction to Forsythe's choreographic ballet style while promoting Forsythe as a choreographer.

The Greatest Dancer: Nureyev and his Market

Even after their death, dancers can be major agents in attracting attention to the ballet market. Those who have succeeded as choreographers have their ballets held by trusts, such as the Balanchine Trust, although the leading dancers for whom a choreography was first made may inherit the performance rights (Wulff 1998). When Rudolf Nureyev died in 1993, a number of European and American foundations were established from his enormous fortune, aiming to provide funding for young dancers, a museum in Paris, and to support dancers with AIDS. Born a poor Tartar in Stalinist Russia, Nureyev had, against all possible odds, not only a brilliant career in the West, but he had also amassed a vast amount of wealth. At a Christie's auction in New York, art works and furnishings from his New York flat, as well as jewellery and costumes he had worn, were sold for $7,945,910, regarded as an extraordinary amount even by the chairman of Christie's America. The record sale was explained by 'Nureyev's personal magnetism and with Christie's ability to market him' (Gladstone 1995: 21). This transnational event took place in Park Avenue in two halls where art collectors, dancers and fans had gathered. In the back room there were two big screens showing what was happening in the other room, the gallery. The crier, who was dressed in a tuxedo and standing in the gallery, was handling bids from abroad via telephone, as well as from the gallery and the back room. He started out carefully with a head-band on a cushion. Then he turned up the tempo: a jacket from the ballet *Don Quixote* was sold for $32,000. Now the audience was excited, and the crier incited them even more. One pair of pink worn-out ballet shoes was sold for $8,000. 'Amazing for sombody else's' (used ballet shoes) the lady next to me, an ex-dancer, was saying. She was shocked, also, because she had obviously been hoping to be able to buy at least a pair of Nureyev's ballet shoes. When the jacket Nureyev wore when he was dancing Albrecht in *Giselle*, one of his major roles, was shown, a flicker went through the audience. People remembered his dancing, both the dancers who danced with him and the ballet lovers and fans who were sad and slightly disgusted over this event; meanwhile, professional and amateur antique dealers predictably behaved in a more businesslike manner.

Much has been written in the press and in popular biographies about Nureyev, his life and his fortune. Dance and theatre writer Otis Stuart (1995) devotes a chapter to 'the Nureyev industry', mentioning the fact that Nureyev had seven homes, including an island. Nureyev was excellent at marketing himself both in the ballet world and outside, which importantly reflected back on his position in the ballet world, increasing his prestige there. Stuart points at the impact of Nureyev's two advisors: one impressario on career matters and one financial advisor on business matters. Dance anthropologists such as Judith Lynne Hanna (1988: 143) have commented how the flamboyant Rudolf Nureyev captured ballet audiences and made 'big bucks', thereby earning respect as well as improving the status of the male dancer. Writing about another Soviet defector who has also made a lot of money, Mikhail Baryshnikov, dance historian Joan Cass (1993) describes how Baryshnikov came to New York in the mid 1970s, acquiring great 'cool' capital by acting in films and on Broadway, and even promoting a line of perfume and cosmetics.

Marketing is one area of heterogeneity in the transnational ballet world. The Royal Swedish Ballet at the Opera House in Stockholm had been instructed to democratize the audience as a part of a government agenda to 'make culture accessible for all citizens irrespective of age, home locality, income or social position'. Written in 1974, during the aftermath of the 1960s radical political ideology but before the commercial boom of the 1980s and subsequent conservative turn, this resolution of the Swedish Parliament stated that 'commercial considerations were not to control what was being offered' (Sandström 1993: 2). This was before corporate sponsoring was accepted at the Stockholm Opera.

In line with Bourdieu's (1993) reasoning, the marketing departments at the Royal Swedish Ballet, as well as at the American Ballet Theatre, were then working to shift ballet from its field of restricted production (the preserve of the cultural elite) towards a field of large-scale production. The latter is less prestigious and succumbs to market forces, but such commercial art can, as Becker (1984) has pointed out, in fact foster a versatile craftmanship in order to meet all kinds of demands. The field of restricted production is also connected to a market, but of a different, smaller kind. So is the experimental, alternative, contemporary work of William Forsythe which is taking place within yet another field of restricted production, although it is at the same time linked to the exclusivity of classical ballet. Forsythe's pieces are danced by classical dancers at many opera houses, among them Covent Garden and the Stockholm Opera.

The Exchange: Ballet and Business

Private, corporate and foundation sponsorship of ballet is well established in New York and London, where it also follows the pattern in other art forms. It is not at all so prominent in Frankfurt, and it is considered marginal in Stockholm at least compared to the hundreds of sponsors and donors in New York and London. Tours, guest performances, new productions and revivals, awards including scholarships for young dancers to train and work with renowned teachers and choreographers abroad take place because of sponsoring mostly from businesses that produce various commodities, such as cigarettes, liquor, matches and automobiles, but also cosmetics, designer fashion and even pharmaceutical appliances. Breweries and banks have moreover provided tax-reducible support. Some of these businesses (American cigarette corporations, for example) operate transnationally both in their business and in their ballet sponsoring. Importantly, this means that representatives of an American cigarette corporation have an impact on the social organization of the transnational ballet world in terms of the distribution of awards and scholarships, as well as influence what companies will come on tour to the United States and their repertory. By sponsoring ballet, cigaretttte corporations can also be said to try to compensate, gain morally as it were, for the fact that they are making a product that is dangerous.

As part of the exchange between sponsors and the ballet world, sponsors also appropriate some cultural capital. Sponsorship is one way to legitimate wealth. A circumstance that tends to be left out in the social anaysis of ballet is the paradox that many dancers do not possess very much cultural capital with respect to their upbringing, and that backstage the ballet world is far from an upperclass institution. In fact, dancers often feel trapped between cultural capital and the market, out of place in both. Another element in the exchange between sponsors and the ballet world is that corporations and private donors are invited to dress rehearsals, premieres, receptions and dinners where they get the opportunity to meet the dancers. The dancers, on the other hand, tend to be rather uncomfortable about these encounters. Post-performance banquets take place when the dancers are exhausted from dancing and acting for three hours. They often feel that they put on an act when they have to answer over and over again well-meaning but uninformed questions about their dancing, diet and career, especially regarding why they started to dance. Expensively dressed donors and their guests make conversation with the dancers and the dancers then often find themselves embarrassed by the fact that they do not remember these people who behave as if they have met them before, often at a previous banquet. This polite 'acting' of the dancers at marketing occasions is talked about in the ballet world in terms of 'spielen' or 'it's all theatre, anyway', as well as 'licking both here and there'. Private donors who the dancers and the management get acquainted with are often respected, even liked, but this is not necessarily the case when it comes to representatives of corporations who can become the targets of ridicule, especially by a dancer, a choreographer or even a ballet director who has just made an effort to charm them. As Ostrower (1995: 135) points out, wealthy donors tend to have a commitment to the organizations they give large sums of money to, but they 'do keep their distance, and remain apart'. This confirms my observations of dancers' experience of meeting patrons.

In general, established dancers or those who were on their way upwards in their career were more favourably inclined to marketing than those who felt that they were in a bad patch, or even realized that they would not get any further than they were now, which usually meant going downhill to minor roles, corps work for soloists, and so-called walking roles (kings and queens who hardly dance at all). George Balanchine, the Russian choreographer in New York, expressed his sense that marketing ballet was important yet also a nuisance by saying: 'you have to go everywhere, give interviews, attend receptions. It's all terrible and tiring. And then you think: after all, it's for the theater, that means it's important, it's good' (Volkov 1986: 59).

It is significant that those at the very apex of the donorship structure are also on boards of ballet companies and opera houses, and thus have a say about ballet politics in terms of repertory, casting, tours and appointments. It is common that donors and corporations that have given large sums of money to a ballet company, in some cases over the course of many years, have certain seats and boxes reserved for them at every performance. There are special lists and advertisments of names of private, corporate and foundation sponsors in ballet programmes, including the information that a certain number 'wish to remain anonymous'. Those who have donated most substantially get their names engraved on brass plates that are exhibited in the foyers of theatres and opera houses. Ballet sponsoring also involves anecdotes like the one about a the wealthy Chicago lady, Mrs Becky D'Angelo, who commissioned the Joffrey Ballet to do the ballet titled *Birthday Variations* as a birthday present for her husband (Drell 1995).

Ballet needs marketing structures to survive and develop, and there is, again, no doubt that the importance of marketing is recognized in the ballet world. Nevertheless, the unease with ballet's relationship with the market remains. It is, as Stuart Plattner has suggested with reference to painters: 'high-art producers live in a value system that is conflicted, not to say schizophrenic, about the importance of selling work' (Plattner 1996: 197). This was most pronounced in Sweden, with its big public sector, including education, health care and the arts, and tradition of welfare and social justice, all provided for by the state. The Royal Swedish Ballet is primarily state-subsidized. It happened that ballet's unease with the market came up at the contemporary Ballet Frankfurt which also relies mostly on state subsidy, but almost never at the Royal Ballet where sponsorship is much more developed, and hardly ever at the American Ballet Theatre, the only company which, except for a very small percentage, was funded entirely by sponsorship. Although dancers are anxious to widen the audience and include all classes, they are reluctant to become part of the artistic field of large-scale production (Bourdieu 1993) because of the alleged impact of commercial forces there. Ballet companies are sometimes concerned that they are linked to business corporations that are accused of 'polluting the environment, making unhealthy products or exploiting their employees' (Wulff 1998: 54). The crux of the matter for ballet companies is that they would not be able to survive without sponsorship. This is so even for those companies that are mostly state-subsidized since that funding is not enough.

Conclusions: Ballet in the Global Marketplace

Although the ballet world has been transnational since Catherine de Medici invited Italian musicians and dance teachers to Paris, the amount and density of communication between ballet centres such as London, New York and Frankfurt-am-Main, and peripheries such as Stockholm, has escalated through intensified touring and guest performances, but also through ballet competitions, festivals and the fact that dancers go abroad to train and work for a few years with other companies. Ballet in media such as video, photography, television, the internet, cd-roms, dvds, as well as press and dance magazines are important for transnational connectivity in the ballet world (Wulff 1998).

This chapter has discussed ballet in the global marketplace, both ballet and its market being Western systems that operate globally even outside the scope of Euro-

America. Although I have used the concept of 'the market' in the singular here in order to signify a transnational entity, it is moored in certain places: old national and new choreographic ballet centres and peripheries. The ballet world is generically transnational with 'a consciousness of the world as a whole' (Robertson 1992: 8) coming up on a daily basis backstage. This refutes the idea that globalization and transnationality necessarily imply deterritorialization. It is also noteworthy that the transnational ballet market in fact consists of multiple interrelated markets that are distinguished in the first place by different funding systems and national ballet cultures that in turn are composed of a vast number of other markets. Those individual agents, famous dancers such as Rudolf Nureyev and Sylvie Guillem, who learn how to create their own markets, also increase the demand for ballet in the global marketplace.

Contrary to much rhetoric about globalization, the ballet world is not controlled from America. Ballet came about in Europe, and Paris and London are still influential ballet centres, as is Frankfurt-am-Main through the choreographer William Forsythe Yet, as I have argued, when it comes to the market, the American ballet companies are the most 'aggressive' promoters. While the European companies in this study are more or less state-subsidized, the American Ballet Theatre gets almost all its funding from corporate and private sponsors. This not only means that business representatives and private donors have an impact on repertory, appointments and tours at the American Ballet Theatre, but since American corporations also contribute to European ballet in the form of awards and support for tours there is thus a certain American influence on European ballet but this does not amount to domination.

Despite unease about ballet's relationship with the marketplace, from the ballet world's point of view, ballet people develop strategies for relating to the market and promotion sometimes with regret, but sometimes with a sense of triumph if they feel that they can manage the market for their own purposes, rather than the other way around. Dancers distrust the market primarily because there is a disagreement over the definition of how the commodity, such as a single performance, should be defined. For dancers, it is the quality of a performance that matters; they want the audience to be 'mesmerized' and 'to go home and really remember'. While the audience may well appreciate the performance, it may also be in the theatre for other reasons besides watching ballet. A great part of the audience, including private and corporate sponsors and donors, buy ballet tickets in order to legitimate economic capital with cultural capital. In her study of the special case of elite philanthropy in the United States, Ostrower found that such donors explain their giving in terms of 'an obligation that is part of their privileged positition' (Ostrower 1995: 12), but that they engage in it mostly with their peers in mind rather than any other people.

At the heart of this situation is the fundamental difference which dancers perceive between an experience of ballet art and the mechanisms of the market. Dancers realize that an experience of ballet art will not happen to the audience, nor the dancers, without the market; neither will it happen during every performance or throughout any one particular performance. Since such exceptional moments cannot be ordered, they happen unexpectedly and irregularly, it is impossible to buy them in advance. Finally, it is interesting to note, in view of dancers' unease with the market, that Jacques Maquet, in his discussion of when an object becomes an art object, concludes that: 'In our society a first criterion, crude but fairly accurate, of art is access to the art market. Objects belonging to that network are art objects' (Maquet 1979: 9). This is to say that ballet companies, stars and performances that are in demand in the global marketplace do have a capacity to touch an audience.

Notes

1. This chapter is a revised version of Wulff, Helena (2005). '"High Arts" and the Market: An Uneasy Partnership in the Transnational World of Ballet', in D. Inglis and J. Hughson (eds), *The Sociology of Art*. Basingstoke: Palgrave, pp.171–82.
2. See also Wulff 2000 and 2002.

References

Becker, H.S. 1984. *Art Worlds*. Berkeley: University of California Press.
Bensman, J. 1983. 'Introduction: The Phenomenology and Sociology of the Performing Arts', in J.B. Kamerman and R. Martorella (eds), *Performers and Performances*. South Hadley, MA: Bergin and Garvey, pp.1–37.
Bourdieu, P. 1993. 'The Market of Symbolic Goods', in *The Field of Cultural Production*. New York: Columbia University Press, pp.112–41.
Bull, D. 1999. *Dancing Away*. London: Methuen.
Bussell, D. with J. Mackrell. 1998. *Life in Dance*. London: Arrow Books.
Cass, J. 1993. *Dancing through History*. Englewood Cliffs, NJ: Prentice Hall.
DiMaggio, P. 1992. 'Cultural Boundaries and Structural Change: The Extension of the High Culture Model to Theater, Opera, and Dance, 1900–1940', in M. Lamont and M. Fournieir (eds), *Cultivating Differences*. Chicago: University of Chicago Press, pp.21–57.
Drell, A. 1995. 'Chicago and the Joffrey'. *Chicago Sun-Times*, 20 January.
Gladstone, V. 1995. 'Nureyev Auction Breaks Records'. *Dance Magazine*, May, 69(5): 21.
Hanna, L. 1988. *Dance, Sex and Gender*. Chicago: University of Chicago Press.
Maquet, J. 1979. *Introduction to Aesthetic Anthropology*. Malibu, CA: Undena Publications.
Ostrower, F. 1995. *Why the Wealthy Give*. Princeton, NJ: Princeton University Press.
Plattner, S. 1996. *High Art Down Home*. Chicago: University of Chicago Press.
Robertson, A. and D. Hutera. 1990. *The Dance Handbook*. Boston: Hall and Co.
Robertson, R. 1992. *Globalization*. London Sage.
Sandström, P. 1993. 'Operan/Kungliga Teatern: En Publikstudie', unpublished report, Stockholm.
Stuart, O. 1995. *Perpetual Motion*. New York: Simon and Schuster.
Taylor, J. 1994. *Irek Mukhamedov*. London: Fourth Estate.
Volkov, S. 1986. *Balanchine's Tchaikovsky*. New York: Anchor Books.
Wulff, H. 1998. *Ballet across Borders*. Oxford: Berg.
―――― 2000. 'Access to a Closed World: Methods for a Multi-Locale Study on Ballet as a Career', in V. Amit (ed.), *Constructing the Field*. London: Routledge, pp.147–61.

―――――― 2002. 'Aesthetics at the Ballet: Looking at "National" Style, Body, and Clothing in the London Dance World', in N. Rapport (ed.), *British Subjects*. Oxford: Berg, pp.67–83.

―――――― 2008. 'Ethereal Expression: Paradoxes of Ballet as a Global Physical Culture', *Ethnography*, 9(4): 519–36.

Chapter 3

'We've Got This Rhythm in Our Blood': Dancing Identities in Southern Italy

Karen Lüdtke

A frequently seen postcard from the Salento, Apulia's southernmost region, shows a woman on the ground arching her spine into a bridge-like pose.[1] Her legs are scarcely covered and the angle chosen by the photographer gives the image an erotic, voyeuristic touch. The position depicted is often seen to characterize rituals of tarantism, used for centuries in southern Italy and elsewhere to treat victims of the tarantula's bite, expressing personal and social crises (De Martino 2005). On the postcard, the group Tamburellisti di Torrepaduli re-enacts elements of a tarantism ritual on the promenade of Gallipoli, a major west-coast tourist destination. In January 2005, I saw this image, magnified a thousand fold, on an electronic billboard suspended some ten metres above the main roundabout leading into Lecce, the Salentine capital, from the northern port of Brindisi. A huge comet-like Christmas star of light bulb strings had only just been removed from above the roundabout and the new year's summer season was already being announced – in the form of spider-driven rituals.

Now proclaimed as extinct, tarantism or tarantolism, involved intense and extensive dancing to the rhythms of the *pizzica*, the Apulian tarantella.[2] For hundreds of years it was widespread in this part of Italy and neighbouring regions. Earliest written documents go back to the thirteenth century, although its precise origins remain a mystery.[3] In the years following the Second World War, tarantism rituals increasingly became a source of shame, clamped down upon by the Church and dismissed as symbols of backwardness and heresy. Nevertheless, recent accounts insist that rituals continued into the 1990s, despite official announcements of their complete extinction (Di Lecce 1994). In the 1970s, moreover, the interest of largely left-wing scholars and musicians led to a gradual revitalization of local traditions.[4] By the 1990s, this groundwork had led to a massive boom in the Salentine music and dance scene, rotating, above all, around the *pizzica* and the symbol of the tarantula spider.[5] Often erroneously seen as synonymous with the variety of music and dance genres associated with this region, the *pizzica* hit the limelight as a symbol of unique Salentine identity and a tourist invite, placing this region on the world-music map. By the year 2000, some fifty groups were playing to the beat of the tambourine, a virtuoso instrument in this context, whilst more established groups, with success in Italy and elsewhere, numbered a dozen or so (Durante 1999; Nocera 2005). An annual mega concert, the 'Night of the Tarantula', having become an icon of this movement, now attracts thousands to this region each August. Renowned musicians of national fame and international calibre have participated and taken the concert on tour. In 2006, a paying audience of fifty thousand attended the concert of the Orchestra della Notte della Taranta in Beijing (Presicce 2006). In 2007, the Salentine group Aramirè played at Zankel Hall, the newest theatre at New York's Carnegie Hall, known for its world, folk and experimental music events.

This chapter looks at how identities are played out against this backdrop. Today, politicians joke that only *pizzica* tunes are permitted if mobiles are left on during conferences or public meetings. Some 100,000 euros of public funding were spent on the 2006 Beijing concert (Presicce 2006), while a decade ago little if any money was put aside for this kind of music (Fumarola 1998). These transformed perceptions, discourses and markets of local Salentine music and dance raise questions regarding the perceived need for a (unique) sense of identity in the modern-day Salento and how this feeds into and off territorial promotions and quests for authenticity. The theoretical approach taken here relies on key studies in the anthropological literature on identity, tourism and performance. A brief overview of Salentine music and dance, focusing on historic, socio-cultural and political contexts and meanings, sets the scene for the exploration of local discourses on identity, and how these may contribute to broader anthropological reflections on this topic.

What emerges is that Salentine dance and music today accentuate as well as alleviate crises and conflicts. They express both anxiety and celebration (Feld 2000: 151–54). In the past, ritual cures of tarantism relied on the aggravation of symptoms through musical rhythms and other sensual stimuli (colours or images, in particular) as an initial phase in the healing process. Victims identified with their aggressors. As the dancing proceeded, other identities came into play: victims became heroes, aggressors acquiescent. A new sense of the self was evoked, enacted and celebrated. Nowadays, concerts bring out more deep-lying discontent, 'anxious narratives' conveying, to quote ethnomusicologist Steven Feld, 'the suspicion that capitalist concentration and competition in the recording industry is always productive of a lesser artistry, a more commercial, diluted, and sellable version of a world once more "pure", "real" or less commodified' (Feld 2000: 152). At the same time, contemporary concerts create celebratory narratives spotlighting a sense of mutual support and communion, as well as 'hopeful scenarios for cultural and financial equity' (Feld 2000: 152).

Experiences of transcending and shifting boundaries in performative contexts throw up, reinforce and mutate identities, stretching or curtailing conceptual boundaries. They hold the potential for fostering not only a reductive sense of identity as limited to specific defining features (the *pizzica* as an emblem of the

Salento), but also an intersubjective sense of identity, based on the assumption that 'we can only understand an other person in terms of ourselves and ourselves in terms of another' (Tankink and Vysma 2006: 3), uniting humanity through its unique expression of differences as embodied in each and every individual (the diverse dimensions accessed and represented through the *pizzica* not only by Salentines and not only in the Salento).[6]

Anthropological Settings

Identity is widely defined in opposition to alterity. This dichotomy has been carefully deconstructed by anthropologists, in an effort to 'discard any essentialized notion of difference, to eschew any over emphasis on identity as sameness and to resist any temptation to moralize about "othering"' (Gingrich 2004: 15).[7] Anthropological studies have highlighted how any group's apparently consolidated identity may involve a cross-boundary struggle for control and contests within the group, challenging the absolute character of discourses on identity and the existence of defining boundaries that are not only a matter of degree but also of kind (Cohen 2000: 1–2). 'Wherever we look in the world, people are fighting back in a struggle for identities which they can regard as more sensitive to themselves, rejecting self-denying generalization and subordination to collective categories' (Cohen 1994: 177). This has led to sensitive and complex debates on rights to identity, and who defines such identities, in the face of imposed matrices of perception. Global media play a crucial role in this context.

Morley and Robins (1995) have considered the implications of such media in reimagining a contemporary Europe 'without frontiers'. Anxieties provoked by shifting and dissolving boundaries and points of reference are soothed by 'calls for the pure (if mythic) certainties of the "old traditions"' (Morley and Robins 1995: 8). Without discarding mass migration in the past, being European (as well as global citizenship more generally) increasingly demands juggling continental, national and regional identities at the same time. It implies negotiating with and a commitment to that which is considered to be different. It implies a world with increasingly porous boundaries, 'an intensification of global interconnectedness' (Inda and Rosaldo 2002: 2), characterized by multiple understandings and realities of 'globalization' with its 'crisscrossing flows and intersecting systems of meanings' (Inda and Rosaldo 2002: 26).[8]

Music, as one of many performance genres, is a key player in this world. 'World music' – a prime label for the *pizzica* – in particular, may be seen as 'today's dominant signifier of a triumphant industrialization of global sonic representation' (Feld 2000: 146). Music is more often than not seen to epitomize places fostering not only marketing strategies, relying on claims to the 'traditional', 'authentic' and 'original', but also music tourism (Connell and Gibson 2003). Meanwhile, spatial coordinates assign credibility and monetary value to music, as music and place reciprocally define each other (Stokes 1994). Attempts at deconstructing such links challenge music's selling power, its mystic appeal and spiritual magnetism. In this sense, Feld points to world music not only as a discourse but as a fundamental zone of activities and representation involving 'intersubjective clashes for musicians, recordists, industry players, journalists and academics' (Feld 2000: 154).

The varying intentions of these diverse actors come into play and conflict, raising accusations of cultural commoditization and theft reminiscent of those expressed in the face of tourism (Kirtsoglou and Theodossopoulos 2004), echoed in much of the literature on this topic. Some stress that 'the tourist is a kind of contemporary pilgrim, seeking authenticity in other "times" and other "places" away from that person's everyday life' (Urry 2000: 9). Such views are reinforced by studies on pilgrimage and healing, showing how typical motivations for curing afflictions, whether of a physical or spiritual nature, are complemented in the animated field of modern-day pilgrimage with those of quests for identity, for 'reassembling the self' and interpersonal connection (Dubisch and Winkelman 2005). Others see tourist aspirations as less enchanted, as thriving on 'pseudo-events' (Boorstin 1961) and, more significantly, have problematized the notion of authenticity as not only existing in various stages (MacCannell 1999) but also as a negotiable and constantly changing point of reference (Chambers 1999). This multi-faceted picture provides a backdrop for a look at the contemporary Salentine music and dance scene.

Dancing Identities in the Salento and Beyond

In July 2004, the Rhythm and Sticks Festival, celebrating percussion music from around the world, brought the *pizzica* to the South Bank Centre, one of London's major arts and culture venues. The well-known Salentine group Ghetonia made its debut in the UK capital, performing its repertoire of songs in the *Griko* dialect and pieces featuring the rhythmic beat of the *pizzica*.[9] The South Bank's Purcell Room, with its black-curtained walls, contrasted sharply with the open-air settings of the Salento, but the concert was a huge success, ending in a standing ovation. A split-second interaction right at the end of the performance struck me: as the musicians returned onstage for an encore, a member of the audience jumped to his feet, in a jack-in-the-box fashion, brandishing a bright red and yellow shawl – the colours of the Lecce football team – which read *Forza Lecce* ('Come on Lecce').

Beyond its comic effect, this gesture seemed to embody the strong sense of (or desire for) belonging of a Salentine émigré in the form of his football scarf. All the more potent in the cosmopolitan setting of London's South Bank Centre and in the context of an international 'world music' festival, this gesture rooted this music and all it entails within the Salento by way of association, creating and shaping not only geographical boundaries but also symbolic and imaginary territories, zones of inclusion and exclusion. It showed, moreover, the importance not only of performers but also of spectators and fans in shaping a sense of belonging (Archetti 2003). Today, the *pizzica* has become a carrier of manifold identities: for many it is simply a fun factor; for others it is a key to their identity, a political tool, a financial asset or a tourist advert. Some perceive it as a potential source of healing and spirituality, while others do not care at all or actively voice their criticisms: *Spegnete i tamburelli e accendete i cervelli!* jokes one cultural project manager – 'Switch off your tambourines and switch on your brains!'

A number of factors have been identified as contributing to the rise in interest in Salentine music and dance in the 1990s. Dance ethnologist Pino Gala (2002: 48) points to the seductive myth and emblematic value of the spider; the psychological impact of rhythmic repetition characteristic of the *pizzica*; increasing interest in complementary medicine as well as esoteric and New Age philosophies; problems of marginalization; the effect of anthropological and related studies as well as cinematographic productions on tarantism; the charismatic influence of well-known Italian musicians (Eugenio Bennato, Teresa De Sio, Daniele Sepe and others); and, last but not least, to generational fashions. A member of the discussion forum on a *pizzica* website takes up this point:

> The success of the pizzica is certainly in part a fashionable and commercial phenomenon, but in my opinion it also represents a response to globalization, currently wanting to force us all to listen to the same music, to eat the same things (perhaps at McDonald's), to think in the same way … With the recovery of popular music, traditions and local identities in general, many are looking for a way to fill a vacuum of values.[10]

In a heated debate about Salentine music and dance during a summer school held in the town of Galatina in 2002, a young male dancer and *pizzica* teacher passionately affirmed 'We wouldn't survive without an identity!' (see Lüdtke 2005a). The need for a sense of identity fed through music and dance appears to be voiced as a matter of life and death, evoking a sense of 'crises of presence', attributed to the *tarantate*, the tarantula's victims, in the past by Italian anthropologist Ernesto De Martino. Such crises, described as a 'failure of subjective identity' by Mariella Pandolfi (1990: 270), were characterized by an individual's sense of disconnection from their social and natural surroundings provoked in the face of extreme hardship, including natural disasters and psychological traumas. Inevitably, however, the notion of 'crises of presence' groups together a vast gamut of circumstances and experiences and, moreover, risks essentializing conceptions of the notion of 'presence' itself.

Keeping this in mind, the socio-cultural fabric of the contemporary Salento – and much of the contemporary Western world – is widely seen to hold the seeds of crises reflected and expressed in, among other things, a need for belonging and identity within a seeming vacuum of points of reference, although these crises may equally stimulate creativity and progress. What is more, the impact of socio-economic development and the introduction of psychiatric care, identified as two key elements to have brought about the end of tarantism, are no safeguard against new problems that have emerged in the modern context of the Salento, such as high unemployment, large-scale emigration rupturing cultural and family ties, and generational differences marking close-knit communities. The Salentine peninsula, moreover, is a roulette wheel of potential identities and fleeting points of reference, having witnessed a history of foreign domination[11] and become a major gateway to Europe for refugees and asylum seekers in recent years, as well as a newly discovered tourist oasis since international cheap flights to Brindisi commenced in 2004.

However, potential comparisons between past and present contexts orbiting around the tarantula spider must, first and foremost, acknowledge evident discrepancies. Whereas in the past tarantism rituals were part of a cultural complex deeply rooted within everyday life, these links have today been cleanly cut. Tarantism and its associations with the *pizzica,* according to social anthropologist Paolo Apolito (2000: 141), appear to be no more and no less than a free-floating spot or slogan that can be put to manifold use. Whereas only a decade or two ago, tarantism was a source of shame, fostering conceptions of Salentines and Apulians as poor and ignorant, this has been reversed today. 'This time it is the Apulians, in particular a cultural group, which is urbanized, critical and postmodern, who claim tarantism as a positive, noble and profound sign of their history and identity' (Apolito 2000: 139). Surfing this wave, De Martino's book *La terra del rimorso* (De Martino 1961) and its English translation *The Land of Remorse* (De Martino 2005), 'often not read and not understood, has become a strong source of interest, dense, just like an emblem, a banner, of local identity' (Apolito 2000: 139). Repercussions of these free-floating images go deeper. In the past the model of tarantism provided a socially acknowledged existential framework, which did not pathologize or stigmatize. The *tarantate* were seen to be 'normal' people, relieved of responsibility for their 'abnormal' behaviour through their link to the tarantula. Past ritual processes relied on the dancers identifying with their perpetrator and the explanatory system of tarantism provided conceptual aid facilitating this process, as affliction was grounded in the physiological reaction to actual spider poisoning. This ensured that the immediacy and embodied reality of individual experience was socially acknowledged, as powers of affliction and cure were located outside the individual and within the social and natural fabric of Salento. In contemporary contexts, meanwhile, football scarves may link performance skills to regional boundaries, in the absence, however, of any commonly accepted belief system. The Salentine music and dance scene has gained immense popularity and may engage with the rhetoric of music's healing power to boost its publicity, but its key motivations may have little, if anything, in common with these claims. Consequently, some performers today have been criticized for creating or re-creating their own explanatory models, engaging in a process of inscribing meaning that inevitably risks incoherence and superficiality. Some have come to define themselves as 'modern' or 'neo-tarantati', on the basis of their own (variously defined) experiences of crises and enhanced well-being, seen to be a consequence of participating in the Salentine music and dance scene (Lüdtke 2009).

Despite widespread criticisms, these views nevertheless suggest that the *pizzica* may serve, as it did in the past, as one possible grounding device – and not only in the Salento.[12] Interestingly, one Italian-American *pizzica* enthusiast tells of how she and others learnt to dance and play the *pizzica* in New York City: 'We were bitten by the beat, if not by spiders, and we used it to counter the disconnect of our stressed-out, over-burdened, spirit-starved modern lives ... We used this music to dance together, to try to heal ourselves, to drive away negative emotions, to invoke the spirits of our ancestors, offer support for each other ... to temporarily break away from our everyday stresses' (personal communication). Here a risk emerges, stressing the importance of a case-by-case analysis, reminiscent of a contradiction inherent in many so-called New Age practices, in which participants 'adopt rituals and other aspects of cultures that depend fundamentally upon collective, communal experience – and sometimes on voiding or subordinating the autonomous self ... put ... in the service of a thoroughly modern world view that takes the self as a thing to be owned, cultivated and coddled – the veritable hub of the universe' (Torgovnick 1996: 176). The above quoted dancer tells about her evolving perspective:

> Looking back, pizzica music served us as a kind of free-standing vehicle that we used like a group of friends might use some other passionate hobby, to bond and relax for a bit. But once I learned about, and better understood tarantism's complex history, I couldn't dress up and throw myself down on the floor anymore. It felt so false. But I did dance even more after that, but always treating it just as a dance, not as a ritual. (personal communication)

A consideration of how motivations and intentions for performing are expressed and legitimized in the Salentine context explores further risks of naturalizing what may in fact be largely cultural constructions.

'We've Got This Rhythm in Our Blood'

'We have it inside' is a widespread tacit conviction suggesting that the *pizzica* and everything associated with it is 'pulsing' in the blood or encoded in the DNA of anyone with Salentine origins, creating a sense of identity sometimes unreflectively voiced in the expression 'We're DOC Salentines!' The label DOC – *denominazione d'origine controllata*, controlled denomination of origin – aiming to assign a guarantee of quality to regionally specific products of the European Union, is ascribed to the people of the Salento as a (perceived) guarantee of originality or official stamp of legitimacy. Such statements are voiced with enthusiasm, becoming almost an expression of modesty, as the ability to dance, play and sing is seen as a gift not only attributed to individual talent, commitment or merit. Instead, the rhythms of music and dance are seen as inscribed in the body, as pumping through the blood. They are essentialized into a biological function, dissociated from cultural influences and, thereby, mystified.

This process of naturalizing a cultural construction has historic parallels in this region, although past rituals may have little, if anything, in common with contemporary performances, keeping in mind the seductive risks of theories insisting on continuity often based on innumerable smaller discontinuities (Horden 2003). In the past, the tarantula's victims naturalized their afflictions through spider poisoning which was widespread in Southern Italy until, as popular opinion states, the advent of pesticides killed off most indigenous spiders. The *tarantate* were often severely criticized for manipulating this link for personal and political reasons. They were accused of collecting money for their own pockets in the name of St Paul, their patron saint; of being exhibitionists; or of faking their illness so as to get time off work or marry someone contrary to their parents' wishes. Likewise, modern fans of the *pizzica* may naturalize their passion for this music and dance on the basis of a belief grounded in modern understandings of the human organism and a genetic conception of the body.

Initially, this belief was rarely questioned or criticized for its inherent manipulative potential. Nevertheless, just like the *tarantate*, musicians and dancers, as well as cultural administrators and intellectuals, have been accused of manipulation, of wanting to enlarge their own name or bank account. Many insist on having been the first to revive this music, claiming a right to others' acknowledgement, if not to copyright. Rather than considering the efforts of various individuals and groups in creating the momentum and popularity which the *pizzica* currently enjoys, energy, words, time and money have, at times, been invested in fighting for 'first place', despite equally insistent claims regarding the ancient and medieval precedents of this style of music and dance, which inherently make them a common inheritance.[13]

Clearly, other issues are at stake. In this sense, social anthropologist Giovanni Pizza has contributed significantly to a critical discourse on this topic. He writes: 'Only the conscious or unconscious incorporation of hegemonic stereotypes, even if widespread among the population, can incite us to consider our sense of belonging to be inscribed in our blood, our flesh or even in our genetic inheritance' (Pizza 2002a: 55). He repeatedly warns against the passive incorporation of stereotypes that are inseparable from existing power structures and ideologies. Just as music was used in the past to aggravate symptoms, today voices, instruments and microphones, not to speak of satellite television, may propagate rivalry just as much as gestures of solidarity and friendship. Every actor in this game faces the choice, Pizza writes, of whether or not to use whatever the *pizzica* brings to the surface as a 'methodological and ethical mirror metaphor' (Pizza 2002a: 53):

> The rhetoric of conserving one's own identity often hides not the fear of looking at 'the other', but the fear of looking into one's own face ... Obscuring the mirror is a precondition for an essentialist discourse that conceives identity as objects, as essences to preserve, as 'intimate' and 'profound' truths; it is a political operation of concealing motivations, intentions and the objectives of one's own discourses and actions. (Pizza 2002a: 52)

What results are automatic reflexes to project onto 'others' (groups, individuals, bodies and so on) everything which the self is not identified with, that which is rejected and condemned. What is more, every minimal glimpse in this mirror may create a further reaction of clinging yet more strongly onto that which is accepted as part of one's self-identity, that which is seen as agreeable and amenable, such as naturalizing explanations diagnosing *pizzica* rhythms in bloodstreams and DNA codes. Apolito (2000: 140) stresses how the myth of the tarantula has taken on religious qualities, all the more potent as this myth is not, like many others, delocalized but has, instead, been reinvented within the region of its apparent origins.

Existing power structures are fully played out in the context of one, or rather *the* major Salentine concert, La Notte della Taranta ('The Night of the Tarantula'), which attracted an estimated 100,000 people in August 2011 according to the local media. Since its inauguration in 1998 this event has, on a symbolic level, turned into a virtual play station screen, with politicians campaigning for popularity and votes, academics and artistic directors jostling with issues of musical authenticity or so-called 'contamination', and with some musicians attaining fame while others boycott the event, arguing that 'culture' cannot be sold and must not be prescribed (Lüdtke 2005a). Some are thrilled by the international interest this music and dance have aroused. Yet others oppose this event as nothing but a form of commercializing the Salento, as the tarantula has switched codes from miracle cure to media miracle.

Beyond Salentine-ness

Local discourses reverberating to the tunes of the Salentine music and dance scene may be indicative of broader currents observed elsewhere: the use of music and dance to create distinct boundaries based on naturalized conceptions which are rarely deconstructed as culturally specific creations. Such a focus on what is perceived as 'local' is observable across Europe, not only as a possible counter-reaction to 'globalization' but also as a result of European funding incentives promoting associations with a united Europe of regions beyond national affiliations. In this context, the *pizzica* reveals itself as a tool for essentializing and naturalizing identities, as well as a key to perceptions of identity as multi-faceted and dynamic.[14]

In light of this, French-Lebanese writer Amin Maalouf (2000) stresses that we have a habit of thought that assumes we must have one major affiliation defining our identity. This, he warns, is a simplistic recipe for massacres on the basis of projections of boundaries distinguishing 'us' from 'them'. Maalouf calls for a new concept of identity not based on the denial of the self versus the denial of the 'other', but instead recognizing that everyone's identity is complex, unique and irreplaceable, that each and everyone is a minority in and of themselves. The modern world situation, often epitomized by the spectre of globalization, inevitably jeopardizes essentializing perceptions of identity, giving rise to feelings of discomfort, loss and fear, if not – to return to De Martino's term – 'crises of presence' or meaning. At the same time, such situations and feelings may also act as an invitation to question essentializing claims.

The case of the *pizzica*, for example, may support such claims to a single, all-defining identity delineated in opposition to others, in line with essentializing and differentiating tendencies widely discussed in terms of Italy's 'Southern question', the issue of deeply rooted differences between Italy's northern and southern regions (Schneider 1998). In his historical study of ritual cycles in the town of Calvello in Basilicata, Hermann Tak (2000: 243) stresses how 'the North' became an imaginary 'other' replacing one time fierce antagonistic inner-town relations. Such juxtapositions also emerge in Christian Giordano's (1992) discussion of a 'culture of superimposition' characterizing regions such as Southern Italy, subjected to hundreds of years of domination by foreign powers, resulting in the internalization of fatalistic attitudes such as the 'image of *miseria*', a belief in poverty as collective fate, or perceptions of the state as hostile and unreliable, expressed in the notion of *governo ladro* (thieving government). Although these concepts are cultural constructions in themselves, cultural self-reification or essentialism in the context of the tarantula's music and dance today is likely to be a way of reaffirming values in the face of these broader socio-economic power structures. Simultaneously, it posits a chance to question these perceptions and values.

Similar processes of identification can be observed in relation to gender issues. Interpretations of tarantism have often been reduced to sexual repression and gender conflicts. Feminist writing, in particular, presents such male/female dichotomies, speaking, for example, of the 'ghostly bite of the tarantula – the invisible yet powerful insect of patriarchal lore, lure and law' (Gilbert 1986: xi). Nowadays, too, the Salentine music scene is heavily marked by gender divisions. Luisa Del Giudice notes: 'One finds few women on concert stages, other than in supporting roles (or as the "pretty face", that is, the singer in the ensemble). "*Stanno lì ... con le mani legate*" (There they stand ... with their hands tied), laments one female musician. They continue, however, to constitute the majority of dancers in the public piazzas, but they are surprisingly absent as cultural activists' (Del Giudice 2005: 250–51). This may be slowly changing with some well-known female singers leading their own bands. Likewise, a shift may be identified in perceptions of the *tarantate*, as embodied by some 'modern' *tarantate*. 'Not only has the stigma been lifted from the tarantata's shoulders, there seems to be a growing positive reevaluation ... of this figure as it undergoes something of an apotheosis. She has become a heroine, passing from something of a feared outcast to shaman' (Del Giudice 2005: 253–54). Clearly, such representations risk being equally essential, posing victim versus hero, glorifying what was stigmatized, while multiple and fluctuating nuances may exist between and beyond these categories.

In this context, Maalouf (2000) presents an invitation to stretch the boundaries of our self-perception to include ever more facets of reality as a key for focusing on the common identity of humanity at large. For this, he argues, it is necessary for everyone to identify a little with the many-faced spectre of globalization, to diminish the power invested in views of globalizing processes as entirely alien. Such a hostile view of the world inevitably reinforces an illusion of hegemony, when in reality those 'on top' are equally subject to the 'uncontrollable' forces of globalization and natural calamities.

An interesting link can be drawn here to the healing ritual of the tarantula cult. A fundamental aspect of the ritual process required the victim to identify with the persecutor – the *tarantata* became the tarantula spider or other poisonous creature that had afflicted it. Such identification was facilitated through music and dance as well as other sensual stimuli, becoming the basis for a renewed sense of identity: for the elimination or pacification of the spider. Along similar lines, music

– especially within the 'world music' scene – may play a powerful role in creating a new, universal, inter-subjective sense of identity in the context of globalization.

Individual experiences of performance situations inevitably mould and are moulded by relations activated in performance contexts, as well as by intentions and interpretations that encourage or inhibit participation. In this sense, the music and dance of the Salento hold the potential not only to accentuate individual afflictions and social conflicts but also to promote well-being and the reintegration of individuals in the larger, global webs of everyday community lives.

In the past, identification with the toxic spider provided a basis for transformation (without any guarantee, however), integrating the spider and all rejected aspects of the self it had come to embody into a new, broader sense of the self. In the same way, identification with that seen to be the perpetrator today – be it globalization, the Italian state, other music groups, the opposite sex or suppressed dreams and desires – may provide a first step towards a shift in experience and perspective. In this context, it comes as a subtle play of irony, to see the Salentine peninsula collapsed into the tarantula on a poster promoting the 2004/5 season of the Lecce football team: above the slogan *Terra di Serie A* ('League A country'), a spider crawls over Italy's heel painted in the team's red and yellow colours, precisely those seen to most provoke the *tarantate* in the past.

Notes

I would like to thank the editors of this volume for inviting me to the 2004 EASA panel 'Meaning in Motion', the EASA committee for an EU travel grant making my participation possible, as well as Dorothy Zinn and Mary Ciuffitelli for valuable feedback on this chapter. Elements of this paper have been previously published in Lüdtke (2005b) and (2009/2011).

1. Postcard by Mediterraneo Productions, A. Morgante, 'Collection 2001'.
2. The *pizzica* is without doubt the most advertised of various forms of *musica popolare* in the Salento, a term denoting traditional musical genres that are orally transmitted within a specific 'ethnic' region or group.
3. For references to the origins, history and earliest cited documentation on tarantism – Sante Ardoini, *Sertum papale de venenis* (1426) – see Lüdtke (2000, 2009) and De Martino (2005).
4. I use the term 'revitalization' here, following Tak (2000: 209), to avoid the term 'revival', which may be misread as the re-establishment of a previously existing situation, discounting the impact of changes in the political economy.
5. Classifications of the *pizzica* are commonly, if reductively and erroneously according to some, divided into three types: *pizzica tarantata, pizzica de core* and *pizzica scherma* (Di Lecce 2001). All are performed in a circle of participants (both musicians and onlookers), known as a *ronda*, and can be linked by broad similarities in rhythm and musical execution, but distinguished by dance steps, rhythmic subtleties and diverging intentions. The *pizzica* marks celebrations and is mostly danced by a man and a woman, although two women (and less frequently two men) may also dance together. In the classic match, the woman dances in small skips and pirouettes. She lures and coaxes, escaping her partner while flirting and inviting him to follow with graceful, seductive gestures of her hands, often waving a handkerchief. The man moves more boldly, fol-

lowing his partner, arms seeking to delimit the space around her in a territorial manner, knees slightly bent, assertive and yet almost in submission (Negro and Sergio 2000). The *scherma*, in contrast, was and to some extent still is used to settle conflicts, to clarify who is the strongest, who has the last say. Two dancers take over the centre of the circle. Right hands gripped in a tight fist, they turn around the axis of this fulcrum, let go and face each other. Index and middle fingers imitate knives, cutting through the air in rotating motions. The aim is to strike the adversary with force and virility. Tensions run high and electricity moves in the circle, creating sparks with every successful hit. Previously this dance was performed exclusively by men and – as many like to tell and others contest – with actual knives. Finally, the *tarantate* danced the *pizzica tarantata* in spider-driven rituals. Despite vast variations in ritual practices, certain dance phases generally marked these events (De Martino 1961). At the outset, the *tarantata* would lie prostrate on the ground until a musical note performed by a small orchestra of musicians moved her into action, bringing her desperation to the surface, into her moves, screams, gestures and grimaces. Her head would move from side to side and her back arch upward. She would roll over and over and eventually jump up to execute elements of the *pizzica* in an ever more frantic manner, before spinning on the spot and collapsing to the ground. Just a short break would provide some rest before another dance cycle with the same dancer was resumed (see Lüdtke 2009).

6. For an in-depth consideration of the notion of intersubjectivity, see Boskovic (2002), Coelho and Figueiredo (2003), and Tankink and Vysma (2006).
7. See Gingrich (2004: 14) for an outline of successive stages in anthropological debates on identity.
8. For a problematization of the notion of globalization, see Inda and Rosaldo (2002).
9. *Griko* refers to the Greek dialects still spoken in an area south of Lecce known as the Grecìa Salentina.
10. Raf, 9 April 2004. Retrieved 19 January 2008 from: http://www.pizzicata.it/index.php?name=MDForum&file=viewtopic&t=106.
11. If we may reduce 2,500 years of local history to a snapshot, the region known as the Salento was inhabited in antiquity by a variety of peoples: the Messapians, Iapygians, Bruttii and Sallentini. These people remained partly independent of the strong Greek colonies of Magna Graecia, but both the Greeks and the earlier inhabitants fell to the Romans during their expansion in the third century BC. Parts of this Roman-held territory were held by the late Roman and Byzantine rulers while the rest was taken by the Longobards from the north. Brief periods of Arab rule in some sites were followed by Byzantine rule in the ninth century AD, succeeded by a Norman conquest in the late eleventh century. These were followed by Swabian, Angevin, Aragonese, Spanish, Austrian Hapsburg and Bourbon rulers, with a brief Ottoman Turkish presence in the fifteenth century. The overlapping conquests, with their attendant changes of language, faith, costume and music, helped define the Salento prior to the unification of Italy in 1861.
12. See Biagi (2004) and Ciuffitelli (2005) for considerations of performances and workshops of the *pizzica* in the US.
13. For valuable reflections on the contemporary music and dance scene in the Salento, see Lamanna (2002), Santoro (2009) and Santoro and Torsello (2002).
14. For a discussion of the Salentine dance and music scene in the context of globalization, see Thayer (2005) and Fumarola and Imbriani (2006). For a consideration of these themes from the perspective of performance studies, see Daboo (2010).

References

Apolito, P. 2000. 'Tarantismo, identità locale, postmodernità', in G. Di Mitri (ed.), *Quarant'anni dopo De Martino.* Nardò: Besa, pp.135–43.
Archetti, E. 2003. 'Playing Football and Dancing Tango: Embodying Argentina in Movement, Style and Identity', in E. Archetti and N. Dyck (eds), *Sport, Dance and Embodied Identities.* Oxford: Berg, pp.217–30.
Biagi, L. 2004. 'Spider Dreams: Ritual and Performance in Apulian Tarantismo and Tarantella', Ph.D. dissertation. New York: New York University.
Boorstin, D. 1961. *The Image.* New York: Vintage.
Boskovic, A. 2002. 'The "Intersubjective Turn" and the Question of the Subject in Contemporary Anthropology: A Review Article', *Campos* 2: 55–65.
Chambers, E. 1999. *Native Tours: The Anthropology of Travel and Tourism.* Longrove: Waveland Press.
Ciuffitelli, M. 2005. 'A Familiar Voice I Never Heard: Discovering and Promoting Pizzica in the US', unpublished paper given at the American Italian Historical Association conference 'Speaking Memory: Oral History, Oral Culture and Italians in America', Los Angeles, 3–6 November 2005.
Coelho, N.E. Jr., and L.C. Figueiredo. 2003. 'Patterns of Intersubjectivity in the Constitution of Subjectivity: Dimensions of Otherness', *Culture and Psychology* 9: 193–208.
Cohen, A.P. 1994. *Self-consciousness: An Alternative Anthropology of Identity.* London: Routledge.
——— 2000. 'Introduction. Discriminating Relations: Identity, Boundary and Authenticity', in A.P. Cohen (ed.), *Signifying Identities: Anthropological Perspectives on Boundaries and Contested Values.* London: Routledge, pp.1–14.
Connell, J., and C. Gibson. 2003. *Soundtracks: Popular Music, Identity and Place.* London: Routledge.
Daboo, J. 2010. *Ritual, Rapture and Remorse: A Study of Tarantism and Pizzica in Salento.* New York: Peter Lang.
De Martino, E. 1961. *La terra del rimorso: contributo a una storia religiosa del Sud.* Milan: Il Saggiatore.
——— 2005. *The Land of Remorse: A Study of Southern Italian Tarantism,* trans. D. Zinn. London: Free Association Books.
Del Giudice, L. 2005. 'The Folk Music Revival and the Culture of *Tarantismo* in the Salento', in L. Del Giudice and N. van Deusen (eds), *Performing Ecstasies.* Ottawa: Institute of Mediaeval Music, pp.217–72.
Di Lecce, G. 1994. *La danza della piccola taranta: Cronache da Galatina: 1908–1993. A memoria d'uomo.* Rome: Sensibili alle foglie.
——— 2001. Tretarante: taranta/pizzica/scherma. Le tarantelle-pizziche del Salento. Nardò: Besa.
Dubisch, J., and M. Winkelman. 2005. *Pilgrimage and Healing.* Tucson: University of Arizona Press.
Durante, D. 1999. 'Pizzica e techno-pizzica', in V. Ampolo and G. Zappatore (eds), *Musica, droga e transe.* Rome: Sensibili alle foglie, pp.167–90.
Feld, S. 2000. 'A Sweet Lullaby for World Music', *Public Culture* 12(1): 145–71.
Fumarola, P. 1998. 'Produzione e riscatto con la musica popolare', *Quotidiano di Lecce* 174: IV.

Fumarola, P., and E. Imbriani (eds). 2006. *Danze di corteggiamento e di sfida nel mondo globalizzato*. Nardò: Besa.

Gala, G. 2002. 'Mitificazioni coreo-musicali e nuovi linguaggi corporei', in A. Lamanna (ed.), *Ragnatele*. Rome: Adnkronos, pp.40–55.

Gilbert, S. 1986. 'Introduction: A Tarantella of Theory', in H. Cixous and C. Clément (eds), *The Newly Born Woman*, trans. B. Wing. Minneapolis: University of Minnesota Press, pp.ix–xviii.

Gingrich, A. 2004. 'Conceptualising Identities: Anthropological Alternatives to Essentialising Difference and Moralizing about Othering', in G. Baumann and A. Gingrich (eds), *Grammars of Identity/Alterity: A Structural Approach*. Oxford: Berghahn, pp.3–17.

Giordano, C. 1992. *Die Betrogenen der Geschichte: Überlagerungsmentalität und Überlagerungsrationalität in mediterranen Gesellschaften*. Frankfurt: Campus.

Horden, P. 2003. 'Continuità e discontinuità nella storia della terapia musicale nel Mediterraneo', in M. Agamennone and L. Di Mitri (eds), *L'eredità di Diego Carpitella: etnomusicologia, antropologia e ricerca storica nel Salento e nell'area mediterranea*. Nardò: Besa, pp.187–97.

Inda, J.X., and R. Rosaldo (eds). 2002. *The Anthropology of Globalization: A Reader*. Oxford: Blackwell.

Kirtsoglou, E., and D. Theodossopoulos. 2004. 'They are Taking our Culture Away: Tourism and Culture Commodification in the Garifuna Community of Roatan', *Critique of Anthropology* 24(2): 135–57.

Lamanna, A. (ed.). 2002. *Ragnatele: tarantismo, danza, musica e nuove identità nel Sud d'Italia*. Rome: Adnkronos.

Lüdtke, K. 2000. 'Tarantism in Contemporary Italy: The Tarantula's Dance Reviewed and Revived', in P. Horden (ed.), *Music as Medicine*. Aldershot: Ashgate, pp.293–312.

———— 2005a. 'Dancing Towards Well-being: Reflections on the *Pizzica* in the Contemporary Salento, Italy', in L. Del Giudice and N. van Deusen (eds), *Performing Ecstasies*. Ottawa: Institute of Mediaeval Music, pp.37–53.

———— 2005b. '"Non si sopravvivrebbe senza un'identità": identificazione e trasformazione', *Melissi* 10/11: 129–31.

———— 2009. *Dancing with Spiders: Crisis, Celebrity and Celebration in Southern Italy*. Oxford: Berghahn.

———— 2011. *Balla coi ragni. La tarantola tra crisi e celebrazioni*. Bari: Pagina.

Maalouf, A. 2000. *On Identity*. London: Harvill.

MacCannell, D. 1999. *The Tourist*. New York: Schocken.

Morley, D., and K. Robins. 1995. *Spaces of Identity: Global Media, Electronic Landscapes and Cultural Boundaries*. London: Routledge.

Negro, M., and C. Sergio. 2000. 'La musica popolare nella reinterpretazione della nuova generazione', in *Tesina di antropologia culturale*. Lecce: Università di Lecce.

Nocera, M. 2005. *Il morso del ragno: alle origini del tarantismo*. Lecce: Capone.

Pandolfi, M. 1990. 'Boundaries Inside the Body: Women's Suffering in Southern Peasant Italy', *Culture, Medicine and Psychiatry* 14: 255–73.

Pizza, G. 2002a. 'Lettera a Sergio Torsello e Vincenzo Santoro sopra il tarantismo, l'antropologia e le politiche della cultura', in S. Torsello and V. Santoro (eds), *Il ritmo meridiano*. Lecce: Aramirè, pp.43–63.

———— 2002b. 'Retoriche del tarantismo e politiche culturali', in A. Lamanna (ed.), *Ragnatele*. Rome: Adnkronos. pp.68–78.

Presicce, C. 2006. 'La Taranta ha gli occhi a mandorla', *Nuovo Quotidiano di Puglia*, 3 May, p.25.
Schneider, J. (ed.). 1998. *Italy's 'Southern Question': Orientalism in One Country*. New York: Berg.
Stokes, M. 1994. *Ethnicity, Identity and Music: The Musical Construction of Place*. Oxford: Berg.
Tak, H. 2000. *South Italian Festivals: A Local History of Ritual and Change*. Amsterdam: Amsterdam University Press.
Tankink, M., and M. Vysma. 2006. 'The Intersubjective as Analytic Tool in Medical Anthropology', *Medische Antropologie: Tijdschrift over Gezondheid en Cultuur* 18(1): 249–65.
Thayer, L. 2005. 'Tarantismo and Neotarantismo: The Transformation of Ritual in the Wake of Globalization in Southern Italy', in O. Pi-Sunyer (ed.), *The Organization of Diversity: Essays on a Changing Europe*. Amherst: University of Massachusetts, pp.261–90.
Torgovnick, M. 1996. *Primitive Passions: Men, Women and the Quest for Ecstasy*. Chicago: University of Chicago Press.
Santoro, V. 2009. *Il ritorno della taranta. Storia della rinascita della musica poplare salentina*. Rome: Squilibri.
Santoro, V., and Torsello, S. (eds). 2002. *Il ritmo meridian. La pizzica e le identità danzanti del Salento*. Lecce: Aramirè.
Urry, J. 2000. *Sociology Beyond Societies*. London: Routledge.

PART II

Tourism, Social Transformation and the Dance

Chapter 4

Performance in Tourism: Transforming the Gaze and the Tourist Encounter at Híwus Feasthouse

Linda Scarangella-McNenly

Introduction

Híwus feasthouse is located on Grouse Mountain in North Vancouver, British Columbia, Canada, on Squamish territory. The First Nations people who work at the Híwus are mainly from the Squamish and Sechelt Nations, both of which are part of the larger Coast Salish 'culture group'.[1] This Salish feasthouse is unlike the usual longhouse, as it is situated within a tourism context. It attracts an international clientele, many of whom arrive as part of a tour group.[2] Upon arrival at Grouse Mountain, tourists ride up on the tram and walk to the chalet where a hostess (or host) waits to bring them to the Híwus. As they trek towards the feasthouse, the hostess shares Squamish and Sechelt legends, such as the 'Hemlock Tree' and 'Queneesh the Whale'. The hostess then stops at the entrance of the feasthouse and shares the meaning of figures carved on the entrance pole. Tourists now have a wonderful photo opportunity, as the hostess thanks guests with a *huy-chexw-aa* stance.[3] Inside the feasthouse, tourists are treated to a traditional meal while Salish performers share their history and culture by recounting their history and legends, which are also embodied through their performances. Lastly, they all dance together as different clans.[4] Through storytelling, song and dance, the Salish at Híwus welcome tourists into their 'family', and offer them a glimpse of ceremonial life and an idea of what it means to be Coast Salish.

Does this tourist-site experience epitomize what MacCannell (1976) refers to as the search for 'staged authenticity', where tourists seek access to the 'backstage' of a Northwest Coast ceremony? Does it seek to satisfy tourists' search for an exotic, mystical Native? Because of the history of colonial representations of the 'other' (Said 1979) and the persistence of stereotypical representations of ethnic 'others,' the tendency has been to view cultural production and reception in tourism as fixed, where indigenous peoples are trapped in discourses that reproduce these stereotypes (see Boissevain 1996; Evans-Pritchard 1989; Meyer and Royer 2001; Lischke and McNab 2005; Yang 2010). Yet the representations produced in tourism are more complex.

Dance, or more generally performance, is often featured in cultural tourism. Studies of dance and performance have contributed to the debates on colonialism and the appropriation and/or production of the 'other' (e.g., Reed 2002). New dance scholarships since 1995 offer insight into our understanding of the politics of culture as well as theories of reception and spectatorship (Reed 1998: 504). Studies of dance and performance also address key concepts of embodiment, representation and the social construction of identities (e.g., Desmond 1997; Chakravorty 2004, 2009). Chakravorty (2009) points out how postcolonial analyses that examine the body in relation to discourses of power may be enriched by drawing on the phenomenological concept of embodiment and by considering indigenous dance practices. While anthropological studies of the performance of culture in tourism have received attention (e.g., Desmond 1999; Senfit 1999; Henry 2000; Bruner 2001, 2005; Tivers 2002; Bruner and Kirshenblatt-Gimblett 1994), a better understanding on how indigenous participants use and transform performance vis-à-vis tourism would offer additional insight into these debates. I situate my analysis along with these and other scholars such as Adams (1995, 1997), Peers (1999, 2007), Ginsburg (2002a, 2002b) and McLagan (2002) who are moving towards investigating dance, media and tourism encounters from the indigenous perspective. My approach is not phenomenological, and while it provides a critique of the representations and discourse at this tourist site, my aim is to show how an examination of indigenous epistemologies and practices can contribute to the study of performance in tourism.

In this chapter, I consider the production and consumption of Coast Salish culture and identity at Híwus feasthouse, a reconstructed Salish feasthouse on Grouse Mountain featuring a 'dinner show'. Following other scholars who have critiqued 'the gaze' (Evans-Pritchard 1989; Laxson 1991; Crang 1997; MacCannell 2001; Chakravorty 2004; Kole 2010), I re-evaluate Urry's (1990) notion of the 'tourist gaze' as a concept for explaining the production and consumption of performances at Híwus. My research shows that Salish performers at Híwus do not view the host–tourist encounter (Smith 1989) as one where tourists consume a commodified culture (cf. Skinner 2006; Yang 2010). Rather, tourists are guests who witness statements of culture and identity. To achieve this relationship, I argue that performances at this tourist site progress as if they were part of a Salish ceremony. Salish performers draw on their ceremonial framework and epistemologies to transform the 'tourist gaze' into an act of witnessing. In doing so, Salish performers negotiate host–tourist interactions, as well as cultural representations and social meanings, via what I call a 'tourism as ceremony' experience. Given this view of tourism interactions, I also question the assumption that local Salish performers are simply conforming to stereotypes of an exotic, mystical Native, or as Francis (1992) writes, an 'imaginary Indian', to meet tourists' expectations. This leads to a brief discussion on the notion of 'authenticity'. My research shows that Híwus also provides a space for the expression and revitalization of Salish song and dance, which embody Salish history, statements of genealogy and connections to their ancestors and land. Significantly, Salish performers wield a great degree of agency in terms of the production of cultural meaning through their performances of oratory, song and dance. Based on six months of ethnographic research conducted in 2001,[5] this chapter provides an example of indigenous agency in performance as Salish performers use the 'tourist gaze' to negotiate interactions in the tourist encounter, and illuminates a more complex reading of the production of 'Native' representations and performances in tourism by highlighting Salish epistemologies and frameworks at work (cf. Nicks 1999; Chambers 2000; Hendry 2005; Scarangella 2004; Peers 2007).

Theorizing the Gaze in Tourism

Foucault's (1977) discussion of the panopticon demonstrates how constant surveillance functions as a form of 'disciplinary power'. Because the panopticon involves a constant state of observation (or perceived observation), it serves as a method of managing, controlling and disciplining the behaviour of those being observed or gazed upon. Foucault's concept of the 'gaze' also applies to the study of medicine, as in his book *The Birth of the Clinic* (Foucault 1973). He argues that the 'medical gaze' objectifies the patient, and by so doing, patients' bodies are transformed into objects for presentation, study and diagnosis (Davenport 2000: 312).

Foucault's ideas on the gaze and objectification, as well as surveillance and control, have been extended to the analysis of social interactions in tourism contexts (e.g., MacCannell 1976, 1992, 2001; Urry 1990; Lutz and Collins 1991). Tourism often involves the objectification of culture and people; it also privileges the visual aspect or 'gazing'. Like the medical body, the exotic 'other' becomes the subject of tourists' gazes. Urry proposes that the tourist gaze emerges from the desire to escape the ordinary and view the 'extraordinary' and exotic (MacCannell 2001: 25). However, this tourist gaze is diverse and contextual, and has changed historically (Urry 1990: 1–2). For example, Urry identifies different types of oppositional tourist gazes: 'romantic/collective, historical/modern, and authentic/inauthentic' (Urry 1990: 135). Lutz and Collins similarly identify various forms of 'gazing' found in the production of *National Geographic*, such as the readers' gaze, the Western gaze and the subjects' gaze (Lutz and Collins 1991: 134). Other studies of dance and tourism have shown how the body is often produced as a primitive 'other', or an exotic (at times sensual) body to gaze upon (Chakravorty 2004; Kole 2010). Kole describes tourism in Hawaii, which promotes the opportunity to gaze upon the primitive/exotic/sensual 'other' via *hula* performances. While the Tahitian *hula* dance in Hawaii continues to be a 'political-economic opportunity by the colonial power' based on commoditizing the exotic body, dancers also engage in auto-exoticization to represent themselves (Kole 2010: 199). These studies highlight the fact that the gaze is in fact complex and multiple, with various viewing positions and possibly multiple interpretations ensuing from these different gazes; moreover, the gaze itself is malleable.

Performers at tourist sites are constantly visible to tourists and hence subject to the constraints of the tourist gaze. However, this constant surveillance is different from Foucault's prison gaze and panopticonism because the performers can verify the constant scrutiny of the tourist gaze.[6] Like the doctor–patient relationship, 'the tourist gaze [is] as socially organized and systematized as is the gaze of the medic' (Urry 1990: 1). Therefore, although the encounter is not 'disciplinary' per se, performers may feel constricted to follow a script or act in acceptable, authentic ways in order to meet tourists' expectations. To a certain extent, interactions between tourists and performers are regulated, and tourists' 'gazing' experiences are choreographed (see Edensor 2001). For example, when tourists arrive at the chalet on Grouse Mountain, the Híwus hostess brings them directly to the feasthouse, where they are not allowed to venture on their own, and the dinner show follows a programme in which tourists have little opportunity to interact with Salish performers in less formalized ways (until the short bus ride back to the chalet, and even then the chance is limited). This is similar to what Edensor found of guided tours in India, which direct and 'choreograph' the tourists' gaze and movements (Edensor 1998: 106). This systemized control of the tourist gaze also becomes a factor in terms of the power to produce knowledge of the 'other'.

According to Foucault, an analysis of power should include an examination of knowledge production because knowledge and power are connected; one stimulates the production of the other. He writes: 'the exercise of power perpetually creates knowledge and, conversely, knowledge constantly induces effects of power' (Foucault 1980: 51–52). To illustrate, Lutz and Collins found that through the process of photography for *National Geographic*, 'knowledge [is] produced through close, constant observation of the subject' (Lutz and Collins 1991: 136). It is clear that *National Geographic*'s 'photography of the other operates at the nexus of knowledge and power' (Lutz and Collins 1991: 136). Tourist sites also involve power relationships because they involve the production of knowledge of the 'other' by the tourist site owners through the production of various forms of representation (guide books, advertisements, brochures and other media) as well as through the tourism performances themselves. These representations of the 'other' are often based on stereotypical or romantic ideals and promote a 'normalizing gaze, a surveillance that makes it possible to qualify and to classify' (Lutz and Collins 1991: 136).

In this case, the Grouse Mountain Corporation[7] creates knowledge of, and a space for gazing upon, the 'other' through the objectification of Salish culture into identifiable visual signs: cedar, totem poles, Northwest Coast masks and performances of exotic dances. Advertisements for Grouse Mountain and brochures for Híwus also depict masked exotic dancers. This type of reification of indigenous cultures into 'identifiable' characteristics and images (and performances) is a common strategy in cultural tourism (e.g., Bruner and Kirshenblatt-Gimblett 1994, 2005; Mason 2004; Yang 2010). In addition, tour operators also play a role in knowledge construction (and knowledge dissemination) of the Salish by providing tourists with brochures and by giving them information about Híwus. Through these visual signs and representations, the Grouse Mountain Corporation constructs its object for the tourists' gaze: an exotic, mystical Native. Consequently, tourists, most of whom arrive as part of an organized tour group, already have certain expectations (cf. Blundell 1995; McGregor 2000: 36; Bruner 2005). Thus under the gaze of tourists, who have preconceived (mis)information and knowledge of First Nations cultures, Salish performers may feel obliged to deliver an 'exotic Native'.

However, Salish performers also produce knowledge of and for themselves. For Foucault, power circulates in a web of strategic relationships interwoven with other social and cultural relationships, and within these relations of power exist possibilities for resistance (Foucault 1980: 142). Key to this understanding of the simultaneous existence of power and resistance is the idea that power is not only a negative (prohibitive) force but also a positive force (productive), with the possibility of creating new relationships (Foucault 1980: 120–21). Therefore, even though Salish performers are working within existing power relations where the Grouse Mountain Corporation produces knowledge of the tourist subject as an exotic 'other', a space for the production of alternative knowledge and social meanings of 'the Native' does exist. In fact, the Salish exercise a fair degree of agency in terms of cultural production: they were involved in the construction of the feasthouse itself and in the development of the programme. Salish performers hence play an active role in the production, expression and experience of Salish culture. Still, Foucault's theories alone are not sufficient for understanding either the process of knowledge production or performances in tourism, nor the agency performers exert. For a more nuanced understanding of performances and host–guest interactions, indigenous epistemologies and practices need to be considered and brought into the analysis.

Using the Gaze: Indigenous Frameworks and Epistemologies

Some scholars (e.g., Turner 1991, 2002; Adams 1995, 1997; Tilley 1997; Hahn 2002; McLagan 2002) have examined how indigenous communities use the gaze in public spectacles, the mass media and the tourism industry. The critical question for this chapter, then, is: How do indigenous communities negotiate the gaze in such spaces of objectification and consumption? First, processes of objectification and self-conscious objectification occur simultaneously. For example, McLagan explains how Tibetans and organizers of the Year of Tibet campaign, engage in 'strategic objectification', taking advantage of the gaze and celebrity interest in Tibetan Buddhism and the Dalai Lama to '[propel] the Tibet issue into public consciousness ... through the staging of spectacles of Tibetan cultural and religious difference' (McLagan 2002: 91, 94). She argues that using spectacle and the gaze does not automatically co-opt Tibetans or Tibetan issues: 'We should not think about the strategic objectification of culture solely in terms of commodification and consumption; rather we need to inflect our analysis with a more complicated understanding of what it means to the various actors involved and what is at stake for them' (McLagan 2002: 106). McLagan further suggests that the Kalachakra deity at this campaign is a positive force in the cultural interchange. Although one could argue that this public spectacle leads to the perpetuation of exoticism,[8] for Tibetan Buddhists, 'rituals such as the Kalachakra achieve their efficacy through audience participation' (McLagan 2002: 106). In other words, the ritual is effective – hence fulfilling Tibetan goals – because audience members witness the spectacle. In the context of cultural tourism, Kole observes the exoticization (as originally proposed by Savigliano 1995) of *hula* dancing in Hawaii as a process that simultaneously co-opts and reifies as it empowers those represented: 'The autoexoticization of "sexy maidens" and the "savage male" … empowers the natives to reclaim and maintain their cultural identity and also creates the exotic "other" on which the survival of the natives rests. Both have been appropriated by the travel industry and reinforced through various acts and performances' (Kole 2010: 199). Therefore, teasing out how performers represent themselves may illuminate performers' perspectives on host–guest interactions, as well as the process of production and consumption of performance in the context of tourism.

Second, some indigenous communities draw on their own frameworks and epistemologies to work through social meanings and cultural exchanges. For instance, Hahn argues that Tongan movie-goers draw on their 'ceremonial framework' by transporting the 'narrator' role from the ceremonial context to the theatre context (Hahn 2002: 261). The narrator does not translate the movie literally, but rather, as in ceremonial contexts, 'embellishes and personalizes the story of the movie, cracks jokes, and makes comparisons with local people' (Hahn 2002: 264). In another example, the Kayapo use their own 'cultural categories and social schemas' in their video productions for the public (Turner 2002: 80). Cultural performances in Kayapo ceremonies gain social value through repetition, and this category of repetition is used in Kayapo video (Turner 2002: 83). Turner argues that Kayapo videos are not only available for the public to 'consume', but that they are also a form of 'social and cultural production' with social value (Turner 2002: 84). Video, in this case, has 'drawn upon powerful Native cultural traditions of representation and mimetic objectification and at the same time extended and strengthened those traditional forms' (Turner 2002: 86).

Given these examples, it would be erroneous to assume that processes of objectification and gazing serve only to perpetuate essentialized images. In some cases, as in the examples above, indigenous people use and transform the gaze. These ethnographically grounded analyses elucidate processes of 'strategic objectification' where indigenous people are seen to manipulate gazes and negotiate complex relationships and interactions between multiple producers and the audience. Significantly, by considering how indigenous people draw upon their own cultural frameworks and epistemologies to negotiate performances, a more complex reading of processes of objectification, gazing and consumption is revealed. Thus, while gazing and consumption occur, I offer a different perspective on the typical understanding of such occurrences. Like the Tongans, Kayapo and Tibetans, Salish performers draw on their own epistemologies and ceremonial frameworks in order to negotiate host–tourist interactions and exotic representations, and in order to transform the tourism context itself into a space for the reclaiming of Salish culture, history and identity.

Tourism as Ceremony: Salish World-views and Witnessing

Performances at Híwus feasthouse go beyond the production of an exotic Native for tourists to gaze upon and consume. An alternative reading would be to view the tourist gaze as an act of witnessing. That is, rather than tourists simply consuming Native culture, Salish performers establish a context whereby tourists witness their cultural claims. To do this, I suggest that Salish ceremonial protocols have been transposed into the tourism context as a way of working through cross-cultural interactions while at the same time providing a way to negotiate the significance and meaning of performances for themselves. In this section, I draw on my own ethnographic research to demonstrate how Salish performers at Híwus feasthouse incorporate their ceremonial framework and protocols to subsequently establish what I call a 'tourism as ceremony' context in order to negotiate representations and interactions at this tourist site. In addition, I show how this tourism context also provides a space for the expression and revival of song and dance, which are the embodiment of Salish history, identity and genealogy. In order to illustrate how the tourist's gaze is transformed from consuming performances into acts of witnessing and thus meaningful experiences of performance for the Salish, an explanation of Salish ceremonial frameworks is required.

Performance – oratory, song and dance – has always been part of the ceremonial, social and political life of First Nations on the Northwest Coast. In Coast Salish communities, performance takes place either in the summer season (secular, usually public) or in the winter ceremonial season (sacred, private performance).[9] Winter ceremonies consist of performances that are considered sacred knowledge. For example, spirit dancing is a special expression of spirit power, and although not everyone can be a spirit dancer everyone has the possibility of getting a spirit helper (see Amoss 1978). These helpers afford 'gifts', such as the ability to fish, carve or cure. The acquisition of spirit power involves ritual preparation, after which a spirit helper reveals itself to that person. The person may acquire a song and/or a dance, which embodies spirit power. Spirit power is significant in the Salish world in that it expresses the relationship that the living share with their ancestors (or spirits) and the landscape (or their territory).

Summer ceremonies by contrast are open to all members of the community, and visitors from other First Nation communities may attend public ceremonies. Even though these performances are public, certain individuals or families 'own' the songs and dances: only certain individuals or families may perform them during ceremonies. As with winter ceremonies, these songs and dances may speak of Salish culture and history, and their relationships with the land and their ancestors. For example, one Stó:lō legend personifies Mount Cheam as a female ancestor; the landscape serves to reference history and Stó:lō relationship with ancestors (Biewert 1999: 39–41).[10] Important for this chapter is the fact that legends, songs and dances, whether private or public, speak of Salish relationships with ancestors and spiritual powers or beings, as well as the rights and privileges associated with an individual, family or lineage.

Delving further into ceremonial participation and performances, ceremonies such as a potlatch have several elements and follow certain protocols.[11] In brief, ceremonies usually include a welcome speech; a statement of rights and genealogies expressed through oratory, song and dance; feasting; the witnessing of claims; and gift exchanges. The family and their kin form a social network that participates in ceremonies, which often take place during potlatches.[12] The popular understanding of a potlatch is as a 'give-away' event or a redistribution of goods, but potlatches are both economic and social exchanges.[13] Gift giving is an integral part of the potlatch for more reasons than just the redistribution of goods and wealth. Accepting gifts is like signing a contract. By accepting the gift, guests acknowledge the giver's claims, which may include statements of history, genealogy and ancestry as well as associated privileges, obligations, and status. Even those who do not receive gifts acknowledge and validate the accuracy of these claims by witnessing the events. This process of the making and witnessing of claims is an important practice in naming ceremonies and funerals, for example, where rights and privileges may be stated and/or transferred. Significantly, these claims are embodied through performance – oratory, song and dance. Performance, therefore, is an integral part of both public and private ceremonies. Now on to the tourist site.

Tourism as Ceremony

Performances at Híwus feasthouse progress in a similar way to those in community ceremonies, which I have just described above, and provide tourists a glimpse of what these Salish ceremonies might be like. I would like to make it clear that the Híwus tourist experience, however, is not a 'recreation' of a Salish ceremony itself. The performers make no such claim of offering a 'backstage' view of Salish ceremonies. Rather, the interactions between the performers and tourists and the programme itself progress *as if* they were part of a public ceremony, and some of the dances at Híwus may be danced at a public ceremony. For this reason, I say that the Híwus provides a 'tourism *as* ceremony' experience. Specifically, I suggest that a ceremonial framework and protocols have been recontextualized and reworked to suit a different context – a tourist site, Híwus feasthouse.

Like (public) ceremonies in Salish communities, the Híwus tourist experience consists of certain elements and protocols, which serve to establish the context and meaning of performances as well as the host–guest relationship and obligations. The performers' explanation of ceremonial protocols at the beginning of the evening provides tourists with a framework for the Híwus experience. Kwel-a-a-nexw (one of the performers) describes a naming ceremony to illustrate the significance of the ceremonial complex for the Salish people. 'When you get your name', he says, 'you stand on three blankets for maybe three hours while people speak and give you advice'. He says that, 'you need to remember your history and ancestry, which is passed down and witnessed at these ceremonies'. Kwel-a-a-nexw then states that, 'you (tourists) are honorary witnesses tonight and will be thanked with a gift box to remember the occasion'. He also outlines the rules of the longhouse, stating that 'today we are all like a family in celebration'. With some of the rules established, the Híwus 'tourism as ceremony' experience continues.

Sxananult, one of the hostesses, welcomes tourists and, as in Salish ceremonies, begins with a testimony of her genealogical relations. She states that she is a fifth generation descendent of Squamish Chief George Capilano, and that she received her ancestral name Sxananult from her grand-aunt, Josephine Paul, wife of Andrew Paul. Later, Kwel-a-a-nexw also announces his genealogy, followed by a number of general and specific claims about Salish culture and history. For instance, he accounts for the endurance of Salish culture and their long-standing occupation of the local area. He states that specific legends expressed through song and dance at Híwus speak of Salish cultural survival. The *Sequalia Slu-lum* ('Sequalia Song'), for example, tells the story of Squamish cultural survival (in terms of tradition and spirituality) in the face of missionization. Besides the evidence presented through this performance, Kwel-a-a-nexw offers scientific evidence of the Nation's prolonged existence. He asserts that archaeologists date their occupation to six thousand years ago and that the Salish may have been there from eight to ten thousand years ago. Like claims made in a community ceremonial context, these claims of genealogy are expressions of enduring connections to the ancestors and the Salish land.

Other protocols integral in ceremonies in the community, such as feasting, exchange, and purification, are incorporated at Híwus. One of the performers will purify the space with burning sweet-grass before the tourists arrive. Later, while Salish performers dance, the tourists enjoy a great feast. Salish performers also lead a feast song to express their thanks for the preparers, servers and cooks, who play an important role in offering hospitality to the guests. As with Salish ceremonies, the 'Owl Song' closes this 'tourism as ceremony' experience. Kwel-a-a-nexw told me that this song informs ancestors that the ceremony is over; the spirits are now free to leave. In addition, tourists receive a mini bentwood-box cup holder adorned with bear and raven designs as a gift. This object is not only a souvenir; it also symbolizes their role as guests and, as Kwel-a-a-nexw says, 'honorary witnesses' of the Salish performers' claims of history, genealogy and connection to their territory.

Performance (oratory, storytelling, song and dance) is one of the feature attractions at Híwus. Tourists witness dances associated with clans such as the Bear, Eagle and Mountain Lion Dance.[14] Some of these dances occur during the video presentation of a legend called 'The Awakening', which recounts the story of the creation of the spirit of Man. In short, these dances mimic the motions and movements of animals. When Kwel-a-a-nexw performs the Bear dance, for example, he raises his arms in a clawing motion, then makes his way to scratch each of the four cedar posts inside the feasthouse. He wears a bear mask and a dark, furry bear suit. The mask seems to meet tourist expectations of Northwest Coast art styles, but the bear costume appears to be a marketing strategy. However, when I asked Kwel-a-a-nexw about it, he spoke of his personal connection to the dance rather than his performance attire. He said that, 'you need to be open to the spirit, follow the way of ancestors, and songs come to us'. Kwel-a-a-nexw told me that he owned a Grizzly Bear, Eagle and Wolf song. He recalled how he had had this Bear dance for thirty years before he danced it for the first time in public at a festival with his son. In another example, Nexwsxía7m performs the Eagle dance wearing a headdress with a wooden eagle head and wings; eagle feathers adorn her arms. She circles the central fire pit, dancing like she is flying through the air. At times, she bows over and bends her knees to be close to the ground, then rises up again. Different people perform the Eagle dance on various nights. It is interesting to note that the night Seapulak performed it, he actually wore a Raven mask. I was told that this was acceptable because he is permitted to wear a Raven mask. Kwel-a-a-nexw also assured me that audiences do not know the difference between an eagle and a raven mask. Kwel-a-a-nexw's and Seapulak's statements about acquiring dances and ownership reveal how only certain public dances may be performed at Hiwus, and only by the owner of the song and dance, just as in the community. More importantly, these dances speak of genealogical and spiritual relationships. That is, these dances embody the performers' relationships with their ancestors and the rights and privileges associated with their lineage.

It is important to point out that besides expressing genealogical ties with their ancestors, rights, privileges and connections with Salish territory, performances at the Hiwus also recount Salish history and legends. One example is the 'entrance song' called *Huphupché*, also known as the song of Chief Simon Baker, or Khot-La-Cha's song. Originally, it was a winter (private ceremonial) song. Kwel-a-a-nexw told me that three chiefs – Chief Cowichan Charley Isipaymilt, Secweqemc Chief Basil David and Squamish Chief Joe Capilano – created this version in honour of their journey to London in 1906 to discuss their conditions and the land question in British Columbia with Edward VII. When they returned, the song and dance was made available for all Squamish people to use. The fact that the song and dance was transformed from a private winter song to one about the chiefs' journey, to a public song for Squamish people in general, is interesting. It shows how songs and dances are always changing and evolving for different contexts. Now, Salish performers dance the *Huphupché* in a tourism context. Tourists may not understand the full meaning and significance of this dance, besides the brief history of the song provided and fact that it is an entrance song. It is not that Salish performers wish to separate 'authentic' from 'tourist' performances, as in the case of Balinese cultural tourism described by Picard (1995), although they do keep winter dances private and do not perform these at Hiwus. Rather, the performance of this history is also personal to the Salish and continues to have meaning outside this tourist site. This counters the argument that 'staged performances' result in a loss of meaning for indigenous performers (cf. Adams 1997). Rather, in this case, the performance leads to the reassertion of history and meaning for Salish performers.

In one of the last performances of the night, tourists dance together with the performers in four different groups representing four different clans: Wolf, Whale, Eagle and Raven.[15] The tourists' role as guests is confirmed through this participation. While other tourist sites are often designed to keep a distance between the tourists and the hosts (see Johnson and Underiner 2001), performers at Hiwus attempt to close this distance by incorporating tourist participation. At this point of the evening, Kwel-a-a-nexw outlines the responsibilities of each of the spirits representing the four clans and explains how they connect with their ancestors. He also reminds us about guests' responsibilities at ceremonies and conveys the importance of feasting. By witnessing, dancing and feasting, Kwel-a-a-nexw says that the tourists have become 'temporary clan members'. Through this final act of tourist participation, where all four clans dance together along with the tourists, Salish performers acknowledge tourists as guests of the Híwus family via this 'tourism as ceremony' experience. As Kwel-a-a-nexw says, 'Once you come in that door, we are all family'. And by dancing together with the performers, tourists' acknowledge Salish claims made via their performances throughout the evening. The mini bentwood-box cup-holder gift finalizes this 'tourism as ceremony' experience and reminds tourists that they were guests at the Híwus and witnessed Salish claims. While tourists may not always understand the full scope of rights and obligations embedded within Salish performances, this 'tourism as ceremony' experience is nonetheless a reaffirmation for the Salish performers. They have witnessed Salish claims of history, territory, genealogy and ancestry in their performances. Moreover, as witnesses of their performances, tourists at the very least acknowledge the presence of Salish people in British Columbia.

On the one hand, performances are integral to the Híwus 'tourism as ceremony' experience because they meet tourists' expectations to see dancing as well as typical masks and Northwest Coast art; on the other hand, these dances represent performers' privileges associated with their clan or lineage, as the performers explain, as well as their relationships with their ancestors and the spirit world, and their connection to the surrounding territory. It is not unusual for this double meaning – in this case, the production of an exotic Native and the representation of Salish history, rights and relationships – to exist at cultural tourist sites, in particular where hosts have some say and control over the performances (see Phillips 1998: 19–20; Mason 2004).

The significance of these performances, therefore, is not the movements of the dances themselves (although they do mimic clan spirits) but rather, how performances speak of Salish rights, history, connection to land and their relationships with ancestors. Performances are not simply movements and songs; performances make claims, and the assertion of claims via performance is only possible in a tourism context because performances follow protocol. Finally, the 'performance' at Híwus encompasses not only the songs and dances themselves, but the entire sequence of events from the welcoming and feasting, to the dancing and gift exchange.

Salish ceremonial frameworks and protocols have been transposed and reworked for the Híwus tourist experience, thereby establishing a suitable context for host–guest interaction and for expressing the meaning of performances. Interestingly enough, Mason (2004) observed a similar (though not identical) process of performance recontextualization in 2001 on Victoria Island, Ottawa, Ontario. In this 'aboriginal experience', the interpreter (performer) similarly engaged tourists in an Iroquoian longhouse with dance demonstrations and oral traditions, including a welcoming song (Mason 2004: 843–44). The welcoming song has been recontextualized in order to educate tourists about aboriginal music 'while respect[ing] the functional integrity of musical forms' (Mason 2004: 844). As with Híwus, interpreters do not perform sacred or ceremonial songs and dances. In addition, tourists participate in an inter-tribal friendship dance, a contemporary social dance that still feels 'genuine' for tourists because of the interpreter's explanation of the music and their interaction (Mason 2004: 847). Mason astutely points out how the passive tourist gaze loses the power to construct the 'other' when the gaze is reflected back through participation (Mason 2004: 847).

More than being reflected back through participation, the gaze is transformed into acts of witnessing at Hiwus feasthouse through the application of Salish ways of being and knowing. To fully understand the nuances of this host–guest interaction and relationship, we need to move beyond Western understandings of gazing, participation and witnessing. Mason's interpretation of 'sound and meaning in aboriginal tourism', for example, forefronts aboriginal 'ways of being, protocols, and forms of interaction' (Mason 2004: 845). Although the interpreter's approach divides 'passive audiences from active performers', Mason explains how the interpreter's style of presentation involves taking on a 'teacher' role by inviting tourists to 'actively listen' to the music and his explanations, rather than 'actively question'; she explains how in many Native American communities, 'listening can be an active way of being and interacting' (Mason 2004: 845–46). Furthermore, the idea that gazing is simply equivalent to seeing or observing from a distance is a deeply entrenched Western perspective. For instance, Chakravorty applies Indian aesthetics of *rasa* in her analysis of classical Indian dance to show how gazing is seeing, knowing, touching and expressing feelings; it is a multi-sensory experience that involves 'returning the gaze of the observer or devotee' so that it is a 'participatory collective experience' (Chakravorty 2004: 9). These examples illustrate the importance of considering indigenous epistemologies. In this case, an understanding of Salish epistemologies, ceremonial framework and protocols informs the analysis of tourism production and consumption beyond a critique at the level of discourse and representation. I have suggested that the gaze is not only returned via participation, but also transformed into acts of witnessing. At Hiwus, participation is more complex than the act of dancing, and witnessing is more than seeing or observing. Witnessing involves establishing a relationship in a context that implies participation and the acknowledgement of claims made by the hosts. In this way, performances at Hiwus feasthouse transpire as 'ceremony'.

Revival and Creativity

The second objective of this chapter is to show how tourism may also facilitate revival and creativity in dance. Due to assimilation policies and the reserve-school system, many songs and dances were 'lost' (see Ellis 1990; Nabokov 1991). In celebration of their connection to Grouse Mountain – their place, their territory – the Salish performers researched and choreographed the Grouse dance as part of the Hiwus programme. Besides the Cocalith (Cannibal Woman) dance, this is one of the most dramatic and spectacular performances at Hiwus. When Kwel-a-a-nexw performs the Grouse dance, he rises from a trap door in the stage floor and is surrounded by a cloud of dry ice. Dizzying lights circle the cedar plank floor and the fire pit as

Kwel-a-a-nexw passionately dances, moving rapidly across the floor using quick, short steps, like a bird, wearing a Grouse mask. The music is an energetic, hip, rock-like soundtrack, of more than 80 beats per minute, or so Kwel-a-a-nexw tells me. A photograph of this dance is also used in promotional materials; the Híwus brochure depicts a performer all shrouded in smoke wearing elaborate regalia and a similar exotic mask.

Delving into this performance further, we see that the dance holds great personal meaning and significance for Salish participants. Although at first this dance appears to once again feed into the trope of an exotic, mystical, Native, this dance again makes explicit statements about Salish connection to place and their ancestors. That is, the Grouse dance speaks of Salish relationships with their land, ancestors and the spirit world. To explain further, the grouse is a bird found on the mountain (hence the name Grouse Mountain), linking the dance directly with Salish territory. The spirit of the grouse is also viewed as an ancestor, Grouse. During the recounting of the legend 'The Awakening' at Híwus, we are told that the Creator asked the Grouse to watch over and guide the new spirit, Man, and that he gladly accepted. The Grouse dance is based on this Sechelt legend; however, the Sechelt Nation, part of the Coast Salish culture group, gave the Salish performers permission to use this dance at the Híwus (another example of adhering to protocol). In sum, the Grouse dance is about Salish connection to the spirit world as well as to the mountain and larger territory.[16] Nexwsxía7m proclaims in an interview: 'This is Coast Salish territory here, there are so many of us – Sechelt there, Musquem here, Stó:lö there'. Even though the Grouse Mountain Corporation relies on images of an exotic, mystical Native like this one to sell the Híwus tourism experience, the Grouse dance (and song and legend) clearly declares their history and continuity: this is our territory and we are here.

Although not part of a strategic 'cultural revival' plan specifically developed for the purpose of making themselves more attractive for the tourism market (cf. Grünewald 2002), the opportunity to revive this dance and make this claim (of connection to the land and cultural continuity) was facilitated by the chance to perform it at Híwus. Kwel-a-a-nexw said that the first time he performed this dance after many years of it remaining unused was at the special opening of Híwus in 1997 for Salish elders. He emotionally recalled how some of the women cried 'because they were so moved to see their legend and culture alive and come to life [again]'. Moreover, Salish community members are proud of what is happening at Híwus. Kwel-a-a-nexw recounted, 'In the winter, we have had native kids, elders, chiefs up here. It was a positive response. One elder, a traditional winter dancer, got up and sang, shook my hand and said to keep up the good work'. When I asked Nexwsxía7m how they felt about Híwus back on the reserve, she told me about the opening of Híwus: 'There were chiefs at the feasthouse, they were proud of the sharing. They put down blankets to honour us. We had to be on the ball though, do things right'. These statements clearly reveal that Salish performers at Híwus and individuals from the community do not view their performances simply as commodities.

Híwus also provides a space to perform new dances, which, although new, are owned and created in the same tradition as other public and private dances, and express personal experiences. One evening, Nexwsxía7m performed what she called the Rediscovery dance. In this dance, Nexwsxía7m moves eloquently in a slow hop one way, then the other, with one hand on her shoulder and the other arm pointing straight out in the direction she is moving as she sings about her 'Rediscovery'. This dance was not part of the regular Híwus programme, so I asked Nexwsxía7m about it.[17] She said that the song was given to her by her mother, and that she danced it for the first time at the 1992 International Youth Conference. She did not reveal much about the meaning of the dance and song to me, except that it is a 'song that speaks of feelings'. But the fact that improvisations occur and new dances are performed at the Híwus is noteworthy. It demonstrates how Salish performers use Híwus as a space to express personal experiences through performance, much like they do in Salish ceremonies outside the tourism context.

I witnessed another case of improvisation one night as Kwel-a-a-nexw and Nexwsxía7m were preparing for the dinner show that evening. Nexwsxía7m asked Kwel-a-a-nexw if he knew the 'Frog Song'. He started to sing it, and Nexwsxía7m joined in. He then said, 'do you want to sing it tonight?' She asked him if they should do this song, since it comes from the Nisga. Then Nexwsxía7m stated that 'they are our neighbours, it should be okay; we can say this song belongs to them'. In the end, they did not perform the 'Frog Song' that night. However, this exchange reaffirms my examples above of the Bear dance and Eagle dance by again illustrating the importance of respecting the ownership of songs and the privileges associated with certain First Nations or lineages. Even though Híwus feasthouse is a tourist site, some Salish individuals view it has one of their longhouses in the sense that interactions and performances similarly follow protocols. In fact, the Lilloet and Squamish Nations used the Híwus feasthouse one night for a meeting. In Sxananult's opinion, however, Híwus is not 'a real feasthouse; pictures would not be allowed in a real feasthouse', she says, 'it's too spiritual a place'. Híwus feasthouse hence occupies a dual space: it is primarily a tourist site, and yet Salish performers at Híwus follow protocol and express Salish claims of history, ancestry, place and genealogy through performances as they would if it were one of their own feasthouses. In the end, attention to protocol is necessary, as Híwus is a public space of cultural interaction, even though it is also a tourist site. These examples show how there is room for revival, innovation, creativity and experimentation in tourism, and that this creativity does not necessarily conflict with the need to meet tourists' expectations or with notions of 'authenticity' (see Kole 2010).

A Word about Authenticity
The notion of authenticity has been much debated in anthropology and in the tourism literature (e.g., MacCannell 1976; Hobsbawm and Ranger 1983; Cohen 1988; Linnekin 1991; Jolly 1992; Gable and Handler 1996; Harkin 1997; Bruner 2001, 2005; Olsen 2002; Scarangella 2010). These debates centre on critiquing the link between authenticity and popular ideas about culture and tradition.

For one, the notion of authenticity leads to the reification, essentialization and objectification of culture. Moreover, tradition is often thought of as something unchanging, old and 'pure' (Mauze 1997: 1–5). These modernist views of culture and tradition as static and homogeneous also frequently consist of dichotomies such as authentic and inauthentic, traditional and modern, spurious and genuine, copies and originals (Handler and Linnekin 1984; Jolly 1992: 49; Bruner and Kirshenblatt-Gimblett 1994: 459; Gable and Handler 1996). Because the notion of authenticity has proved to be problematic, scholars have suggested alternative conceptions of culture in terms of 'hybridity' (Clifford 1997) or 'invented tradition' (Hobsbawm and Ranger 1983). In addition, scholars have moved from focusing on the appearance of aesthetic forms and tradition to discourses of authenticity about aesthetics and traditions, which leads to discussions of power and agency (Bruner 2005; Scarangella 2010).

Without a doubt, the Grouse Mountain Corporation is interested in promoting the authenticity of its site and performances in order to attract tourists, and is concerned with providing an overall authentic experience. This is evident from their brochure, which promises an 'authentic West Coast Native experience',[18] and their customer satisfaction survey, which asks tourists to 'rate the authenticity of the performance'. But what does the Grouse Mountain Corporation mean by authentic? They appear to be referencing multiple discourses of authenticity here. Like the New Salem site that reproduces Abraham Lincoln's town (see Bruner 2005: 149–50), the Grouse Mountain Corporation claims that Híwus is authentic in terms of 'verisimilitude' and 'genuineness' – these are real Natives presenting a credible reproduction of Native culture; it is just like the real thing. To this end, they involved Salish individuals in the development of the programme. It is also authentic in terms of 'originality' (Bruner 2005: 150) – Salish individuals made the feasthouse, entrance pole and masks. If we view authenticity in terms of a discourse, then Grouse Mountain Corporation's meanings are clearly visible.

On the other hand, the Salish performers do not view their performances in terms of purity or some measurable variable, or in terms of a credible reproduction. Their views of authenticity are more experiential. When I asked Nexwsxía7m what she thought of the survey question, she replied: 'How can you say what is authentic? It's authentic because we speak the truth'. Neither do performers say that their performances are 'invented' or stereotypical representations of an 'Imaginary Indian'. Such scholastic conceptions do not resonate with performers. Upon reviewing a draft of my master's dissertation (Scarangella 2002), for example, Kwel-a-a-nexw commented that Salish culture is not 'invented'; the Salish have a long-standing tradition and cultural continuity. Grünewald similarly writes that the Pataxó Indians do not recognize a process of 'invented traditions' but 'prefer to communicate a "cultural revival"' of traditions for tourism (Grünewald 2002: 1012). Nonetheless, what can be said is that these Salish performers (like the Pataxó, the Tibetans described by McLagan, and the Tana Toraja described by Adams) are indeed active producers of culture who exert agency. Salish performers at Híwus reframe tourism images of an exotic Native into meaningful performances embodying Salish claims, and negotiate the tourism encounter itself into a space for cultural exchange, based on their own epistemology and frameworks.

I also find it useful to think of tradition not in terms of a 'continuity of manifest cultural practices' but as 'a measure of the effectiveness of symbols, and especially their ability to constitute and motivate a group' (Harkin 1997: 100). This highlights how traditions may change, but may also continue to have (new) meaning for the group (see also Skinner 2006). Key to this notion of authenticity in terms of effectiveness is the 'ritual reframing of cultural symbols' (Harkin 1997: 98). Applying this perspective to Híwus, Salish performers reconfigure their ceremonial framework and protocols in order to negotiate meaning and the significance of performances for a different context. From this perspective, one could argue that the performances in the tourist encounter at Híwus are 'effective' rather than 'authentic'. The notion of 'tourist realism' as an alternative to authenticity similarly relates to 'virtuality and its effects', but this idea does not fully encapsulate the performances at Híwus, as it emphasizes the experience as being effective for the tourist (Bruner and Kirshenblatt-Gimblett 1994; Bruner 2005). More appropriately, the notion of 'cultural integrity in lieu of authenticity ... shifts the focus away from appearances and onto practices in appropriate contexts', including tourist sites, as they are active sites of negotiation and interaction (Mason 2004: 848–49). Salish performers maintain the cultural integrity of their performances by adhering to Salish protocol while recontextualizing performances for a tourism context.

In addition, the concept of 'staged authenticity' is problematic because, first, Salish performers do not attempt to replicate a ceremony, and second, the notion of staged authenticity implies that tourist performances are of no significance to the Salish. This is clearly not the case at Híwus. For one, although the brochure appears to suggest it, Salish performers do not attempt to recreate an 'authentic ceremony'. Rather, performers draw on their ceremonial framework and rework it for this tourist site. It makes sense that a public gathering, tourist site or not, follows local protocol. Performances are not superficial or 'staged' in the sense that they give tourists 'backstage access' to an authentic ceremony, even though it progresses like a ceremony and follows particular protocols. While the line between what these Salish individuals do at Híwus and what they do for themselves is not so clear, the distinction between what they do in tourism and what they do in private ceremonies is maintained; that is, the distinction between private and public is maintained (see Picard 1995: 56–59). Even back on the reserve, differences exist between public and private ceremonies, public and private dances, and who can dance what. While the brochure and related media refer to Híwus generically as 'Northwest Coast', the tourism experience specifically represents Coast Salish (specifically Squamish and Sechelt) songs, dances, masks, entrance poles and so forth. Híwus is not a 'model culture', as described by Stanton (1989) of the Polynesian Cultural Center, where identifiable characteristics of different First Nations are chosen to construct one non-existent 'Native' representation because it is not an attempt to produce a facsimile or 'mimic' an actual ceremony. I have argued that, in this case, tourism is experienced 'as Salish' – as a Salish ceremony.

Furthermore, as Adams (1997: 316, 317) found for the Tana Toraja in Indonesia, cultural productions of rituals in tourist contexts do not necessarily result in a loss of meaning for indigenous people.[19] And as with the Tibetan example, performing in a tourist context does not diminish meaning. In the case of Híwus feasthouse, the recontextualization and reinterpretation of ceremonial protocol and performing for tourists do not result in a loss of meaning of the performances. Rather, performances at Híwus relate to personal experiences, Salish history, Salish relationships with their land and ancestors, and to the rights and privileges associated with their lineage. Performances at Híwus are more complex than the production of an exotic 'other' in that their meaning and significance are maintained. Híwus hence may be viewed as a space to express these Salish claims through performance. In sum, discourses of authenticity and staged authenticity underestimate the importance of these spaces for local communities. I agree with Taylor (2001: 16, 24), then, who argues that we should view these types of cultural interactions as the 'sincere' communication of local identities. As such, Salish performers exert agency in the process of cultural production for tourists, despite tourism apparently being a context for gazing upon the exotic Native.

Conclusions

This chapter contributes to ongoing debates in the anthropology of dance about the centrality of performance for negotiating the tourist encounter as well as the production and consumption of cultures and identities. At the beginning of this chapter, I asked if the Híwus tourism experience is an example of what MacCannell (1976) refers to as the search for 'staged authenticity'. The tourism media for Híwus feasthouse promises tourists an authentic Northwest Coast experience, and the Grouse Mountain Corporation appears to produce an exotic, mystical Native for tourists to gaze upon and consume. While Urry's concept of the 'tourist gaze' offers insight into the interactions at Híwus, including the objectification and knowledge production of 'Native culture', an analysis focused exclusively on the gaze tends to emphasize consumption and the passivity of the hosts. This chapter offers another perspective on host–tourist interactions and the production, performance and consumption ('gazing') of the 'other' by considering indigenous epistemologies. I have argued that Salish performers transform the tourist gaze into acts of witnessing by adhering to protocols and recontextualizing a Salish ceremonial framework for a tourism context in order to engage with a non-Native audience. Ceremonial protocols that have been transposed into the Híwus tourism experience include expressions of genealogy, performance (oratory, song and dance), feasting, gift exchange and guest participation, including the act of witnessing. Performances in this 'tourism as ceremony' experience speak of Salish claims in terms of their history and culture, rights and privileges, and their continuous connection to their land and ancestors. Viewed from this perspective, I have suggested that, rather than being authentic, performances are 'effective' and maintain 'cultural integrity'. The tourists' gaze, therefore, may be viewed as a meaningful form of witnessing these claims, once this interaction is contextualized within Salish ceremonial frameworks and epistemologies. This is an indigenous perspective of witnessing that moves beyond Western notions of simply observing and seeing. For these Salish performers, the fact that tourists witness their claims and take them back home, either through the retelling of their experience and what they heard or through photography, does not simply result in the consumption of an exotic Native. Rather, gazing fulfils the tourists' obligations as witnesses in a process of cultural interaction and exchange.

Notes

1. It is important to note that although this culture group belongs to the larger Northwest Coast culture area, there is socio-cultural variation among the different culture groups and various First Nations. Furthermore, the history of colonialism affected different Nations at different times to varying degrees. This chapter does not attempt to provide a comprehensive account of Coast Salish experiences or world-views.
2. Tour groups often consist of tourists from Australia, Germany or France (and other European countries), mainly couples or friends ranging in age from their late twenties to their forties. Very few children or elderly attend. On one night, there was a tour group from Japan.
3. *Huy-chexw-aa* means 'thank you' and is expressed by raising your arms, elbows bent and palms facing you at heart level. This gesture is also used to thank the Creator.
4. I use the term 'clan' here because this is the word performers use at Híwus. The term that would be used in anthropology to describe the grouping (non-corporate) of Salish extended families would be lineage.
5. Thank you to all the participants of this research project – my teachers at Híwus – and to the Grouse Mountain staff for their cooperation. Ethnographic research included participant-observations at the tourist site, semi-structured interviews with performers, informal conversations and discourse analysis of advertisements and various media related to Híwus feasthouse.
6. Although Foucault might argue that the presence of the gazer does not need to be verified in order for it to be a controlling force, this face-to-face contact and interaction between tourists (gazers) and performers (subjects) should not go unstated.
7. The Grouse Mountain Corporation is run by a board of directors without Salish representation.
8. McLagan writes: 'having the Dalai Lama sitting on an elaborate throne with a fringed yellow hat and talking to an audience through a series of esoteric visualizations ... would merely create images of the Tibetan leader that would reinforce exotic stereotypes about Tibetans, confuse his political supporters, and produce feature stories about the celebrity Buddhists in attendance instead of generating hard news coverage of the Tibetan situation' (McLagan 2002: 101–2).
9. See Jenness (1955), Kew (1970, 1978) and Biewert (1999) for discussions on ceremonial life during the winter.
10. This legend acts as a teaching guide to relationships. Place and landscape figure prominently in oral history, as both are agents of power. That is, power is located in place and ancestral beings, and history lives through the landscape. For an in-depth discussion on 'figures of power' and place, see Biewert (1999).
11. Kew (1970) provides a detailed account of winter ceremonials, and the different elements and phases, describing how ceremonial processes constantly shift. That is, there is not one identifiable way of doing things for everyone and all contexts.

12. The family is the main social unit in the Salish world. Following Suttles (1987) and Elmendorf (1993), who recognized the importance of family relationships, Miller (2001: 3, 8) elaborates that these family relationships formed networks that are both temporary and corporate.
13. For more views and discussion on the potlatch, see Kan (1986, 1989) and the essays by Boas, Barnett, Codere, Drucker and Garfield gathered in McFeat (1997).
14. The following discussion does not describe the entire one-and-a-half-hour Híwus programme. There are other dances that take place that I do not discuss here. For a more detailed ethnographic description and analysis, see Scarangella (2002).
15. Masks representing these four clans and other spirit animals adorn the walls of the feasthouse.
16. For a more detailed discussion on the significance of 'place' at Híwus feasthouse, see Scarangella (2004).
17. I witnessed this dance on two occasions in the process of conducting fieldwork.
18. The Híwus brochure reads 'experience authentic West Coast Native Culture in its natural setting'; 'inside you are welcomed by a ritual of Native song and dance' (Grouse Mountain Resorts Ltd, 'Supernatural Híwus, Grouse Mountain, The Peak of Vancouver', 2001).
19. On the other hand, Greenwood (1989) argues that these productions do result in a loss of ritual meaning.

References

Adams, K.M. 1995. 'Making-up the Toraja? The Appropriation of Tourism, Anthropology, and Museums for Politics in Upland Sulawesi, Indonesia', *Ethnology* 34(2): 143–54.
———— 1997. 'Ethnic Tourism and the Renegotiation of Tradition in Tana Toraja (Sulawesi, Indonesia)', *Ethnology* 36(4): 309–21.
Amoss, P. 1978. *Coast Salish Spirit Dancing: The Survival of an Ancestral Religion*. Seattle: University of Washington Press.
Biewert, C. 1999. *Brushed by Cedar, Living by the River: Coast Salish Figures of Power*. Tuscon: University of Arizona Press.
Blundell, V. 1995. 'Riding the Polar Bear Express, and "Other" Encounters Between Tourists and First Peoples in Canada', *Journal of Canadian Studies* 30(4): 28–51.
Boissevain, J. 1996. 'Introduction', in J. Boissevain (ed.), *Coping With Tourists: European Reactions to Mass Tourism*. Oxford: Berghahn, pp.1–26.
Bruner, E.M. 2001. 'The Maasai and the Lion King: Authenticity, Nationalism, and Globalization in African Tourism', *American Ethnologist* 28(4): 881–908.
———— 2005. *Culture on Tour: Ethnographies of Travel*. Chicago: University of Chicago Press.
Bruner, E.M., and B. Kirshenblatt-Gimblett. 1994. 'Maasai on the Lawn: Tourist Realism in East Africa', *Cultural Anthropology* 9(4): 435–70.
———— 2005. 'Maasai on the Lawn: Tourist Realism in East Africa', in E.M. Bruner, *Culture on Tour: Ethnographies of Travel*. Chicago: University of Chicago Press, pp.33–70.
Chakravorty, P. 2004. 'Dance, Pleasure and Indian Women as Multisensorial Subjects', *Visual Anthropology* 17(1): 1–17.
———— 2009. 'Moved to Dance: Remix, *Rasa*, and a New India', *Visual Anthropology* 22(2): 211–28.
Chambers, E. 2000. *Native Tours: The Anthropology of Travel and Tourism*. Illinois: Waveland Press.

Clifford, J. 1997. *Routes: Travel and Translation in the Late Twentieth Century*. Cambridge, MA: Harvard University Press.

Cohen, E. 1988. 'Authenticity and Commoditization in Tourism', *Annals of Tourism Research* 15(3): 371–86.

Crang, P. 1997. 'Performing the Tourist Product', in C. Rojek and J. Urry (eds), *Touring Cultures: Transformations of Travel and Theory*. London: Routledge, pp.137–54.

Davenport, B.A. 2000. 'Witnessing and the Medical Gaze: How Medical Students Learn to See at a Free Clinic for the Homeless', *Medical Anthropology Quarterly* 14(3): 310–27.

Desmond, J. (ed.) 1997. *Meaning in Motion: New Cultural Studies of Dance*. Durham, NC: Duke University Press.

―――― 1999. *Staging Tourism: Bodies on Display from Waikiki to Sea World*. Chicago: University of Chicago Press.

Edensor, T. 1998. *Tourists at the Taj: Performance and Meaning at a Symbolic Site*. London: Routledge.

―――― 2001. 'Performing Tourism, Staging Tourism: (Re)producing Tourist Space and Practice', *Tourist Studies* 1(1): 59–81.

Ellis, C. 1990. '"Truly Dancing Their Own Way": Modern Revival and Diffusion of the Gourd Dance', *American Indian Quarterly* 14(1): 19–33.

Elmendorf, W.W. 1993. *Twana Narratives: Native Historical Accounts of a Coast Salish Culture*. Vancouver: Univeristy of British Columbia Press.

Evans-Pritchard, D. 1989. 'How "They" See "Us": Native American Images of Tourists', *Annals of Tourism Research* 16: 89–105.

Foucault, M. 1973. *The Birth of the Clinic: An Archaeology of Medical Perception*. London: Tavistock.

―――― 1977. *Discipline and Punish: The Birth of the Prison*. New York: Pantheon.

―――― 1980. *Power/Knowledge: Selected Interviews and Other Writings, 1972–1977*, trans. and ed. C. Gordon. New York: Pantheon.

Francis, D. 1992. *The Imaginary Indian*. Vancouver: Arsenal Pulp Press.

Gable, E., and R. Handler. 1996. 'After Authenticity at an American Heritage Site', *American Anthropologist* 98(3): 568–78.

Ginsburg, F. 2002a. 'Screen Memories: Re-signifying the Traditional in Indigenous Media', in L. Abu-Lughod, F. Ginsburg and B. Larkin (eds), *Media Worlds: Anthropology on New Terrain*. Berkeley: University of California Press, pp.39–57.

―――― 2002b. 'Mediating Culture: Indigenous Media, Ethnographic Film, and the Production of Identity', in K. Askew and R.R. Wilk (eds), *Anthropology of Media: A Reader*. Malden, MA: Blackwell, pp.210–35.

Greenwood, D.J. 1989. 'Culture by the Pound: An Anthropological Perspective on Tourism as Cultural Commoditization', in V.L. Smith (ed.), *Hosts and Guests: The Anthropology of Tourism*. Philadelphia: University of Pennsylvania Press, pp.171–85.

Grünewald, R.A. 2002. 'Tourism and Cultural Revival', *Annals of Tourism Research* 29(4): 1004–21.

Hahn, S. 2002. 'The Tongan Tradition of Going to the Movies', in K. Askew and R.R. Wilk (eds), *Anthropology of Media: A Reader*. Malden, MA: Blackwell, pp.258–69.

Handler, R. 1988. *Nationalism and the Politics of Culture in Quebec*. Madison: University of Wisconsin Press.

Handler, R., and J. Linnekin. 1984. 'Tradition, Genuine or Spurious', *Journal of American Folklore* 97(385): 273–90.

Hanson, F.A. 1997. 'Empirical Anthropology, Postmodernism, and the Invention of Tradition', in M. Mauze (ed.), *Present is Past: Some Uses of Tradition in Native Societies*. Lanham, MD: University Press of America, pp.195–214.

Harkin, M. 1997. 'A Tradition of Invention: Modern Ceremonialism on the Northwest Coast', in M. Mauze (ed.), *Present is Past: Some Uses of Tradition in Native Societies*. Lanham, MD: University Press of America, pp.97–111.

Hendry, J. 2005. *Reclaiming Culture: Indigenous People and Self-representation*. Basingstoke: Palgrave Macmillan.

Henry, R. 2000. 'Dancing into Being: The Tjapukai Aboriginal Cultural Park and the Laura Dance Festival', *Australian Journal of Anthropology* 11(3): 322–32.

Hobsbawm, E., and T. Ranger (eds). 1983. *The Invention of Tradition*. Cambridge: Cambridge University Press.

Jenness, D. 1955. *The Faith of a Coast Salish Indian*. Victoria: British Columbia Provincial Museum.

Johnson, K.N., and T. Underiner. 2001. 'Command Performances: Staging Native Americans at Tillicum Village', in C.J. Meyer and D. Royer (eds), *Selling the Indian: Commercializing and Appropriating American Indian Cultures*. Tucson: University of Arizona Press, pp.44–61.

Jolly, M. 1992. 'Specters of Inauthenticity', *Contemporary Pacific* 4(1): 49–72.

Kan, S. 1986. 'The 19th-century Tlingit Potlatch: A New Perspective', *American Ethnologist* 13: 191–212.

⸺ 1989. *Symbolic Immortality: The Tlingit Potlatch of the Nineteenth Century*. Washington, DC: Smithsonian Institution Press.

Kew, J.E.M. 1970. 'Coast Salish Ceremonial Life: Status and Identity in a Modern Village', Ph.D. dissertation, Department of Anthropology. Seattle: University of Washington.

⸺ 1978. 'Central and Southern Coast Salish Ceremonies since 1900', in W. Suttles and W. Sturtevant (eds), *Handbook of North American Indians*, Vol.7: *Northwest Coast*. Washington, DC: Smithsonian Institution, pp.476–84.

Kole, S.K. 2010. 'Dance, Representation, and Politics of Bodies: "Thick Description" of Tahitian Dance in Hawai'ian Tourism Industry', *Journal of Tourism and Cultural Change* 8(3): 183–205.

Laxson, J.D. 1991. 'How "We"' See "Them": Tourism and Native Americans', *Annals of Tourism Research* 18: 365–91.

Linnekin, J. 1991. 'Cultural Invention and the Dilemma of Authenticity', *American Anthropologist* 93(2): 446–49.

Lischke, U., and D.T. McNab (eds). 2005. *Walking a Tightrope: Aboriginal People and Their Representations*. Waterloo: Wilfrid Laurier University Press.

Lutz, C., and J. Collins. 1991. 'The Photograph as an Intersection of Gazes: The Example of National Geographic', *Visual Anthropology Review* 7(1): 134–49.

MacCannell, D. 1976. *The Tourist: A New Theory of the Leisure Class*. New York: Schocken Books.

⸺ 1992. *Empty Meeting Grounds: The Tourist Papers*. New York: Routledge.

⸺ 2001. 'Tourist Agency', *Tourist Studies* 1(1): 23–37.

McFeat, T. (ed.). 1997. *Indians of the North Pacific Coast: Studies in Selected Topics*. Ottawa: Carleton University Press.

McGregor, A. 2000. 'Dynamic Texts and Tourist Gaze: Death, Bones and Buffalo', *Annals of Tourism Research* 27(1): 27–50.

McLagan, M. 2002. 'Spectacles of Difference: Cultural Activism and the Mass Mediation of Tibet', in F. Ginsburg, L. Abu-Lughod and B. Larkin (eds), *Media Worlds*. Berkeley: University of California Press, pp.90–111.

Mason, K. 2004. 'Sound and Meaning in Aboriginal Tourism', *Annals of Tourism Research* 31(4): 837–53.

Mauze, M. 1997. 'On Concepts of Tradition: An Introduction', in M. Mause (ed.), *Present is Past: Some Uses of Tradition in Native Societies*. Lanham, MD: University Press of America, pp.1–5.

Meyer, C.J., and D. Royer (eds). 2001. *Selling the Indian: Commercialization and Appropriating American Indian Cultures*. Tuscon: University of Arizona Press.

Miller, B. 2001. *The Problem of Justice: Tradition and Law in the Coast Salish World*. Lincoln: University of Nebraska Press.

Nabokov, P. (ed.). 1991. *Native American Testimony: A Chronicle of Indian–White Relations From Prophecy to the Present, 1492–1992*. New York: Viking.

Nicks, T. 1999. 'Indian Villages and Entertainments: Setting the Stage for Tourist Souvenir Sales', in R.B. Phillips and C.B. Steiner (eds), *Unpacking Culture: Art And Commodity in Colonial and Postcolonial Worlds*. Berkeley: University of California Press, pp.301–15.

Olsen, K. 2002. 'Authenticity as a Concept in Tourism Research: The Social Organization of the Experience of Authenticity', *Tourist Studies* 2(2): 159–82.

Peers, L. 1999. '"Playing Ourselves": First Nation and Native American Interpreters at Living History Sites', *Public Historian* 21(4): 39–59.

———— 2007. *Playing Ourselves: Interpreting Native Histories at Historic Reconstructions*. Lanham, MD: Altamira Press.

Phillips, R.B. 1998. *Trading Identities: The Souvenir in Native North American Art from the Northeast, 1700–1900*. Seattle: University of Washington Press.

Picard, M. 1995. 'Cultural Heritage and Tourist Capital: Cultural Tourism in Bali', in M.-F. Lanfant, J.B. Allcock and E.M. Bruner (eds), *International Tourism: Identity and Change*. London: Sage, pp.44–66.

Reed, S. 1998. 'The Politics of Dance', *Annual Review of Anthropology* 27: 503–32.

———— 2002. 'Performing Respectability: The Berava, Middle-class Nationalism, and the Classicization of Kandyan Dance in Sri Lanka', *Cultural Anthropology* 17(2): 246–77.

Said, E. 1979. *Orientalism*. London: Routledge.

Scarangella, L. 2002. 'Reclaiming Symbols and History in Multiple Zones: Experiencing Coast Salish Culture and Identity Through Performance at Híwus Feasthouse', M.A. dissertation. British Columbia: University of British Columbia.

———— 2004. 'Narratives and Counter-narratives of "Nativeness" in Tourism: Re-claiming Place at Híwus Feasthouse', *Anthropology in Action: Journal for Applied Anthropology in Policy and Practice* 11(2/3): 9–21.

———— 2010. 'Indigeneity in Tourism: Transnational Spaces, Pan-Indian Identity, and Cosmopolitanism, in M.C. Forte (ed.), *Indigenous Cosmopolitans: Transnational and Transcultural Indigeneity in the Twenty-first Century*. New York: Peter Lang, pp.163–88.

Senfit, G. 1999. 'The Presentation of Self in Touristic Encounters: A Case Study from the Trobriand Islands', *Anthropos* 94: 21–33.

Skinner, J. 2006. 'Modernist Anthropology, Ethnic Tourism and National Identity: The Contest for the Commodification and Consumption of St Patrick's Day,

Montserrat', in K. Meethan, A. Anderson and S. Miles (eds), *Tourism, Consumption and Representation: Narratives of Place and Self.* Oxford: CAB International, pp. 253–71.

Smith, V. (ed.). 1989. *Host and Guests: The Anthropology of Tourism*, 2nd edn. Philadelphia: University of Pennsylvania Press.

Stanton, M.E. 1989. 'The Polynesian Cultural Center: A Multi-ethnic Model of Seven Pacific Cultures', in V.L. Smith (ed.), *Hosts and Guests: The Anthropology of Tourism*. Philadelphia: University of Pennsylvania Press, pp.247–62.

Suttles, W. 1987. *Coast Salish Essays.* Vancouver: Talonbooks.

Taylor, J.P. 2001. 'Authenticity and Sincerity in Tourism', *Annals of Tourism Research* 28: 7–26.

Tilley, C. 1997. 'Performing Culture in the Global Village', *Critique of Anthropology* 17(1): 67–89.

Tivers, J. 2002. 'Reforming Heritage: The Use of Live "Actors" in Heritage Presentations', *Leisure Studies* 21: 178–200.

Turner, T. 1991. 'The Social Dynamics of Video Media in an Indigenous Society: The Cultural Meaning and the Personal Politics of Video-making in Kayapo Communities', *Visual Anthropology Review* 7(2): 68–76.

——— 2002. 'Representation, Politics, and Cultural Imagination in Indigenous Video: General Points and Kayapo Examples', in F.D. Ginsburg, L. Abu-Lughod and B. Larkin (eds), *Media Worlds.* Berkeley: University of California Press, pp.75–89.

Urry, J. 1990. *The Tourist Gaze: Leisure and Travel in Contemporary Society.* London: Sage.

Yang, L. 2010. 'Ethnic Tourism and Cultural Representation', *Annals of Tourism Research* 33(2): 561–85.

Chapter 5

Movement on the Move: Performance and Dance Tourism in Southeast Asia

Felicia Hughes-Freeland

An important area of investigation for understanding dance culture in its broadest sense is the pattern of relationships between performers, audiences and students of dance, and the transformations of these relationships. When dance forms lose their traditional patrons and venues, performers trained in these forms have to adapt in different ways to new cultural and political conditions. In Southeast Asia, for instance, traditional performance contexts have included the village, the temple, the court and spaces where other special ritual or ceremonial events are held. Nowadays, performers in such regions have had to adapt to changing social and political circumstances that led to changes in the patronage of dance and the need to cater to international audiences (Hughes-Freeland 1993, 2001, 2008a). Performance venues in Indonesia and elsewhere in Asia nowadays normally include hotels, heritage shows, arts-and-culture festivals, national and religious holidays, carnivals, and documentation and revival projects.

The relationship between tourism and performance has been an important theme since Graburn's (1976) seminal discussion. Initially the tourist's role tended to be conceptualized as that of spectator (Urry 1990), but soon moved to 'consumption' (Urry 1994). In the past decade that theoretical framework has extended to performance and participation or what is sometimes called 'embodied tourism'. This is also explained with reference to notions of immersive and existential experience, and includes the sensorium and the process of sense-making (Little 2007), as well as key notions of 'belonging' and 'inhabiting' in the tourist experience (Harrison 2010). Meanwhile, performance has generated an analytical vocabulary which structures an extended typology of 'tourism as performance' (Edensor 2001). In contrast to Edensor's metaphorical use of performance, this chapter addresses actual cultural 'performances as performances', with particular attention to audience–performer relationships in a wide range of tourist venues. This concern reflects a trend for 'outsiders' to a tradition, be they national or international tourists, to experience actively 'other' forms of dance by participating in different ways. Such participation may be short or long term interactions. As I explain, variations in the limited interactions between performer and short-term tourist become more complex in the long-term exchange relationships of teacher and student. The longer-term examples raise questions about how we conceptualize cultures on the move and cultural encounters on a continuum from the conventional understanding of tourism as short-term visits to longer engagements, such as field research. Dance research has started to examine the creative outcomes of performers' responses to the challenges of tourism (Daniel 1996). My argument extends the discussion of dance and tourism by addressing the social and interactive emergent qualities of performance as the result of interaction between performers, patrons and audiences, and treats dance culture itself as social production (Buckland 1999: 3). Instead of approaching dance in the tourist context as a product or commodity which is transacted, we need to examine the relationships which organize the many kinds of transactions that are found within the process of dancing across cultures.

Using examples of the different kinds of relationships I discovered during my research in Southeast Asia, I present these interactions and relationships as they are determined by two variables: by the location, which in this chapter refers specifically to the extent to which the different participants can be said to be 'at home'; and by the duration of the exchange, which takes us beyond the conventional timescale of tourism when understood as the consumption of other cultures. I argue that these two variables are crucial for analysing two-way cultural flows, and for exploring how dance moves across cultural spaces in a series of interactions that have different extents, in terms of locations and durations.

Before presenting the examples, I set the scene by considering arguments which present tourism in terms of participation rather than spectatorship. These arguments provide a rationale for conceptualizing dance tourism as including a wider range of temporal variations in dance interactions and transactions than it has done.

From Spectatorship to Participation in Tourism

Although 'tourism' has referred to consumption in the context of leisure in a different spatial zone from everyday life, 'the tourist' is increasingly recognized as a heterogeneous category which may be relatively local or international. Tourism itself may be short or long term. It involves physical participation to the extent that the tourist moves physically to another location, but this of course is not the deep immersion of participation experienced by the anthropological fieldworker. Nor are all tourists 'international' or 'overseas'. What may be a distant 'other' to the international tourist is a closer albeit 'exotic other' for metropolitan 'locals' who journey to provincial cities and rural sites in their 'own' country. Once in this holiday zone, tourists have been conceptualized as consuming 'culture' as observers or spectators, for instance, gazing at dance from a seated and immobile position.

It has been claimed that as a category tourists 'are not participants; tourism is largely a spectator sport' (Hannerz 1990: 242). In contrast to the cosmopolitan, characterized by a 'willingness to engage with the Other' (Hannerz 1992: 252), the tourist retains their own cultural identity, whereas the cosmopolitan 'possesses it, it does not possess him [sic]' (Hannerz 1990: 240). The grounds for Hannerz's contrast have been challenged by attention to increased forms of participation by tourists. In the past decade or so, scholarly interest has turned from the analysis of tourism as a form of spectatorial consumption based on Urry's 'tourist gaze' (Urry 1990) to active participatory experience. The concept of performance theory generated metaphors to analyse tourist behaviours, as in the case of pilgrimage (Coleman and Elsner 1998). The interface between pilgrimage and tourism continues to challenge the spectatorial or visual domination of tourism (Ebron 2000; Rountree 2010).

Among the growing number of researchers of dance tourism, there are also some who try to go beyond the gaze to consider the role of embodiment in tourist participation. A pioneering attempt in this regard is Desmond's (1999) analysis of dance tourism in Hawai'i, and animal tourism in other areas of the United States. Desmond emphasizes 'the kinaesthetic dimensions of tourism' and the 'analysis of the relationship between bodily display and bodily actions (who does what, how, with whom, and why)' (Desmond 1999: 146, 252) – in other words, she prioritizes the relational, transactional approach which I am advocating here. For example, Desmond discusses *hā lau* ('hula') dance shows in Waikiki as spectacles for consumption by tourists, performed by locals who are usually Filipino or Portuguese Chinese, not native Hawai'ians. She compares this to another cute tourist-pleaser which involves a moment of physical participation, in the form of nose-rubbing kissing (Desmond 1999: 22–25) – something which is not limited to Hawai'i, as I observed the same kind of physical encounter in 2002 at the Maori cultural centre in Rotorua in New Zealand. Desmond suggests that while there are omissions and stagings in these performances, there is nonetheless a continuum between the 'real thing' and the 'tourist shows'. These shows are not simply a genre of tourist art; by promoting stereotypes, they deny the possibility of a reflexive understanding of how history has shaped contemporary practice (Desmond 1999: 264). There are different kinds of tourist performances which go beyond stereotypes. Native Hawai'ians Roland and Robert Cazimero produce performances which include large middle-aged performers to challenge the physical stereotype of the 'hula girl' (Desmond 1999: 260–61). More radically, the Cazimeros give dancing lessons held at a shopping centre (Desmond 1999: 28–33). These events are dialogic, involve participation, and serve to challenge the stereotypes of Hawai'i.

Desmond's analysis shows how important it is to ask 'who is producing what for tourists?', but it is also important to recognize that participation alone does not necessarily generate cross-cultural understanding. When outside tour companies try to set up dance holidays, they can seriously misjudge the cultural appropriateness of what they offer the tourists. The company 'Dance Holidays' offered dance packages to learn tango, salsa, Indian and Arabic, flamenco, ceroc and jive, line dancing, or Modern and Latin ballroom. However, the ceroc dance classes for holidaymakers in Cuba 'did not suit the salsa environment and it did not meet the expectations of the visiting tourists' (Skinner n.d.: 4, 15). One problem with participation is that even if tourists who go on dance holidays may not be looking for cross-cultural understanding, participation is no guarantee of a satisfactory outcome, aesthetically, culturally or socially. What determines the nature of the cross-cultural encounter and the effectiveness of the exchange is the provision and management of participation.

A second problem in analysing participation is the risk of slipping back into discourses of disembodiment. For instance, Desmond (1999: 30) writes that 'the image of Hawai'i gets rewritten'. This textual metaphor is at odds with her emphasis on embodied participation. Attempts to restore fleshly presence to physical action are often undermined by such metaphors of inscription. Participation may be more accurately characterized by Crouch's (2002: 207) phrasing: 'shared spaces ... transformed by the presence and practice of bodies ... a combining of sensed and social encountering'. Crouch's article comes from Coleman and Crang's edited collection which highlights 'a dynamic sense of embodied and performed, as well as visualized and textualized, engagement with places and tourist activities' (Coleman and Crang 2002: 1). It is one of a number of papers that go 'beyond the visual to performance' (Coleman and Crang 2002: 11), a further example of the move from visualist idioms of observation to participation in analytical frameworks. These two problems mean that we have to be careful when we use the concept of participation neither to assume that it inevitably produces easy cross-cultural encounters, nor to slip back into representational idioms which imply culture as product rather than as productive process.

Despite these problems of theorization, dance tourism is indisputably among one of the many niche markets that are moving from what I will call 'observational' consumption to 'participant' consumption. These two categories of course refer to the classical method of data collection in anthropology. Indeed, early in the anthropology of tourism, Malcolm Crick suggested that anthropologists themselves are a species of tourist (Crick 1985). During my own research on tourism in Yogyakarta in 1989, I was disconcerted to discover that foreign residents are classed as tourists (*pariwisata*), or specifically as overseas tourists (*wisman*) (in contrast to local tourist, *wisnu*),[1] Despite Crick's comparison, I felt unhappy to be classed along with holidaymakers spending a few days in the city before going on to Bali. Whether I liked it or not, being a participant-observer did not free me from the stigma of tourism in the eyes of the locals. But whether research visits constitute tourism or what Davis called 'leisure imperialism' (cited in Crick 1985: 80), by recognizing that tourism is a broader category of activity than the classic two- to three-week annual package holiday, it becomes possible to identify a diversity of transactions and interactions for exploring dance in terms of the social production of what Pedregal (2007) refers to as 'culture in tourism environments'.

I now turn to examples from my long-term research in Indonesia and latest project in Laos. I present a series of situations or spatially defined spheres of transaction which include participation in both long- and short-term tourism and dance learning. This transactional and interactive approach leads to a re-examination of the hosts–guest model for relations. This brief survey also yields some preliminary suggestions about whether or not explicitly embodied participant consumption of different kinds results in the production of new dance steps or intercultural forms.

Short-term Participation in Dance Tourism

My first examples refer to the more conventional schemes of tourism associated with a shorter period of travel away from home, and include cases of tourists with different degrees of knowledge about the host country. I illustrate this with data about 'local' tourists to show how their participation varies, even within a relatively short encounter. Attitudes to social dancing as a form of participation also vary according to attitudes towards interactions between men and women in public, and the type of embodied displays that are deemed appropriate. Within Southeast Asia, participation in social dancing is acceptable in Laos but problematic in Indonesia. Indonesian perceptions of what might appeal to overseas tourists have resulted in changes in the visibility of social dancing which was formerly marginalized.

Participation by 'Local' Visitors

On Christmas Eve 2002, I was filming the dance show put on for diners at the Lane Xang Hotel in Vientiane, the capital of Laos. This grand socialist hotel continues to be used by official delegations. It happened that a Vietnamese delegation, guests of the Lao Women's Association, was staying at the hotel over Christmas. During our meal we were treated to a series of 'folk' dances, purportedly from the different minorities and regions of Laos. They were performed by five highly trained male and female dancers from Vientiane's National School of Music and Dance (Natasin), one of whom had an impressive history of performing overseas.[2] An ensemble of five male musicians and two female singers accompanied a programme of 'ethnic' dance which was as notable for the variety of costumes as the similarity of the choreographies. As one of my travelling companions remarked, 'They're all the same'. After the first dance from Mahasae district in Khammaun Province performed by three women, members of the Lao Women's Association, some wearing Vietnamese dress to express solidarity with their guests, sang a *lamwong* song. This was followed by a courtship dance performed by two couples, accompanied by the *khaen*, a bamboo reed pipe often described as the Lao bagpipe and a core symbol of Lao ethnicity, which were also carried by the two male dancers who pretended to play them. Next was a Vietnamese song for the group, a strange but compelling birdsound impersonation, and a dance with three girls representing Hmong, Lalum and Latung minorities. Then the singer performed another *lamwong* song, and was presented with a rose by the Vietnamese ambassador. When she started to sing a third *lamwong* song, the entire delegation jumped up from their seats and began to dance together.

Despite acknowledgements of this delegation being built into the performance, this dancing appeared to be a spontaneous response to the singer performing the song. This was followed by more 'ethnic dance', with two couples performing a dance from Phounxaly Province. By now, members of the VIP element of the audience were no longer interested in spectating, and were determined to become the chief participants in the event, to the amusement of the other guests. After another *lamwong* dance, the Vietnamese took over the stage and sang as a way of thanking their Lao hosts. This was followed by the song 'Tealong', rarely performed these days, which accompanies the Saravahn dance from the region of the same name in southern Laos. The four costumed dance professionals on stage were joined by the delegation in what is best described as disco, Southeast Asian style (see fig. 5.1). What was particularly striking was the way in which the dancers suddenly crouched down at a certain point in the song.

The closest comparison is a similar move during the twist in French nightclubs in the 1960s where, according to my parents (I was too young to observe this), there would be competitions to see who could twist their body closest to the floor. In the Saravahn the competitive element was absent, but the general hilarity and energy were similar. The evening came to a close with an interlude of *khaen* music: a reassertion of Lao national identity, which transcended the cultural pluralism of the minority dances.

It is noteworthy that the participatory element of dance tourism. *Lamwong* and Saravahn normally occur at Buddhist festivals. In this hotel, an ostensibly 'tourist' package had been transformed into an impromptu and unstaged participatory social event among some of the guests. Of course, there was clearly an arrangement with the hotel that the delegation would be involved in the songs, but the other tourists, including myself, were not party to this. We thought that we were paying for an evening of entertainment, and so none of us joined in. The visitors who participated, and hijacked the event, were 'informed outsiders'. This social dance tradition has its counterparts in Vietnam and elsewhere in mainland Southeast Asia, so the participation of the visitors was based on familiarity, not strangeness.

Figure 5.1 Guests participate in the Saravahn dance in Vientiane, Laos. Photo courtesy of Irwin Tsieng.

This moment of culture contact opened a door for me on to the much wider issue of neighbourly alliances and alienations which has characterized mainland Southeast Asian politics. The performance had been a microcosmic instance of a wider pattern of the cultural politics of the Association of Southeast Asian Nations (ASEAN), in this case the delicately balanced relationships between Laos and its neighbours.

The event was also striking as a contrast to findings from my thirty years of research in Java, Indonesia. Here, social dance is less common, for a wide range of 'cultural' reasons which includes an avoidance of men and women dancing together socially. Following the dramatic curtailment of Indonesia's postcolonial left-wing agenda in the 1960s and '70s, the government attempted to ban social dancing (Hughes-Freeland 1997). In rural Java, social dancing occurs at harvest thanksgiving rites and rites of passage in *tayuban*s, which are social dance events in which men take turns to pay two or three professional female singer-dancers (*ledhek*) to dance with them alone or with several companions (Hughes-Freeland 2008c). Urban Javanese people as well as Indonesian and overseas scholars have regarded *tayuban* as uncharacteristically un-Javanese orgies of uncontrolled indecency, but intensive research in two provinces in central Java proved that this reputation was at odds with the evidence. Far from being occasions for unleashed sexual misdemeanours, the *tayuban*s I observed were highly ordered, and made visible the social hierarchies of the village, revealed in the sequence of dance turns which were determined by age and status.

Tayuban also involve providing hospitality, and are intended to entertain visitors to the community. During a second visit to a *tayuban* in a highland community in the Special Region of Yogyakarta, the dancing was opened by a village elder, who performed briefly but with great vigour before forcing my reluctant research assistant to take the floor. He did so with considerable embarrassment, never having participated in a *tayuban* before. Indeed, he had attended his first ever *tayuban* only five years earlier because of my research. He had no choice but to perform, in order to fulfil his obligation as an honoured guest. Later in the evening, other visitors from the city of Yogyakarta arrived. Among them was the artist, Joko Pekik, who has attended *tayuban*s all over central Java and often represents *ledhek*s in his paintings. He arrived with a party that included a Japanese visitor, and they were soon disporting themselves with the *ledhek*s (see fig. 5.2).

These two examples of social dancing show different responses to participation by local tourists in cultural contexts which are close to home, but not necessarily familiar in their everyday life. The Vietnamese visitors to Laos found common cultural ground for moments of meaningful participation. At the Javanese *tayuban*, outsider participation was received with mixed feelings by members of the host community: it brought status to the senior male organizers of the event while annoying the younger males in the community who wanted to have their turns. There was a sense of adventure and transgression for the urban visitors and their guest from Japan who came up the hill from the city of Yogyakarta to the village in search of authentic village ritual. Local leaders and cultural brokers have been attempting to capitalize on a perceived outside interest in *tayuban*, as my next case will show.

Participant Tourism Away from Home

In spite of cultural reservations about men and women dancing together socially in Indonesia, many entrepreneurs and troupe managers have realized that social dancing will attract national and international tourists. Most hotels in the Special Region of Yogyakarta offer programmes of shortened classical-style dance and Ramayana ballets of different lengths and scales as performances for tourists to watch (Hughes-Freeland 2008a). During the 1990s, tourism policy makers and hotel managers were trying to find other forms of dance event to provide a diversion from the endless rounds of Ramayana ballets. Enterprising leaders in villages situated near heritage sites with their own stages and productions also hoped that *tayuban* would attract international visitors to their communities. In general these hopes have not been realized, but a few individual enterprises have successfully managed Indonesia's neglected social dance forms, to get the tourists dancing.

One example was the Javanese dancer and choreographer Didik Nini Thowok's collaboration with a small-scale Dutch travel company during the late 1980s. The company catered for small, exclusive groups of international tourists and commissioned performances which often took place in the homes of well-known choreographers and performers. The tour group came to Didik's relatively small house located in the rice fields to the west of Yogyakarta. After a simple meal, there was a dance performance by Didik and his students, followed by a mock *tayuban* in which guests were invited by the dancers to join in (see fig. 5.3).

Figure 5.2 Urban visitors participate in a rural tayuban *in Java. Photo by the author.*

There was none of the structure and material exchange associated with village *tayuban*s. The financial transactions occurred offstage, and as far as the Javanese were concerned, the status of the tourists was irrelevant.

In both these cases of participation in *tayuban*s, the performance of the stranger, whether domestic or international, becomes an object for the gaze of the skilled performers and local guests, eliciting responses which can range from amusement to mockery. Participation does not entail acceptance and belonging (see also Bruner 2005). Instead it manages the potential hostilities which might arise when strangers come into a community to dance, as has been graphically demonstrated by Schieffelin (1976) in his account of social relations in the *Gisaro* dance among the Kaluli of Papua New Guinea.

Figure 5.3 Overseas visitors participate in tourist tayuban *in Java. Photo by the author.*

Participant Tourism at Home? Unequal Local Exchanges

My final example of participation away from home shows unequal transactions between skilled and knowledgeable locals, and unskilled outsiders without any knowledge of local dance practices. This inequality of relationship and knowledge can also be found in festivals organized for audiences who are 'at home'. My example here is from the Tayuban Festival, a one-evening event organized by four journalists at Taman Budaya ('The Garden of Culture') in Solo, Central Java, in 1989. The organisers intended this event to be both provocation and education, as a challenge to the urban ambivalence in Java about *tayuban*.

The festival provided an opportunity for townspeople to see something of an event that, as already explained, survives in rural communities but has acquired a reputation for indecency among urban Indonesians. But what they saw was something modern, created for the festival. Four troupes from Java performed, including two from the district of Sragen where I had been doing intensive research. Sragen's Ngarum group, lead by Karno KD performed a ten section creation dubbed 'Ta-la-dut'. The 'Ta' was a *tayuban* choreographed as if at a wedding ceremony. 'La' was an act in which five young men, including four in brightly coloured satin shirts, sang popular Javanese rock songs (*lagu*). This was followed by 'dut', the conventional use of comic humour (*badut*) by male dancers performing with female dancers. Next came a 'modern' *tayuban* in which the rockers danced with the two *ledhek*s (see fig. 5.4). Audience participation was encouraged in a closing section in which members of the audience came on stage to take the dance scarf, much as they would in a village event. These were mostly young men, although at one point a young couple joined in, and the woman

Figure 5.4 Locals join in at the Tayuban Festival in Java. Photo courtesy of Didik Teha.

found herself dancing on her own as her boyfriend turned his attention to the professional dancers.

This festival was extremely popular but as it was considered to be outside the bounds of acceptable order, it was not instituted as a regular cultural event. Although it succeeded in giving a young generation of urbanites a chance to experience a version of the disappearing rural *tayuban*, innovations like this have negative impacts on performers. By making their dancing respectable, their low-status livelihoods are at risk of being converted into high-status honorariums which are not enough to live on. This problem is also faced by academically trained classical dancers in Indonesia because dancing has not yet acquired an economic niche which makes it professionally sustainable (Hughes-Freeland 2001). In the last fifteen years, *tayuban* dances have been increasingly performed by academically trained dancers from secondary and tertiary dance schools, and rural dancers have been less able to find willing apprentices among the younger generations.

A final point needs to be made about festivals. In contrast to the case of the *tayuban* festival discussed above, it is relevant to note that festivals vary in the form of transactions they produce. Equal transactions do occur at big international festivals where dancers from many countries come together, and where some will be 'at home'. In the ASEAN region, these include the Ramayana Festival, first held in Panandaran, East Java, in 1971 (Brandon 1972) and subsequently around the region (Devi 2002); the Singapore Arts Festival, since 1977; and the Bali Arts Festival, since 1979 (Foley and Sumandhi 1994). In contrast to the previous category, these events produce long-term impacts on costume and choreography. Innovations such as these have to be understood in relation to transnational intercultural exchanges. They also raise questions about wider issues about the cultural politics of heritage and associated intellectual property rights, implied in some of my examples but beyond the scope of this chapter.

Diplomatic and Cultural Tours

Diplomatic and cultural tours are events which may overlap with regional dance exchanges at international festivals, but they differ because they are usually spectacles for consumption. For example, in 1989 the Indonesian Embassy sponsored two very different tours: the classical troupe from the Mangkunagaran palace in Central Java Province, and traditional dances by the Asmat of West Papua (Hughes-Freeland 1989).

Cultural tours increasingly include workshops which allow members of the host society to participate in dance classes and experience different forms of performance with their bodies, not just with their eyes. London's The Place (formerly the Contemporary School of Dance) started to produce this kind of event in the early 1980s, when I attended a Balinese dance workshop. The Balinese dance master soon spotted that I had previous experience of Balinese dance, and took advantage to demonstrate the required turn-out by making me lie on the floor and walk on my thighs. In 2003, when The Place hosted a mini festival of cross-gendered Asian dance (from India, China, Japan and Indonesia) presented by the Japan Foundation with support from the Asia House and Japan Airlines, there were also four workshops, each one led by a participating dancer, and attended by a number of British dance ethnographers. Didik Nini Thowok performed *Beskalan Putri*, a piece inspired by an Indonesian female ritual dance he had learned from a traditional practitioner in East Java (Hughes-Freeland 2008b). Although the performer was away from home, many members of Didik's audience were from closer to home than he might have expected: at the performance I attended, a large proportion of the audience was made up of young Asian men and women.

This discussion has demonstrated how performance events extend the concept of social dancing to a broader range of participants in different ways. Whether or not the participants will learn the steps, or even wish to, is not the issue. The effect of participation is a sense of involvement, a moment of interaction which breaches the spectacular experience of tourists and brings them into a shared movement space with their hosts. Participating in social dancing thus creates a moment of shared experience, a microcosmic exchange across cultural boundaries. This is very different from the longer-term acquisition of skilful dance steps, to which I now turn.

Long-term Participation: Cultural -Political and Educational-Academic

I now consider a second set of exchange situations which arise from cross-cultural dance participation in the longer term. The importance of this perspective was emphasized by James R. Brandon, the well-known practitioner and scholar of Asian theatre and Emeritus Professor of Asian Theatre at the Department of Theatre and Dance at the University of Hawai'i at Manoa. During his keynote address at an Asian performance conference at Leiden in 2000, Brandon (2000) argued that the usual analytical triad of performer, patron and audience needs to be extended to include a fourth element, the 'foreign' (*sic*) student or scholar-performer. Here, the characterization of tourism is extended to include longer visits and interactions which involve visitors in work and education, not simply leisure and pleasure. The performances that we encounter in these situations are normally elaborated 'high art' performance in which dance steps normally comprise one feature of dance theatre, such as Javanese *wayang wong* and Japanese *noh*.

By including this fourth relationship in the production of performance, Brandon argues that we can develop new perspectives on cross-cultural dance exchanges. The dance forms encountered in these circumstances are usually art dance. One example he discusses is Japanese *kabuki*, which has been practiced in Hawai'i for over a century (Brandon 1996: 51). This kind of dance scenario has led him to prefer to use the term 'multiculturalism' (Brandon 1996: 55) instead of what others call 'intercultural' work. Schechner (1996: 48–49) has classed dance which requires more extended training to achieve a minimal competence due to the complexity of movement style and choreography as being on an 'east–west' axis, in contrast to a 'north–south' classificatory axis which refers to popular and social performance of the kind discussed in my examples of short-term participation. Schechner's classifications are developed in his discussion of interculturalism which occurs at the 'deep structural level' in respect of audience relations, performance duration and extraneous elements, and acting styles (Schechner 1996: 43–44), with interculturalism consisting of the encounter of the modern with the modern (Schechner 1996: 47). Brandon prefers to characterize this form of encounter as long-term 'multicultural' dance interaction, where the 'dance scholar' becomes involved in projects to 'replicate ... high art Eastern forms' (Brandon 1996: 51–55). More recently Brandon (2000) has conceded that culturally hybrid forms are a way of reaching out to the audience interculturally and intraculturally. Nonetheless, he still insists that cultures are not homogeneous. Internal variation – the strangeness and diversity within – should never be forgotten. This is particularly relevant to the postcolonial idea that particular arts are no longer the property of a particular culture.

While it is crucial to recognize the importance of longer-term participation in dance which goes beyond the common resonance of 'dance tourism', it is also important to recognize the range of situations under which these interactions and exchanges can occur in different cultural locations and configurations. Not all longer-term dance interactions across time and space involve the formal academic structures experienced by Brandon's students in Hawai'i. My research findings in Java identified four different versions of longer-term participation, as follows.

Long-term Dance Participation in Learning Javanese Dance in Different Locations

Firstly, local dance teachers teach local students at home. In this situation, the teacher trains local students from within and without the immediate cultural sphere. Some are the children of dancers who receive a tradition and replicate it. For instance, in Yogyakarta close relatives of the sultan who are mostly cousins and other members of aristocratic families run dance associations to preserve what has come to be identified as a distinctive local court aesthetic. Meanwhile, lower status courtiers are often involved in court-sponsored dance associations which perform new choreographies with a traditional look (Hughes-Freeland 2008a). And then there are those from outside court circles and outside the Province of Yogyakarta who are able to train in national performance academies and acquire the skill to develop the traditions, and make new choreographies. Our previous example of the Javanese choreographer, Didik Nini Thowok, comes from the Province of Central Java. He trained in Yogyakarta's Academy of Performing Arts (then ASTI) and since set up a dance school where he teaches his own dance forms. His practice is to travel around other parts of the island learning different local traditions with elderly practitioners. In this respect he is a dance ethnographer, but his aim is to create new choreographies which he then performs at high-status venues and teaches to pupils to earn his living (Hughes-Freeland 2001, 2008b, 2010). An example of his famous 'Two Face Dance' (*Tari Dwimuka*) can be seen on YouTube (http://www.youtube.com/watch?v=obITUpe-eWg).

These local teachers also teach non-local students who come from outside the locality to study, either in private lesson or in regular group classes. Normally these outsiders are dance researchers pursuing scholarly or educational projects for a year or more. There have been Indonesian postgraduate scholarships for foreigners wishing to pursue musical training. Dance students from Southeast Asian departments in universities in Hawai'i and the Netherlands often come to Indonesia for further training in state and private associations as part of exchange schemes or postgraduate programmes.

During my doctoral research into classical Javanese dance, I joined the beginners' class at Pamulangan Běksa Ngayogyakarta, a dance association managed by the court official, Rama Sas (K.R.T. Sasmintadipura) at the Pudjokusuman residence. He was regarded by many as the most creative of the classical choreographers, but his innovations were not approved of by all aristocrats. Among his students was Garrett Kam, who had previously trained in Hawai'i. He had became a skilled performer, and in 2006 was able to raise considerable amounts of money by giving Javanese dance performances around Southeast Asia to help repair the devastation inflicted by a major earthquake on the Pudjokusuman dance pavilion where he had formerly trained (Kam 2011). Kam has also been researching and performing Okinawan dances, and having noticed important gestural commonalities with Javanese dances, since 2008 he has been choreographing and performing a hybrid that he calls Oki-Jawa, available as a YouTube clip (http://www.youtube.com/watch?v=aYb893vcQ1w). I also studied with Mbak Kadar, a cousin of the current sultan of Yogyakarta. She happened to mention a Western dancer who used to take lessons with her regularly for a short period each summer. This 'student' turned out to be the well-known Belgian contemporary choreographer, Anne Teresa De Keersmaeker, although the work of her company, Rosas, has not (yet) explicitly referenced her encounters with Javanese dance. My third teacher, Bu Yuda, the former sultan's sister-in-law, was the leading choreographer of women's court dance. She taught at her nephew's dance association, and also at the Indonesian Academy of Arts (ISI). She also gave private lessons in her home to foreigners, particularly those with an interest in the ceremonial court *běžhaya* dances.

Normally, foreign dance students did not participate in performances for tourists, but there have been a few exceptions. During the 1980s, two young women from the Netherlands and the United States who studied with Rama Sas's dance association performed fighting duets at the regular concerts he produced for tourists. The Korean-American dancer Jeannie Park, who studied with Rama Sas and Bu Yuda, and since the late 1990s has been permitted to perform in the court, the only foreigner I am aware of who has been privileged to do so; in 2001 she danced alongside two of the sultan's daughters in *Běžhaya Sang Amurwabumi*. She established the Wahyuning Kuswala dance company in Yogyakarta with her husband, Lantip Kuswala Daya, and since 2007 has also promoted dance culture as executive director of the Bagong Kussudiardja Foundation, which builds on the legacy of the late choreographer of modern Indonesian-Javanese dance (see also below). She and her husband can be seen performing as Dewi Trijatha and Hanuman in a section of the Ramayana in LosAngeles in 2005 on YouTube (http://www.youtube.com/watch?v=MTapGD-eflM). This demonstrates that longer-term dance tourism can lead to the most extreme form of moving to another place –

migration – although in Indonesia it is normally difficult to secure a permanent residence permit, even if one is married to an Indonesian citizen.

A third variation is when a local teacher teaches non-local students away from home. There is a similar process of exchange when the dance teacher exports their expertise. Many of Rama Sas's students had already gained dance skills at home in their own countries before coming to Yogyakarta to further their competence. The Department of Theatre and Dance at the University of Hawai'i at Manoa, already noted in connection with Professor Brandon, has played a major role in developing courses in Asian performing arts, and there has been a proliferation of Javanese music and dance courses in institutions across the United States. Universities and embassies also host visiting or longer-term resident dance experts to run courses or workshops. In Britain, Indonesian music and puppetry have received more attention than dance, but since the mid 1980s the Indonesian embassy in London has also employed dance teachers, allowing for greater participation in dance training than before.

Finally, there is the case of the teacher who studies with an overseas teacher away from home. This example of participation on the move is when choreographers and teachers study overseas. It should be considered as a highly specialized and under-researched category of dance tourism. For instance, Indonesian performers often go to Japan to study, producing influences as varied as cabaret. In the early 1980s, dancer and entrepreneur Hamzah spent time in Japan, and produced a cabaret called *Glass and Dolls* which included new choreographies inspired by cabaret acts he had seen in Japan. In the past decade there have been a growing number of collaborations between Indonesian and Japanese choreographers, and long-term outsiders. For example, in 2000, Didik Nini Thowok went to Japan to study *noh* for three months with Master Gujo Onagata. He also studied with Richard Emmert, who has lived in Japan for over thirty years, and has a deep understanding of *noh* drama of the Kita School. He is one of a very small number of non-Japanese certified performers of *noh*. On his return to Java, Didik produced a new form of the traditional *bĕdhaya* court choreography for women, in collaboration with Emmert, Bu Yuda and the Chinese-American gamelan expert, Alex Dea. This dance, *Bĕdhaya Hagomoro*, used masks and fans for all the dancers and kimonos for the main protagonists, as well as songs and drumming patterns from *noh* (Hughes-Freeland 2010). This example raises questions about the concept of interculturalism which is outside the brief of this chapter.[3]

These four situations are an indication of dance flows in our 'glocalized' world. Other examples include classical ballet, which is a long-standing case of transnational performance (Wulff 1998). The Ballet Russe company based in Swansea, Wales, for example, compounds its transnational character through regular collaborations with the Temma Ballet School in Japan. Such longer-term cross-cultural encounters make it clear that while learning about regional styles is a crucial aspect of dance ethnography, we have to recognize that local steps span greater spaces. Learning dance across cultures spans a continuum, from short-term encounters by local and overseas tourists to long-term encounters where the tourist is transformed into a student or scholar, and reveals the complexity of cross-cultural encounters and exchanges.

Participant Consumption and Interculturalism

I now return to the question of whether explicitly embodied participant consumption of different kinds results in the production of new steps or intercultural forms.

Two issues that have arisen from the discussion of dance tourism may help to develop the debates about interculturalism and transnational performance. Firstly, embodied participation helps to challenge stereotyping which comes from looking at bodies and ignoring how bodies are shaped by histories of cultural practices: 'Only by historicizing these encounters and thus disrupting the physical foundationalism in which they rest can we envision a future of tourism as more than its past' (Desmond 1999: 266). In Indonesia the cultural position of colonially founded performance traditions in Java has ensured their survival into the postcolonial world, but has also accelerated their transformation into classical Indonesian dance in the last decades of the twentieth century. Indeed, Schechner has gone so far as to argue that Java court performance practices that became formalized in the colonial period survive only because they are taken up by foreign scholars (Schechner 1993: 196). This is an exaggeration, as many local students learn court dance forms in secondary and tertiary state educational institutions and at privately-run dance associations.

Secondly, it is important to examine the degree of equality within the exchange relationship, as well as its temporal depth. I would argue that enduring intercultural or cross-cultural performance work cannot arise from short-term engagement between very different actors. The case of festivals illustrates this. Festivals of experts sharing with other experts can produce long-term innovations, as in the ASEAN Ramayana festivals. But festivals have also been criticized by scholars for being international in a 'banal' rather than 'intercultural' way (Pavis 1996: 5). For example, the large multicultural Los Angeles Festival in 1990 was criticized for merely 'restaging sources', and ultimately for 'banalizing difference' instead of enabling a 'shared experience' (Kirshenblatt-Gimblett 1995: 239–40, 247–50). It would seem that more attention needs to be paid to the micro-exchanges which are taking place within performance events of this kind.

On the basis of the examples presented in this chapter, I would propose that intercultural forms can be produced only when local practices have already been disrupted in some way, and started to undergo what Evans (1998: 129–40) has called 'customization'. This supports Schechner's point discussed earlier that interculturalism arises from an encounter of the modern with the modern. The exchange or transaction must be equal and coeval, sharing the same time. In this sense, instead of thinking of cultural practices such as rituals, political ceremony and other forms of collective representation as being inventions or re-inventions of tradition, customization recognizes that practices are often altered or adjusted in many small ways to fit the needs of the situation.

Distinctiveness articulated in 'high art' dance is originally about social differentiation and power. Cultural distinctiveness may then follow in a nationalist context. So art dance is always designed to be exclusive, even when it is open to all who have the required ability. This means that it is not easy to learn, nor is it easily reproducible. Art dance is what it is because it is not transactable or transformable in an obvious way. This does not mean that it is unchanging. For example, I have already mentioned Rama Sas, the well-known Javanese court choreographer who ran a very successful dance school and tourist show business. In his shows, 'classical' dance was simplified and speeded up but maintained the costume and music of court dance, so that non-practitioners would not know the difference (Hughes-Freeland 2007). Such choices met with criticism by insiders, but were less controversial than the 'new choreographies' (*kreasi baru*) by Bagong Kussudiardjo when they were first performed in the 1960s and 1970s because people were confused about what they were watching. These hybrid forms remained beyond the pale of 'classical Javanese dance' until they were performed for the first time in the court for the sultan's birthday in the early 1990s, replacing the hitherto customary 'traditional' court dance forms.

In performance situations, customization also arises from a desire to please a wider or different audience; this has been the case with the innovative work of Javanese choreographer and performer Didik Nini Thowok, discussed above. This is consistent with Brandon's (2000) argument that hybridization is a way of reaching out to audiences, and also with Schechner's (1996) point about mutual modernity within the exchange. In other words, there is an intention to attract, often in order to sell the performance; commoditization is at work. Generally speaking, art dance is less amenable to cultural appropriation and reinvention unless the context is radically different. Festivals and heritage performances offer scope for large-scale modern art-dance performances called *sendratari*. These are classical dance ballets, which work intraculturally within Indonesian traditions, rather than interculturally. Performed on a larger scale to larger audiences, they become spectacular. In Indonesia these dance ballets are often performed at tourist sites, such as the well-known Ramayana Ballet, which is produced on a massive scale outside the Lara Jonggrang temple in central Java. These newest versions of formerly exclusive art dances are widespread in Southeast Asia, but they vary in the extent to which the dances are customized or transformed. In Laos, for example, at the opening of a UNESCO heritage site in 2003, traditional steps were simply done by many more people.

Conclusion

The analysis of dance exchanges in relation to tourism allows us to understand the pattern of the transactions that arise in transcultural movements and flows. It is possible to map more closely the pathways of cultural transmission and reproduction of dance as social production and socio-cultural exchange by extending the idea of tourism beyond short-term leisure package holidays to other kinds of cultural encounters and by focusing on embodied practice and participation instead of spectacle and the tourist gaze. Participation thus moves us away from consumption models of society to models which privilege action and creative exchanges. It also invites further questions about temporal variations in how we analyse different ways of being a guest, whether as a short-term visitor, longer-term student or worker, and permanent migrant guest.

As noted at the beginning of this chapter, other cases of the category of 'unequal exchange' for overseas tourists include 'tourist' shows with or without participation: home shows, away tours and dance holidays in Cuba and Spain, currently marketed in Europe to capitalize on the current revival of Latin dance, but not always very effectively. I am not aware of any dance holiday packages in Asia, but there could be a niche for dance to be incorporated into the latest form of participatory tourism: health-and-beauty tourism, for example, includes spa holidays in Bali, and the 'Ayurvedic' massage treatments offered in heritage and luxury hotels in India.

Both short- and long-term participation in dance tourism may result in transformed styles of embodiment and personhood. Dance traditions and practices such as an 'Indian dance class' are now being packaged as 'exercise' for British tourists 'at home' (Miller 2004). This new packaging of dance as an activity conducive to well-being suggests that dance tourism research will need to include new forms of practice which go beyond theatrical intercultural hybrids and innovations. This kind of practice was pioneered by Sue Jennings, whose research into the ritual performances of the Senoi Temiar in Malaysia led to her developing drama therapeutic practices (Jennings 1995: 186–92). These steps for healing have had an impact beyond purely leisure activities, on personal healing and social regeneration at home.

For emergent short-term dance tourism packages in Asia, it is more feasible to offer the chance to participate in social or folk dance styles and rhythms. Art dance is not accessible in a regular 'world music' way: Javanese art dance rhythms are difficult because they are very slow and attenuated; Balinese dances are difficult because of syncopation and variable speed; Laotian art dance has a more regular rhythm but difficult gestures. Access to social dance which comes from folk traditions is greater, although its simplicity is of course deceptive. It is ironic that despite the greater accessibility and rhythmic similarities of many folk traditions, these forms have tended not to attract the interest of choreographer-tourists. Thus, in Indonesia dancers and choreographers study Martha Graham technique in performance academies, not folk dances such as morris dancing or square dancing.

It may well be the case, however, that Desmond and other researchers have been over-optimistic about the lasting educational force of short-term participation in dance tourism. Nonetheless, even if their effects are fleeting and involve both misunderstanding and understanding, we can still hope that by trying out the dance steps of others, however briefly, it may be possible to achieve shared moments of sociality with those for whom those steps have come to seem natural, and to understand that what may appear natural is an aspect of culture.

Notes

1. *Wisman* is a compression of *wisata mancanegara*; local or domestic tourists are *wisnu*, a compression of *wisata nusantara*.
2. The dancer concerned, 'Chanmaly', had performed in Vietnam, Cambodia, Thailand, China, Japan, India and France (personal communication, 24 December 2002).
3. For further discussion of this issue, see Hughes-Freeland (2010: 39–42).

References

Barker, C. 1996. 'The Possibilities and Politics of Intercultural Penetration and Exchange', in P. Pavis (ed.), *The Intercultural Performance Reader*. London: Routledge, pp.247–56.

Brandon, J.R. 1972. 'First International Ramayana Festival', *Educational Theatre Journal* 24(2): 200–1.

────── 1996. 'Bridging Cultures: 101 Years of Kabuki in Hawai'i', in C. Brakel (ed.), *Performing Arts of Asia: The Performer as (Inter)Cultural Transmitter*. Leiden: International Institute for Asian Studies, pp.47–60.

────── 2000. 'The Performance Triangle: Whole or Unholy', unpublished paper given at the conference 'Audiences, Patrons and Performers: The Performing Arts of Asia', Leiden, 23–27 August.

Bruner, E.M. 2005. *Culture on Tour: Ethnographies of Travel*. Chicago: University of Chicago Press.

Buckland, T.J. 1999. 'All Dances are Ethnic, but Some are More Ethnic than Others: Some Observations on Dance Studies and Anthropology', *Dance Research* 17(1): 3–21.

Coleman, S., and M. Crang. 2002. 'Grounded Tourists, Travelling Theory', in S. Coleman and M. Crang (eds), *Tourism: Between Place and Performance*. Oxford: Berghahn, pp.1–17.

Coleman, S., and J. Elsner. 1998. 'Performing Pilgrimage: Walsingham and the Ritual Construction of Irony', in F. Hughes-Freeland (ed.), *Ritual, Performance, Media*. London: Routledge, pp.46–65.

Crick, M. 1985. 'Tracing the Anthropological Self: Quizzical Reflections on Field Work, Tourism, and the Ludic', *Social Analysis* 17: 71–92.

Crouch, D. 2002. 'Surrounded by Place: Embodied Encounters', in S. Coleman and M. Crang (eds), *Tourism: Between Place and Performance*. Oxford: Berghahn, pp.207–18.

Daniel, Y.P. 1996. 'Tourism Dance Performances: Authenticity and Creativity', *Annals of Tourism Research* 23(4): 780–97.

Desmond, J.C. 1999. *Staging Tourism: Bodies on Display from Waikiki to Sea World*. Chicago: University of Chicago Press.

Devi, H.R.H. Princess Norodom Buppha. 2002. 'The Ramayana Festival, the Intangible Heritage of Angkor', *Museum International* 54(1/2): 82–84.

Ebron, P.A. 2000. 'Tourists as Pilgrims: Commercial Fashioning of Translatlantic Politics', *American Ethnologist* 26(4): 910–32.

Edensor, T. 2001. 'Performing Tourism, Staging Tourism: (Re)producing Tourist Space and Practice'. *Tourist Studies* 1(1): 59–81.

Evans, G. 1998. *The Politics of Ritual and Remembrance: Laos since 1975*. Honolulu: University of Hawaii Press.

Foley, K., and I.N. Sumandhi. 1994. 'The Bali Arts Festival: An Interview with I. Nyoman Sumandhi', *Asian Theatre Journal* 11(2): 275–89.

Graburn, N. 1976. *Ethnic and Tourist Arts*. Berkeley: University of California Press.
Hannerz, U. 1990. 'Cosmopolitans and Locals in World Culture', in M. Featherstone (ed.), *Global Culture: Nationalism, Globalization and Modernity*. London: Sage, pp.237–52.
_____ 1992. *Cultural Complexity: Studies in the Social Organization of Meaning*. New York: Columbia University Press.
Harrison, J. 2010. 'Belonging at the Cottage', in J. Scott and T. Selwyn (eds), *Thinking Through Tourism*. Oxford: Berg, pp.71–92.
Hughes-Freeland, F. 1989. 'Indonesian Image Enhancement', *Anthropology Today* 5(6): 3–5.
_____ 1993. 'Packaging Dreams: Javanese Perceptions of Tourism and Performance', in M. Hitchcock, V.T. King and M.J.G. Parnwell (eds), *Tourism in South-East Asia: Theory and Practice*. London: Routledge, pp.138–54.
_____ 1997. 'Art and Politics: From Javanese Court Dance to Indonesian Art', *Journal of the Royal Anthropological Institute* 3(3): 473–95.
_____ 2001. 'Performers and Professionalization in Java: Between Leisure and Livelihood', *South-East Asia Research* 9(2): 213–33.
_____ 2007. 'Tradition and the Individual Talent: T.S. Eliot for Anthropologists', in E. Hallam and T. Ingold (eds), *Creativity and Cultural Improvisation*. Oxford: Berg, pp.207–22.
_____ 2008a. *Embodied Communities: Dance Traditions and Change in Java*. Oxford: Berghahn.
_____ 2008b. 'Cross-dressing across Cultures: Genre and Gender in the Dances of Didik Nini Thowok', Working Papers Series 108, Asia Research Institute. Singapore: National University of Singapore.
_____ 2008c. 'Gender, Representation, Experience: The Case of Village Performers in Java', *Dance Research* 26(2): 140–67.
_____ 2010. 'Creativity and Cross-cultural Collaboration: The Case of Didik Nini Thowok's *Bedhaya Hagoromo*', in L. Noszlopy and M.I. Cohen (eds), *Southeast Asian Arts in Transnational Perspective*. Newcastle upon Tyne: Cambridge Scholars Publishing, pp.25–46.
Jennings, S. 1995. *Theatre, Ritual and Transformation: The Senoi Temiars*. New York: Routledge.
Jeyifo, B. 1996. 'The Reinvention of Theatrical Tradition: Critical Discourses on Interculturalism in the African Theatre', in P. Pavis (ed.), *The Intercultural Performance Reader*. London: Routledge, pp.149–61.
Kam, Garrett. 2011. 'Rising from the Ruins', *Indonesia and the Malay World* 39: 115, 445–54.
Kirshenblatt–Gimblett, B. 1995. 'Confusing Pleasures', in G.E. Marcus and F.R. Myers (eds), *The Traffic in Culture: Refiguring Art and Anthropology*. Berkeley: University of California Press, pp.224–55.
Little, K. 2007. '"Paradise is as Paradise Doesn't": Arresting Images and Visual Embodiment in a Tourist Encounter in Belize', unpublished paper given at the ASA conference 'Thinking through Tourism', London Metropolitan University, 10–13 April.
Miller, F. 2004. 'Ready, Get Set, Go …: Indian Summer', *Guardian* ('Weekend' section), 24 July, p.47.
Pavis, P. (ed.) 1996. *The Intercultural Performance Reader*. London: Routledge.
Pedregal, A.M.N. 2007. 'An Anthropological Dilemma: Facing the Patrimonialisation of Culture in Tourism Contexts', unpublished paper presented at the ASA conference 'Thinking through Tourism', London Metropolitan University, 10–13 April.

Rountree, K. 2010, 'Tourist Attractions, Cultural Icons, Sites of Sacred Enconter: Engagements with Malta's Neolithic Temples', in J. Scott and T. Selwyn (eds), *Thinking Through Tourism*. Oxford: Berg, pp.183–208.

Schechner, R. 1993. *The Future of Ritual: Writings on Culture and Performance*. New York: Routledge.

―――― 1996. 'Interculturalism and the Culture of Choice', in P. Pavis (ed.), *The Intercultural Performance Reader*. London: Routledge, pp.41–50.

Schieffelin, E.L. 1976. *The Sorrow of the Lonely and the Burning of the Dancers*. New York: St Martin's Press.

Skinner, J. n.d. 'Packaging and Consuming Niche Tourism: The Case against Ceroc Dance Tourism in Cuba', unpublished paper.

Urry, J. 1990. *The Tourist Gaze: Leisure and Travel in Contemporary Society*. London: Sage.

―――― 1994. *Consuming Places*. London: Routledge.

Wulff, H. 1998. *Ballet across Borders*. Oxford: Berg.

Chapter 6

Dance, Visibility and Representational Self-awareness in an Emberá Community in Panama

Dimitrios Theodossopoulos

The community of Parara Puru in Chagres National Park, Panama, a two hour drive from Panama City, is an Emberá community with many talented and skilled dancers. The members of this community – women, men and children – dance for consecutive groups of tourists day after day. They dance traditional Emberá dances, some of which were used in the past in curing ceremonies, while others were used purely for entertainment. Due to their full-time involvement with tourism, the residents of Parara Puru have numerous opportunities to perfect their skills as individual performers and to spontaneously improvise or explore the details of dance as an expressive medium. Their daily engagement with Emberá dancing, and the enactment of dances in front of audiences of outsiders, has encouraged local dancers to develop a strong interest in the authenticity and history of their dance, the details of the choreography, and its importance as medium of representation. Overall, the practice of dancing for tourists has emerged as an act of wider significance for the Emberá, contributing not only to the global visibility of this ethnic group, but also to the knowledge and awareness of local dancers about their own culture.

This chapter embarks upon an exploration of Emberá dance, which has three aims. First, I seek to chart ethnographically the details of this tradition, which had been in decline over the later part of the twentieth century, but has – since the introduction of tourism fifteen years ago – been revitalized. Given that previous ethnographic testimonies on this topic – however valuable these may be – are short and do not provide a thorough description of the particular dances (see Torres de Araúz 1966: 131–35; Reverte Coma 2002: 273–82), I attempt here to fill a gap in the anthropological record.[1] Thus, taking inspiration from the developing field of the anthropology of dance (Spencer 1985; Reed 1998; Royce 2000; Wulff 2001;

Grau 2007), I describe the particular form and practice of Emberá dance as enacted in the context of indigenous tourism, but also the circumstances by which Emberá dance contributes to the wider politics of Emberá cultural representation.

The issue of visibility understood in terms of cultural representation at the national and international level is my second concern in this chapter. With the introduction of tourism, the renewed interest of the Emberá in their dancing tradition is paralleled by an increased visibility of Emberá culture more widely. It is in this respect, I argue, that Emberá dancing makes a contribution to Emberá cultural representation more generally. Dance provides a communicative medium that is immediate, non-verbal and easily transmissible to heterogeneous audiences (Daniel 1996). Through presentations that involve music and dancing, Emberá individuals dressed in traditional attire have succeeded in captivating the imagination of Western audiences. Undoubtedly their success involves turning pre-existing stereotypes about indigenous rainforest dwellers to their advantage; and in this regard, the Emberá, like other indigenous groups in the Americas, engage with the exoticized images projected by the global community (Turner 1992, 2006; Conklin 1997, 2007; Ramos 1998; Ewart 2007; Bunten 2008). Indeed, asserting such stereotypes can have positive political implications, explains Guerrón-Montero (2006b: 658), writing about the music of the Afro-Antillean community of Panama; and in the case of the Emberá, as with indigenous groups in the Amazon (e.g., Conklin 2007), exotic stereotypes can be an asset to cultural visibility.

My third aim is related to the second and concerns the notion of authenticity, and the proliferation of what Gow (2007: 54–55) describes as a Western aesthetic about the appearance and life of Amerindian inhabitants of the rainforest; an aesthetic that expects indigenous communities to be uncontaminated by Western civilizational elements (Ramos 1998; Ewart 2007). According to this Western aesthetic, Emberá dancing performances can be accused of inauthenticity, a perspective prevalent in the expectations of some tourists who visit Parara Puru.[2] An extensive body of anthropological literature, however, has confronted the essentialist foundations of the authenticity/inauthenticity divide, especially as this becomes apparent in the tourist context (Smith 1989; Selwyn 1996; Abram, Waldron and MacLeod 1997; Coleman and Crang 2002; Bruner 2005; Franklin 2003; Leite and Graburn 2009; Skinner and Theodossopoulos 2011). The concept of inauthenticity entails the potential of denigrating certain cultural performances in comparison to other imagined or actual performances or simply in juxtaposition with one's expectations. From an analytical point of view, it makes more sense to move beyond the divide of authenticity/inauthenticity – unless such a problematic is directly introduced by the social groups under study – and approach cultural presentations for tourists as dynamic cultural processes that may involve experimenting with new possibilities beyond or in addition to Western expectations (Bruner 1993, 2005; Skinner and Theodossopoulos 2011).

Thus, I will consciously refrain from referring to Emberá dance performances for tourists as 'staged', 'authentic' or 'inauthentic' and I will employ instead a more useful conceptual distinction used by Nahachewsky (1995) to discuss dance specifically: that between participatory and presentational dance. The former takes place at social events, such as community celebrations, while the latter relates to dance performances that involve some cultural distance between performers and audience. As Nahachewsky herself demonstrates, these 'two conceptual categories are idealisations', and in fact 'specific dance traditions may operate within any range on this conceptual axis' (Nahachewsky 1995: 1). This is the case of the Emberá dance tradition, which is enacted in both participatory and presentational contexts, and represents a single dance genre to be followed in both tourist and non-tourist occasions. In this respect Emberá dance can be contrasted with other examples of dancing for tourists, such as the case of Bali described by Picard, where separate categories of dance have been set – albeit with a certain degree of confusion – to distinguish between which dances are suitable for the entertainment of tourists and which are not (Picard 1996: 155–63).

Having made the above clarifications, I will now proceed with a description of the Emberá dancing tradition as I have witnessed it in Parara Puru, my primary fieldwork site, a community that specializes in indigenous tourism. I use ethnographic material collected during six periods of fieldwork in Panama, carried out between 2005 and 2011 and totalling seventeenth months, during which I have also visited several other Emberá communities, which, unlike Parara Puru, do not receive tourists on a frequent basis. My experiences among these communities have provided me with a wider perspective on the effects of tourism on the wider politics of Emberá representation (see Theodossopoulos 2007, 2010), which informs my discussion in this chapter. In the section that follows, I draw a sketch of the community of Parara Puru and its involvement with tourism. Then, I continue with a description of the various types of dance performed in cultural presentations for tourists, and I give a representative example of such a presentation. I conclude by underlining the importance and contribution of dance performances for tourists to Emberá cultural representation, but also to the self-awareness of local dancers about their own culture. 'Dance and movement are not only shaped by society', argues Helena Wulff, 'dance and movement also shape society' (Wulff 2001: 3212).

The Community and Its Involvement with Tourism

The Emberá, until thirty or forty years ago, preferred to live in dispersed settlements (see Faron 1962; Herlihy 1986; Kane 1994). They built their thatched-roof houses on stilts, preferably close to a river, and used the rivers as transport avenues to travel, transfer their horticultural produce, and migrate.[3] When faced with trouble – for example, external threat, internal disagreement or lack of resources – they would disassemble the wooden components of their houses and move to a new location in the rainforest. This is how their ancestors dealt with European penetration in the colonial past (Williams 2005) and the assimilation policies of the Latin American nation-states that later emerged. Following this steady and gradual pattern of migration – usually from one river sector to the next – the Emberá, and a culturally related ethic group, the Wounaan, have expanded from Choco in Colombia to south-eastern Panama, and more specifically to the relatively inaccessible region of Darien (see Wassén 1935; Faron 1962; Kane 1994; Tayler 1996; Velásquez Runk 2009; Colin 2010). In the last fifty years groups of Emberá have established themselves in locations closer to Panama City and the Panama Canal, such as the wider area surrounding the River Chagres.

In Chagres, the Emberá were initially settled in their preferred dispersed manner. At first they relied on horticulture and hunting, but later, in 1985, the creation of a national park in the area prohibited systematic cultivation and hunting. To survive under these restrictions, the Emberá living in the park explored the option of cultural tourism. Gradually, and with some external help,[4] the Emberá learned how to share the profits generated from tourism, keep their accounts, meet the necessary safety regulations, and make links with tourism agencies interested in organizing tourist excursions. The agencies provided the infrastructure for advertising and transporting the tourists, while the Emberá offered the knowledge of the rainforest and the 'tourist spectacle' (see Urry 1990). The entertainment offered to the tourists focused on visual and easily communicable aspects of Emberá cultural tradition, such as for example dance, that could be conveyed to outsiders during short visits.

The success of the experimental introduction of cultural tourism encouraged the Emberá in Chagres to form concentrated settlements, villages that specialize in the development of tourism and are prepared to carry out cultural presentations for outsiders on a frequent, almost daily basis. The social and political nucleus of the new communities was composed primarily of Emberá individuals who had been born in Chagres, although some marriage partners came from distant communities in Darien. The new communities were all set up close to a river (according to Emberá tradition), and all constructed in a careful manner so that they adhered to the rules and stylistic conventions of Emberá architecture.

It is also important to note that the flexible manner with which the communities were composed and organized, and the overall decision to establish concentrated settlements, is part of a much more widespread process. Since the late 1950s, the Emberá and the Wounaan living in Panamanian territory started resettling in concentrated communities (Herlihy 1986, 2003; Kane 1994; Velásquez Runk 2009; Colin 2010). The government provided schools and medical care, and in some regions a certain degree of regional autonomy,[5] while the members of the new communities elected leaders to represent them politically. Although Parara Puru, the community I examine in this chapter, was founded only fourteen years ago, its foundation was part of a wider process of resettlement in concentrated communities that started fifty years earlier in Darien.

Since its foundation the community has come to receive tourists on an almost daily basis during the high season and approximately two to three times a week during the low season.[6] The tourists arrive in small or large groups[7] at designated embarkation points at Lake Alajuela – at the edge of Chagres National Park – and continue their journey to the community by motorized canoe navigated by the Emberá. The great majority of the tourists come from either exclusive resorts situated in the wider Canal area or cruise ships that are passing through the Canal. Each visitor contributes to the community a standard fee, which is determined by the size of the group.[8] The residents of Parara Puru share this income with each other according to an organized formula that takes into account how many members of each family participate in work invested in tourism and the nature of their contribution. The overwhelming majority of local residents work full-time in tourism and directly communicate their satisfaction with this type of work, which they find more rewarding than cultivating the land or labouring for wages outside the community.

Seen from this wider perspective, the development of cultural tourism in Chagres emerged as a new economic strategy that the Emberá successfully explored, without radically departing from more generally established patterns of migration, residence and social organization. As I have argued elsewhere, the Emberá who now engage with tourism adhere to the basic principles of post-concentrated-community organization, while they experiment with new economic opportunities (Theodossopoulos 2010). In this respect, their engagement with tourism can be seen as a new adaptation strategy, but one that encourages the Emberá to work more closely with and develop a strong interest in their own indigenous traditions. Among the latter, dancing in particular has emerged as a daily practice in the Emberá communities that have developed cultural tourism.

A representative selection of Emberá dances is always included as a standard constituent of the cultural presentations carried out for the tourists and, in this manner, dance performances have become an integral part of the 'cultural package' advertised and made available. In fact, it is fair to say that the dance performance is the culmination of the cultural presentations, the part that the tourists most enthusiastically photograph and video, and the one in which they are invited to participate most actively. Dance, as Daniel has argued, has the advantage of being 'a holistic and multisensory phenomenon that often communicates to tourists and performers at a fundamental level' (Daniel 1996: 781–82). Apart from the dances, the standard cultural package for visiting tourists involves a short speech on the history of the community and the methods of Emberá artefact construction, a traditional meal of fish and fried plantains, body-painting with the black juice of the *jagua* fruit, and a canoe ride to the nearby waterfalls.

In most cases the dancing is introduced towards the end of the above activities and requires the cooperation of a larger group of Emberá performers. The dances are performed in special spaces designed for cultural displays, surrounded by rows of wooden benches for the audience. Parara Puru has two such specially designated dance areas, two enormous thatched roofed houses (without walls), which the local residents refer to as communal houses.[9] Unlike all other houses in the community, the communal houses in Parara Puru are not built on stilts and the dances are executed on the earth floor. The most recent and smaller communal house accommodates the overflow of parallel tourist groups during the peak of the tourist season. The older and larger communal house – apart from the benches surrounding the dance area – shelters wooden tables with traditional Emberá artefacts (*artesania*), such as hand-woven baskets, masks and wood sculptures, which are made available for display and purchase. The dance performances, therefore, take place in a setting surrounded by Emberá material culture, the *artesanía*, inside the communal houses themselves, which comprise representative examples of Emberá architecture.

The Animal Dances

There are two categories of dance that the inhabitants of Parara Puru recognize as part of the Emberá tradition: dances which usually carry the name of an animal (or less frequently a plant or an object), and couple dances such as the rumba Emberá and cumbia Emberá. The animal dances are danced by a line of women, or young girls, who imitate the movements and characteristics of the animal (or plant) in question. These dances were part of healing ceremonies in the past, and were danced by young girls under the guidance of a shaman (*Jaibaná*). During those ceremonies the *Jaibaná* would choose which animal dance to perform, inviting the animal spirit to either expel the 'bad' spirit that afflicted the patient or seduce it to willingly depart. The same dances were also performed on other occasions that called for the protection of spirits, such as the inauguration of a new canoe, a new house or an important gathering, and during ceremonies that focused on communication with the spirit world (Torres de Araúz 1966; Tayler 1996; Reverte Coma 2002; Ulloa 1992). The Emberá argue that this practice has not been completely discontinued, although nowadays there are only a handful of practicing *Jaibanás* left in Panama.

Since the establishment of concentrated settlements in Darien, the animal dances have been performed in festivals commemorating the foundation of a new community. In some of those festivals, groups of women from neighbouring communities will compete with which other, each group performing one or two animal dances of their choice. Occasions like these provided the women in Darien with an incentive to continue practising the dances during a period when traditional dancing had been in decline. Before a competition the women will rehearse the dance, perfect their skill, and add new elements to the dance – such as new movement patterns in imitation of the particular animal in question – but without altering completely the general structure of the choreography, which is transmitted from one generation of women to another.

Stephanie Kane, an anthropologist who worked in Darien during the 1980s, reports that animal dances were performed during formal occasions, 'political congresses and international events of cultural exchange sponsored by the government', such as when Emberá communities were entertaining government and military officials during the regime of Manuel Noriega (Kane 1994: 167). José Manuel Reverte Coma (2002), who published a detailed ethnographic account of Emberá culture based on fieldwork in Darien during the 1950s and 1960s, mentions that the *Jaibanás* in Darien would not hesitate to ask young girls from their community to dance for a non-Emberá visitor, such as the anthropologist himself. These examples demonstrate that the animal dances in the past, as in the present, were an aspect of Emberá culture that the Emberá saw as appropriate for performing in order to honour outsiders, such as government officials, foreign visitors, and, nowadays, tourists.[10]

Nowadays, the Emberá animal dances are an indispensable constituent of cultural performances for tourists. They are enacted by groups of women that move in single file and in a synchronized manner, with energetic jumps and dramatic movements that imitate the familiar imagery of particular natural species. Very often, the women hold the dancer in front of them by their skirt (*paruma*), forming – as Krieger describes commenting on a rare photograph from the early part of the twentieth century – 'an unbroken encircling chain' (Krieger 1926: 128, plate 34). During the dance, however, this 'unbroken chain' may be temporarily divided up or become a closed circle, always depending on the choreographic arrangement.

In preparation for the dance the women form a line led by the dance leader who holds a small drum, the *tonóa*. This instrument provides the basic rhythm, and in the absence of musicians accompanying the performance, a small group of girls can practise the dance by simply relying on the rhythm set by the leading performer. When men support the dance performance with musical accompaniment, they play the *chirú*, a small 10 to 12 cm flute, in a manner that reinforces the rhythm established by the *tonóa*. While dancing, the main line of dancers can form circles or snake-like wavy patterns. Sometimes it is divided into two lines only to reunite later in the same dance. The leading dancer can occupy various positions according to the choreographic demands of the particular animal-imitation theme. For example, in the flower dance (*ártoto karí*) – one of the dances not named after an animal – the dance leader might act as the stamen of the flower, encircled by her fellow dancers who represent the petals; in the dance of the snake (*damá karí*) the dance leader traces a wavy line, leading the other women to follow her, one behind the other mimicking the movement of a snake.

Many animal dances are accompanied by songs, which are chanted by the women while dancing. The lyrics of these songs emphasize or praise some of the most visible qualities of the species after which the dances are named. In some cases, the same animal dance has two versions, each with a different song, or one with a song and one without. It is technically impossible to compile an exhaustive list of all animal dances, since each community practises an extensive but not exactly identical variety of dances, and because new dances are introduced with the passage of time. Flexibility and a certain degree of improvisation lies at the heart of this type of dancing, which relies on the imitation of a particular species that has captured the imagination of the performers or has, in the past, been recommended for its power by a shaman. Theoretically every natural species – animal or plant, and in some cases also significant objects, such as the cross or the canoe – can provide the inspiration for one of these dances. They will then acquire the name of this species (or object) and the suffix *-karí*, meaning 'dance' in Emberá.

Rumba and Cumbia Emberá

The animal dances are not the only 'traditional' Emberá dances recognized in Parara Puru. Rumba and cumbia Emberá, despite their evidently non-indigenous names, are considered by the Emberá to be an indispensable part of their musical tradition. Throughout living memory they have been danced by the Emberá during community celebrations and festive occasions. 'The Emberá had been dancing rumba and cumbia since ancient times', I was told emphatically by several respondents, 'our grandparents danced them and the parents of their grandparents'. The residents of Parara Puru also juxtapose rumba and cumbia Emberá (which are considered as 'traditionally' Emberá) with *típico*, a popular musical genre in Panama, which some of the members of the community find attractive and dance during more personal occasions (such as an adolescent's birthday) or festivals outside the indigenous community (for example, in the neighbouring Latino towns). Emberá music, I was told in Parara Puru, is unlike the music of the Latino peasants (*los campesinos*), because it is not performed with the accordion and the guitar, instruments considered by many Emberá as emblematic of *campesino* music,[11] and also because it is distinctive in melody and style.

Previous anthropologists, such as Reina Torres de Araúz (1966) and Reverte Coma (2002), both of whom conducted fieldwork in Darien in the 1960s, identify Western and African influences in the music of the Emberá. Both scholars describe how the Emberá enjoyed listening to music in general, including Latino music that they heard during occasional visits to small provincial towns or villages in Darien. When the Emberá visited those communities, usually to sell their plantain produce, they spent considerable time in the cantinas of the Afrodarienitas – the black inhabitants of Darien – listening carefully to various types of non-Emberá music from jukeboxes and the radio (Torres de Araúz 1966: 131–35; Reverte Coma 2002: 273). Furthermore, the two ethnographers report, some Emberá men in Darien owned and played their own accordions and guitars (Torres de Araúz 1966: 135; Reverte Coma 2002: 279), instruments that my respondents in Parara Puru strongly associate with non-Emberá music.

The difficulty with tracing the exact details of the history and origins of rumba and cumbia Emberá is a general characteristic of research of this type (cf. Wade 2000: 231). Wade, in his work on Colombian music, further observes general tendencies to project styles into the past, the many local variations in musical styles, the movement of music across the country–city divide, and the combinations of African, indigenous and European elements (Wade 2000). It is safe to speculate, considering the strong musical interests of the Emberá described by Torres de Araúz (1966), Tayler (1996) and Reverte Coma (2002), that at various points in the past the ancestors of the Emberá were exposed to diverse exogenous musical influences – including music from other neighbouring indigenous groups, or even church chanting introduced by missionaries in previous centuries (Bermúdez 1994: 232). Cumbia, a major Colombian musical genre (Wade 2000), has influenced Panamanian music,[12] including related Panamanian rhythms such as cumbia-*chorrerana* and *típico*. I should also stress that 'rumba' in Panama does not refer to the particular Cuban style (see Daniel 1995) or the rumba danced in international dance competitions; it is rather a generic term referring to all types of loud party music, ideally of a cheerful and rattling type, such as the music that the grandparents of the contemporary Emberá encountered in their short visits to Colombian and Panamanian Latino towns.

Thus, it is fair to say that rumba and cumbia Emberá are the end product of a long process of cultural mixture or 'transculturation' (Chasteen 2004). This process has resulted in a new and unique musical style, which, as with most other living music traditions, is subject to change, variation and improvisation. The confidence of the Emberá in the old or ancient quality of their music indicates that any external musical influences were introduced to the Emberá gradually, and over a long period of time, allowing ample opportunities for consolidating new elements within established indigenous – that is, Amerindian – musical themes and traditions. What is also important to stress in the context of this analysis is that in Parara Puru and in other communities that entertain tourists, rumba and cumbia Emberá have been introduced to the presentations for tourists as representative examples of Emberá dancing and Emberá culture.

In terms of the order of presentation during presentations for tourists, rumba and cumbia Emberá always follow the animal dances, and provide a joyful, party-like conclusion to the cultural presentations. Since they are danced in couples – man and woman – they provide the Emberá with an opportunity to invite tourists of the opposite sex to participate, through the medium of the dance, in Emberá cultural tradition. In Parara Puru, the two dances, cumbia and rumba, follow different choreographic arrangements: the cumbia is danced in a procession of pairs, each couple holding hands and following one another in a line, while the rumba is danced by pairs, once again holding hands but moving more freely around in a circle. In this last respect, rumba Emberá with its less orderly arrangement pays tribute to its name, that is 'rumba' in the Panamanian sense, a loud party-like music.

The two dances are accompanied by music played by Emberá men. A well-organized group of musicians – such as the ones formed in Chagres – can have a flute (*chirú-dromá*) which is the lead musical instrument, a large drum (*el tambor grande* or *caja* or *chim-bom-bom*), a smaller drum beaten with sticks (*la requinta*), and some (or all) of the following percussion instruments: churuca (*chogoró*), maracas and turtle drums (*chimpigí*). The flute player introduces the main musical theme, and also engages in virtuoso improvisation, often repeating the refrain several times. In Parara Puru the music is not usually accompanied by lyrics, but in other Emberá communities some men sing while performing rumba Emberá.

Dancing with Tourists in Parara Puru

The two main categories of dance that I have described so far have become indispensable parts of Emberá dance performances for tourists. This is not only the case in Parara Puru and in the general Chagres area, but also in communities that do not receive regular visits from tourists (see Theodossopoulos 2007). This standardization, my respondents in Parara Puru explained, is related to the desire of the Emberá to present a representative selection of their dancing tradition. This should ideally include one or two animal dances, a cumbia Emberá and a rumba Emberá, although often the Emberá choose to present two rumbas (and no cumbia); 'the rumba', they say, 'is easier for the tourists to dance'. The relative standardization of the structure of performances is also related to comparisons with different Emberá communities and the attempt of the Emberá to follow what has so far proved a successful formula of entertainment: 'when we do something successfully', one of the leaders of Parara Puru explained, 'they [other Emberá communities] want to do it as well'.

As I mentioned previously, during the last dance, which is usually a rumba, the Emberá dancers ask their visitors to join in. Most tourists are pleasantly surprised by the invitation, and many accept. Those who do not dance enjoy the performance or take photographs of their friends or family dancing with the Emberá. How many tourists join in depends on the size of the tourist group. Tourists visiting Parara Puru in smaller groups have more opportunities to participate in the dance, as there are proportionally more indigenous dancers to partner them. However, even those tourists who do not dance share the cheerful atmosphere generated by the music, the dance and the dancing of the other tourists in their group.

A typical dance performance for tourists in Parara Puru is introduced as a dimension of Emberá culture. The women form a line, waiting for the first to beat her *tonóa* (the small drum), the signal for the start of the dance. Then they execute two animal dances, imitating with their movements or with the arrangement of their bodies the movements of particular animals. In the hummingbird dance (*impisú karí*), for example, the single line of dancers forms a circle, a formation that represents a flower. The leading dancer then enters the circle, imitating a hummingbird drinking nectar. The dancers sing a short verse about the hummingbird, moving their arms up and down in imitation of the bird's wings and in time to the rhythm of the *tonóa*. At the end of the short song, the circle is dissolved and then forms again on the other side of the communal house, closer to another part of the audience. After a thirty-second break to catch their breath, the women execute a second animal dance, followed by the warm applause of the tourists.

The Emberá take the stage once more, in pairs of men and women holding hands, in procession. The pairs form a circle, moving to the rhythm of the cumbia Emberá. At the end of the cumbia performance, individual dancers walk towards the audience stretching their hands out to invite the tourists to join them in rumba Emberá. Emberá children – usually little girls – reproduce the same gesture employed by the adults, successfully encouraging tourists (of the same or opposite sex) to join them in the dance. The adult Emberá more conventionally invite a single partner of the opposite sex. The musicians play rumba Emberá and the Emberá couples, as well as the mixed tourist–Emberá couples, fill the dance stage in an upbeat mood.

Very often the end of the dancing coincides with the departure time for the visitors, especially for tourists from cruise ships, who are always on a tight schedule. Other groups might stay in the community a bit longer browsing the selection of artefacts. By the end of the last dance performance the local dancers are physically exhausted, as they often have to dance several times for different groups, especially during the high season. All dancers contribute to the overall tourism endeavour from more than one position of responsibility. For example, some of the men who either play the music or dance the cumbia and the rumba had previously devoted considerable effort navigating the canoes that bring the tourists to the community.

After the dance they have to navigate the canoes on the return journey. The women dancers make general preparations earlier in the day, such as cooking the food – fried fish and fried plantain chips – that the tourists consume, or cleaning the surroundings before their arrival. Very early in the morning, before they join their efforts in collective activities, they deal with routine domestic activities, while additional chores are waiting for them in the late afternoon after the departure of the tourists.

Considering these detailed aspects of daily labour in Parara Puru, it is not surprising that dance performances require careful organization and planning. This is the case for most jobs that relate to the hosting of tourists, and also most other communal undertakings. The Emberá in Parara Puru share a strong communal ethos of sharing jobs and responsibilities, and they often do so based on a work plan that involves the rotation of tasks. Dancing for tourists requires prior organization of this sort, as the leaders of the community have to take care that a sufficient number of dancers and musicians are available for each particular performance. This task is made somewhat easier by the fact that the overwhelming majority of the local inhabitants, men and women, children and senior individuals, are able to dance and – unless already exhausted by other jobs – welcome an opportunity to do so. As the Emberá themselves put it, dancing for tourists is enjoyable; indeed, it is more enjoyable than other responsibilities related to the hosting of tourists, and much more than wage labour outside the community. 'When we work for tourism', the Emberá explain, 'we work with our culture'.

Visibility and Representational Self-awareness

I have already described how dance has become a central part of cultural presentations for tourists in the community of Parara Puru. The dancing, more than any other cultural practice that is made available in the particular presentations, is an expressive medium that captures the imagination of the visiting audiences, and has been so far very successful in enhancing the visibility of Emberá culture more generally. Photographs of Emberá women and men performing are frequently displayed on the publicity generated by national tourists campaigns and tourism agencies. Images of Emberá dancers are often supported by some description explaining Emberá culture, or at least refer to the Emberá by their politically correct self-designation – that is, 'Emberá' – as opposed to the stereotyped descriptive *Chocoes* (the people from Choco, in Colombia), which refers to the place of origin of their ancestors, but has been used in Panama to discriminate against the Emberá and the Wounaan as people who are not properly Panamanian.

This wider visibility of Emberá culture is, however, a very recent phenomenon, realized in the last ten or fifteen years. During colonial times, but also later, after the establishment of the Latin American nations, the Emberá struggled to avoid social assimilation, maintain their language and their distinctive way of life (Williams 2005). Stereotyped as *indios* (Indians) they occupied, along with other Amerindian groups, one of the lowest positions in the Panamanian social hierarchy. The introduction of tourism has changed this history of discrimination significantly

(Theodossopoulos 2010, 2011). It was first the Panamanian government, via the Panamanian Institute of Tourism (IPAT), which encouraged cultural tourism and created a plan for its development (see Guerrón-Montero 2006a, 2006b). Images of the Emberá and of their better-known neighbours, the Kuna (on whom, see Salvador 1976; Swain 1989; Tice 1995), were included in national advertising campaigns for tourism. Now that indigenous tourism has taken off, the tourists themselves are disseminating information about Emberá culture.

Some tourists, after their return home, feel a strong desire to share the experience they had while visiting some remarkable people in the Panamanian rainforest, the Emberá. They publish their photos and short videos on the internet, along with descriptions of what they learned from the Emberá and their overall experiences. In the last five years, the rate of this wider dissemination on the internet has increased exponentially. It is paralleled by the creation of new webpages advertising trips to particular Emberá communities, or explaining facets of Emberá culture. This increasing publicity has contributed in enhancing the overall profile of the Emberá nationally, presenting them as people who contribute actively to the economy of Panama and are respected by tourists from economically powerful nations. Internationally, they have gained recognition as an indigenous group with a culture increasingly known worldwide.

Although very few Emberá have access to the internet, the admiration of the international public is communicated to the Emberá by the tourists themselves, most of whom do not hide their enthusiastic reception of Emberá culture during their visits to particular communities. The strong interest of the tourists for things indigenous is expressed in the questions they ask (see Theodossopoulos 2011), their participation in the dancing, their gestures of thanks and their overall gratitude, which is not only conveyed verbally but also by small monetary donations. On a few occasions, Westerners who had been captivated by Emberá culture during their short day trips made more significant donations to the community, such as laptop computers, digital cameras and a new, 'modern' toilet for visiting tourists.

From the point of view of the Emberá, the positive attention of the outside world is a new phenomenon. The adult residents of Parara Puru, for example, were raised with the expectation – originating from the wider Panamanian society – that they should learn Spanish, dress in modern clothes and adopt Western practices. In the context of previous discrimination and stereotyping in Panama, Emberá culture was caricatured as 'primitive' or 'uncivilized'. With the introduction of tourism, however, the Emberá are receiving the message that their culture is now respected by the international community, and by individual tourists or travellers who come from countries more powerful and wealthier than Panama. This realization is now encouraging the Emberá to forge a stronger identification with their indigenous identity, and project their indigenous identity to outsiders more confidently. Instead of hiding away from the non-Emberá world, an adaptation strategy that served them well in the past (Williams 2005), they are now reaching out to the international community, and gradually take advantage of the new representational opportunities offered by an increasingly globalized world (Theodossopoulos 2009).

With greater visibility, however, comes greater responsibility: the inhabitants of Parara Puru now desire to become even better hosts to their visitors. Not only do they wish to perform, but also to guide their visitors in their cultural practices. Central to this desire is the realization of the Emberá that a successful engagement with indigenous tourism involves a certain degree of control of the tourism exchange by the indigenous community. As some of them clearly explain, they prefer to receive the tourists in their community, instead of dancing for them in hotels or on cruise ships. It is also important, they add, to provide their guests with an explanation of Emberá culture, instead of merely dancing or selling arefacts. 'Tourism', one of the leaders of Parara Puru explained, 'is an opportunity to tell foreigners about Emberá culture', to make Emberá traditions more widely known. So, with respect to their dance tradition, the Emberá of Parara Puru do not only aspire to improve their performative skill but also to learn additional details about the dances and their histories. Gradually, their engagement with their dances has contributed to an increasing awareness of what the local dancers themselves see as constituting an Emberá identity.

Against this background, the relative lack of abundant information about the dance practices of the past motivates the dancers to explore less frequently practised aspects of their own tradition. For example, the women in Parara Puru regularly introduce new animal dances into the dance repertoire of their community by bringing together memories of dances they remember from their childhood. Those women who have married into the community introduce new variations or animal dances with different names, drawing on their own memories and experiences of these dances in the communities of their parents. All residents of Parara Puru – the women who are interested in animal dance variations, but also the men who are interested in rumba and cumbia musical themes – have become increasingly interested in the performances of other communities, and in the overall history of their dance and music tradition.

This renewed interest in the history of their dances, and in Emberá traditions more generally, has enhanced the representational awareness of the inhabitants of Parara Puru. It is in this respect that the manner of presentation, but also the explanation of the presentation, become acts of ever increasing consequence. In Parara Puru, as its residents explain, dances are performed not merely for the enjoyment of the tourists but also for the sake of their own 'education'. Thus, the animal dances, and rumba and cumbia Emberá, are enacted as representative examples of an indigenous culture that has survived – despite the discrimination experienced in the past – and now claims its rightful place in the contemporary world. As such, the revival of Emberá dance in the present can be seen as emblematic of the resilience of Emberá culture itself.

Conclusion

The introduction of tourism into Emberá communities such as Parara Puru has brought about an intensification of Emberá cultural practices, which are now watched and admired by audiences of international tourists. Emberá dance is one of the most visible of these cultural practices and provides an easily communicated medium for representing Emberá culture to the outside world. In this respect, the dance adds to the visibility of Emberá culture, and through this visibility it provides the Emberá with new opportunities to represent themselves. As I have argued elsewhere (Theodossopoulos 2009), marginalized communities around the globe are taking advantage of globalization in order to reach out to the world, represent their culture, and make new allies among international audiences (cf. Conklin and Graham 1995; Conklin 1997; Turner 2002; Strathern and Stewart 2009). These potential allies include tourists from the economically privileged nation-states of the North who bring with them currency and, often, a strong appreciation of indigenous cultural practices.

In many cases, the warm reception of Emberá culture by their international tourist audience is the by-product of an essentializing gaze, which is based on previous Western preconceptions about the exotic. These revolve around static images of 'an unspoiled and irrecoverable past' (Herzfeld 1997: 109), an unreflexive expectation to meet people untouched by modernity, expressed through 'the lament for things lost' (Howe 2009: 249). Rosaldo (1989) refers to this sentiment – or sentimental pessimism (Sahlins 2000) – as 'imperialist nostalgia': the children of modernity mourn what was lost by the dominating impact of their own societies. So they search among indigenous people, such as the Emberá, to discover and satisfy their Western aesthetic of premodern authenticity (Conklin 1997; Ramos 1998; Ewart 2007; Gow 2007; Santos Granero 2009). The Emberá, their appearance and their dances happen to coincide with this particular Western expectation (see also, Theodossopoulos 2012).

So, undoubtedly the tourism exchange has had an effect on Emberá culture and Emberá dance, but one that has been, so far, constructive rather than destructive. Tourist imaginaries, 'reembedded in new contexts' and built 'on local referents' – such as the exotic appearance of the Emberá and their dances – 'help in (re)creating peoples and places' (Salazar 2010: 15). The Emberá in the communities that receive tourists have seized the opportunity for improving their financial situation, but also for making their culture more widely known. From their perspective, the positive attention of their international audience positively contrasts with the stereotyping that they experienced in the past, especially in the context of relating to the wider society of their own nation. Images of Emberá dancers are now part of official national tourism campaigns, while photographs and short videos of their performances are posted on the internet by the tourists themselves. This unprecedented – by Emberá standards – publicity entails a small but positive transformation of status, nationally and internationally.

At a local level, the new visibility of Emberá culture has encouraged the local dancers to engage with their indigenous tradition and its representation in a more systematic manner. Some of them feel responsible for perfecting their skill in performing traditional dances; others express a strong interest in learning more about the history of those practices, and constantly introduce new versions and variations of dances into their repertoire. I argue that this renewed interest of the Emberá in the details of their own culture represents a new, emerging representational self-awareness; it encourages the accumulation of new knowledge about their culture and, more importantly, a more confident articulation of this knowledge during communication with outsiders. Bunten (2008: 381) has referred to this type of self-representation as self-commodification, the construction of a marketable identity to employ in the tourism encounter, but one that does not seem alienating to the indigenous host. Thus, by becoming guides to their own culture, the Emberá in Parara Puru educate others about themselves and, more importantly, they do so in a way that they have chosen by themselves.[13] Dance is an influential representational medium in this emancipatory process.

To appreciate fully the representational self-awareness of the Emberá, we would benefit from a less static and more flexible conceptualization of authenticity (see Selwyn 1996; Abram, Waldren and Macleod 1997; Coleman and Crang 2002; Franklin 2003; Lindholm 2008; Theodossopoulos 2012). With reference to indigenous tourism in particular, Bruner (2005) has underlined the importance of seeing host indigenous communities for what they are: authentic indigenous performers. Seen from this perspective, the Emberá are authentic and true to themselves when they perform Emberá dances since they are (and remain) Emberá for the duration of their performance. Likewise, any cultural improvisations that may occur during the dances represent new possibilities for an authentic Emberá culture, which, in the same way as all cultures, is subject to change. In the case of expressive mediums such as dance, authenticity is even harder to circumscribe and narrowly define: 'movement is a primary not secondary social "text" – complex, polysemous, always already meaningful, yet continuously changing' (Desmond 1993: 36). While certain choreographic patterns may disappear over time, the possibilities for new variations are immense. This element of originality, embedded in the nature of dance, can complicate or challenge our view of staged dance performances as artificial reconstructions (Ness 1997: 81).

This is why dance in tourist settings does not always involve a loss of authenticity; on the contrary, it may reaffirm artistic freedom and encourage 'a contemporary manifestation of inventiveness within traditions and among styles' (Daniel 1996: 781–82). Indigenous dances, with their variations and improvised styles, can be seen as creative practices, that promote reflexivity and embody 'indigenous cultural meaning and values" (Citro 2010: 365, 381). Inventiveness and improvisation in this context can lead to new or alternative types of dance authenticity: the Emberá performances of animal dances, rumba and cumbia Emberá encourage a certain degree of performative improvisation, and are developing, through continuous everyday practice, to become fluid but dynamic manifestations of contemporary Emberá culture. They are – to refer to Nahachewsky's (1995) useful conceptual distinction – participatory as much as they are presentational: the former dimension provides a large repository of opportunities for improvisation, while the latter presents novel possibilities for enhancing Emberá cultural representation. More importantly, in the case of Emberá, the presentational aspect of dance enhances participatory involvement, but also an awareness of the cultural significance of dance.

In Parara Puru, during quiet intervals between consecutive visits of tourists or on days without tourists, it is relatively common to see six- to twelve-year-old girls dancing the animal dances. They approach this practice as a game and enjoy imitating the moves and choreographic variations performed by their mothers during presentations for tourists. Their elder sisters, who are more experienced dancers, might step in and dance with them, remind them of a verse in the lyrics of a song or demonstrate a particular move or pattern of a dance. In moments like these, Emberá dance is not performed or rehearsed for tourism; it is a game, a familiar set of embodied experiences, a part of these children's childhood and identification with Emberá culture and identity. At the end of the first decade of the new millennium Emberá dance is embedded in everyday life in Parara Puru and the other Emberá communities that have developed indigenous tourism. This is good news for those Western romantics who perceive with idealized admiration the resilience of indigenous practices, but also for the Emberá themselves, who seize the opportunities of the global tourist industry to experiment with and enhance their self-presentation.

Notes

I would like to thank Hélène Neveu Kringelbach, Jonathan Skinner and Andrée Grau for their comments and valuable suggestions, and the inhabitants of Parara Puru for teaching me the secrets and beauty of their dancing tradition. I would also like to thank Keith Alport for providing me with valuable video clips of Emberá dances from Darien, the two anonymous reviewers for their comments and suggestions, and the Economic and Social Research Council (ESRC, RES-000-22-3733) for supporting the research upon which this chapter is based.

1. In comparison to the scarce ethnographic description of Emberá dance, the literature on the dance practices of the Kuna, the neighbours of the Emberá, is more developed; see in particular the work of Sandra Smith (1984, 1997), but also (Holloman 1969, Margiotti 2009).
2. For more details about tourist expectations in Parara Puru, see Theodossopoulos (2011). Suffice to say, not all tourists suspect Emberá performances of lacking authenticity. Some acknowledge the nuanced interface of tradition and modernity, while (ethnic majority) Panamanian tourists are sometimes happy to realize that Emberá share with them common tastes and experiences as citizens of the same nation.
3. Rivers are used as points of reference for defining where one (or one's family) comes from (see Faron 1962: 19), or for mapping social relationships more generally (see Isacsson 1993: 15–23; Velásquez Runk 2009: 459).
4. Initial help came from the Panamanian Institute of Tourism (IPAT), NGOs based in Panama City, and some tourist agencies.
5. For example, the two semi-autonomous reservations in Darién, Comarcas Emberá-Wounaan I & II.
6. The high period of tourist activity in Parara Puru lasts from late December to late March, which coincides with the Panamanian summer or dry season. After the middle part of April, the number of visitors gradually declines and remains low until October. Tourist numbers steadily increase from November.

7. Group size ranges from four or five to eighty or ninety visitors, with groups of over a hundred being rare. There are also occasional independent travellers, very often a couple of individuals, or sometimes, Panamanian visitors who visit with their families.
8. Smaller groups of tourists pay a higher entrance fee per person to justify the mobilization of the local community on their behalf.
9. Although constructed for the purpose of accommodating tourism, the communal houses have become focal points of the community in which community meetings take place during times outside the timetable of tourism activities.
10. It is interesting to note that in the mid-twentieth century, the Kuna, the neighbours of the Emberá, formed dance societies (Holloman 1969: 480; Smith 1984: 191–94) and developed a variety of secular dancing (from traditional roots) which was made available to visiting foreigners, and later, tourists (Smith 1984: 257–58; Howe 2009: 181). Nowadays, these dances are considered as part of the Kuna tradition.
11. In Darien, I have met Emberá who own accordions, an instrument used to play both indigenous and non-indigenous music. Reina Torres de Araúz also observed the use of accordions by the Emberá during her fieldwork in the 1960s (Torres de Araúz 1966: 135).
12. Panama gained its independence from Colombia only in 1903.
13. I mentioned earlier that, during its initial stage, Emberá involvement with indigenous tourism was encouraged by the Panamanian state and facilitated by some infrastructural assistance provided by Panamanian NGOs. The Emberá have, however, been responsible for the content of their cultural presentations, and all cultural aspects of these presentations.

References

Abram, S., J. Waldren and D.V.L. Macleod (eds). 1997. *Tourists and Tourism: Identifying with People and Places*. Oxford: Berg.

Bermúdez, E. 1994. 'Syncretism, Identity, and Creativity in Afro-Colombian Musical Traditions', in G.H. Béhague (ed.), *Music and Black Ethnicity: The Caribbean and South America*. Miami, FL: University of Miami North–South Center Press, pp.225–38.

Bruner, E. 1993. 'Epilogue: Creativity, Persona and the Problem of Authenticity', in S. Lavie, K. Narayan and R. Rosaldo (eds), *Creativity/Anthropology*. Ithaca, NY: Cornell University Press, pp.321–34.

——— 2005. *Culture on Tour: Ethnographies of Travel*. Chicago: University of Chicago Press.

Bunten, A.C. 2008. 'Sharing Culture or Selling Out? Developing the Commodified Persona in the Heritage Industry', *American Ethnologist* 35(3): 380–95.

Chasteen, J.C. 2004. *National Rhythms, African Roots: The Deep History of Latin American Popular Dance*. Albuquerque: University of New Mexico Press.

Citro, Silvia. 2010. 'Memories of the "Old Aboriginal Dances": The Toba and Mocoví Performances in the Argentine Chaco', *The Journal of Latin American and Caribbean Anthropology* 15(2): 363–86.

Coleman, S., and M. Crang (eds). 2002. *Tourism: Between Place and Performance*. Oxford: Berghahn.

Colin, F.-L. 2010. '"Nosotros no solamente podemos vivir de cultura": Identity, Nature, and Power in the Comarca Emberá of Eastern Panama', Ph.D. dissertation. Ottawa: Carleton University.

Conklin, B.A. 1997. 'Body Paint, Feathers, and VCRs: Aesthetics and Authenticity in Amazonian Activism', *American Ethnologist* 24(4): 711–37.
―――― 2007. 'Ski Masks, Veils, Nose–rings and Feathers: Identity on the Frontlines of Modernity', in E. Ewart and M. O'Hanlon (eds), *Body Arts and Modernity*. Wantage: Sean Kingston Publishing, pp.18–35.
Conklin, B.A., and L.R. Graham. 1995. 'The Shifting Middle Ground: Amazonian Indians and Eco-politics', *American Anthropologist* 97(4): 695–710.
Daniel, Y. 1995. *Rumba: Dance and Social Change in Contemporary Cuba*. Bloomington: Indiana University Press.
―――― 1996. 'Tourism Dance Performances: Authenticity and Creativity', *Annals of Tourism Research* 23(4): 780–97.
Desmond, J.C. 1993. 'Embodying Difference: Issues in Dance and Cultural Studies', *Cultural Critique* 26: 33–63.
Ewart, E. 2007. 'Black Paint, Red Paint and a Wristwatch: The Aesthetics of Modernity among the Panará in Central Brazil', in E. Ewart and M. O'Hanlon (eds), *Body Arts and Modernity*. Wantage: Sean Kingston Publishing, pp.36–52.
Faron, L.C. 1962. 'Marriage, Residence, and Domestic Group among the Panamanian Choco', *Ethnology* 1(1): 13–38.
Franklin, A. 2003. *Tourism: An Introduction*. London: Sage.
Gow, P. 2007. 'Clothing as Acculturation in Peruvian Amazonia', in E. Ewart and M. O'Hanlon (eds), *Body Arts and Modernity*. Wantage: Sean Kingston Publishing, pp.53–71.
Grau, A. 2007. 'Dance, Identity, and Identification Processes in the Postcolonial World', in S. Franco and M. Nordera (eds), *Dance Discourses: Keywords in Dance Research*. London: Routledge, pp.189–207.
Guerrón–Montero, C. 2006a. 'Tourism and Afro-Antillean Identity in Panama', *Journal of Tourism and Cultural Change* 4(2): 65–84.
―――― 2006b. '"Can't Beat Me Own Drum in Me Own Native Land": Calypso Music and Tourism on the Panamanian Atlantic Coast', *Anthropological Quarterly* 79(4): 633–63.
Herlihy, P.H. 1986. 'A Cultural Geography of the Emberá and Wounaan (Choco) Indians of Darien, Panama, with Emphasis on Recent Village Formation and Economic Diversification,' Ph.D. Dissertation. Louisiana State University.
―――― 2003. 'Participatory Research Mapping of Indigenous Lands in Darien, Panama', *Human Organisation* 62(4): 315–31.
Herzfeld, M. 1997. *Cultural Intimacy: Social Poetics in the Nation State*. New York: Routledge.
Hoerburger, F. 1968. 'Once Again: On the Concept of "Folk Dance"', *Journal of the International Folk Music Council* 20: 30–31.
Holloman, R.E. 1969. 'Developmental Change in San Blas,' Ph.D. dissertation. Evanston, Illinois: Northwestern University.
Howe, J. 2009. *Chiefs, Scribes, and Ethnographers: Kuna Culture from Inside and Out*. Austin: University of Texas Press.
Isacsson, S. 1993. *Transformations of Eternity: On Man and Cosmos in Emberá Thought*. Göteborg: University of Göteborg.
Kane, S.C. 1994. *The Phantom Gringo Boat: Shamanic Discourse and Development in Panama*. Washington: Smithsonian Institution.
Krieger, H.W. 1926. *Material Culture of the People of Southeastern Panama*. Washington: Smithsonian Institution.

Leite, N., and N. Graburn. 2009. 'Anthropological Interventions in Tourism Studies', in M. Robinson and T. Jamal (eds), *The Sage Handbook of Tourism Studies*. London: Sage, pp.35–64.

Lindholm, C. 2008. *Culture and Authenticity*. Oxford: Blackwell.

Margiotti, M. 2009. 'Kinship and the Saturation of Life among the Kuna of Panamá', Ph.D dissertation. St Andrews: University of St Andrews.

Nahachewsky, A. 1995. 'Participatory and Presentational Dance as Ethnochoreological Categories', *Dance Research Journal* 27(1): 1–15.

―――― 2001. 'Once Again: On the Concept of "Second Existence Folk Dance"', *Yearbook for Traditional Music* 33: 17–28.

Ness, S.A. 1997. 'Originality in the Postcolony: Choreographing the Neoethnic Body of Philippine Ballet', *Cultural Anthropology* 12(1): 64–108.

Picard, M. 1996. *Bali: Cultural Tourism and Touristic Culture*. Singapore: Archipelago Press.

Ramos, A.R. 1998. *Indigenism: Ethnic Politics in Brazil*. Madison: University of Wisconsin Press.

Reed, S.A. 1998. 'The Politics and Poetics of Dance', *Annual Review of Anthropology* 27: 503–32.

Reverte Coma, J.M. 2002. *Tormenta en el Darien: Vida de los Indios Chocoes en Panama*. Madrid: Museo Profesor Reverte Coma.

Rosaldo, R. 1989. *Culture and Truth: The Remaking of Social Analysis*. London: Routledge.

Royce, A.P. 2002[1977]. *The Anthropology of Dance*. Bloomington: Indiana University Press.

Sahlins, M. 2000. '"Sentimental Pessimism" and Ethnographic Experience; or, Why Culture IS NOT a Disappearing "Object"', in L. Daston (ed.), *Biographies of Scientific Objects*. Chicago: University of Chicago Press, pp.158–202.

Salazar, N.B. 2010. *Envisioning Eden: Mobilizing Imaginaries in Tourism and Beyond*. Oxford: Berghahn.

Salvador, M.L. 1976. 'The Clothing Arts of the Cuna of San Blas, Panama', in N.H. Graburn (ed.), *Ethnic and Tourist Arts: Cultural Expression from the Fourth World*. Berkeley: University of California Press, pp.165–82.

Santos-Granero, F. 2009. 'Hybrid Bodyscapes: A Visual History of Yanesha Patterns of Cultural Change', *Current Anthropology* 50(4): 477–512.

Selwyn, T. (ed.). 1996. *The Tourist Image: Myths and Myth Making in Tourism*. Chichester: Wiley.

Skinner, J., and D. Theodossopoulos. 2011. 'Introduction: The Play of Expectation in Tourism', in J. Skinner and D. Theodossopoulos (eds), *Great Expectations: Imagination and Anticipation in Tourism*. Oxford: Berghahn, pp. 1–26.

Smith, S. 1984. 'Panpipes for Power, Panpipes for Play: The Social Management of Cultural Expression in Kuna Society,' Ph.D. Dissertation. Berkeley: University of California.

―――― 1997. 'The Musical Arts of the Kuna', in M.L. Salvador (ed.), *The Art of Being Kuna: Layers of Meaning Among the Kuna of Panama*. Los Angeles: UCLA Fowler Museum of Cultural History, pp. 293–309.

Smith, V.L. (ed.). 1989. *Hosts and Guests: The Anthropology of Tourism*. Philadelphia: University of Pennsylvania Press.

Spencer, P. 1985. 'Introduction: Interpretation of Dance in Anthropology', in P. Spencer (ed.), *Society and the Dance: The Social Anthropology of Process and Performance*. Cambridge: Cambridge University Press, pp.1–46.

Strathern, A., and P.J. Stewart. 2009. 'Shifting Centers, Tense Peripheries: Indigenous Cosmopolitanisms', in D. Theodossopoulos and E. Kirtsoglou (eds), *United in Discontent: Local Responses to Cosmopolitanism and Globalization*. Oxford: Berghahn, pp.20–44.
Swain, M.B. 1989. 'Gender Roles in Indigenous Tourism: Kuna Mola, Kuna Yala and Cultural Survival', in V.L. Smith (ed.), *Hosts and Guests: The Anthropology of Tourism*. Philadelphia: University of Pennsylvania Press, pp.83–104.
Tayler, D. 1996. *Embarkations: Ethnography and Shamanism of the Chocó Indians of Colombia*. Oxford: Pitt Rivers Museum, University of Oxford.
Theodossopoulos, D. 2007. 'Encounters with Authentic Embera Culture in Panama', *Journeys* 8(1): 43–65.
——— 2009. 'Introduction: United in Discontent', in D. Theodossopoulos and E. Kirtsoglou (eds), *United in Discontent: Local Responses to Cosmopolitanism and Globalization*. Oxford: Berghahn, pp.1–19.
——— 2010. 'Tourism and Indigenous Culture as Resources: Lessons from Emberá Cultural Tourism in Panama', in D.V.L. Macleod and J.G. Carrier (eds), *Tourism, Power and Culture: Anthropological Insights*. Bristol: Channel View, pp.115–33.
——— 2011. 'Emberá Indigenous Tourism and the World of Expectations', in J. Skinner and D. Theodossopoulos (eds), *Great Expectations: Imagination and Anticipation in Tourism*. Oxford: Berghahn, pp.40–60.
——— 2012. 'Indigenous attire, exoticisation and authenticity: dressing and undressing among the Emberá of Panama', *Journal of the Royal Anthropological Institute* 18(3): 591–612.
Tice, K.E. 1995. *Kuna Crafts, Gender, and the Global Economy*. Austin: University of Texas Press.
Torres de Araúz, R. 1966. *La Cultura Chocó: Estudio Ethnológico e Historico*. Panama: Centro de Investigaciones Antropológicas, University of Panama.
Turner T. 1992. 'Defiant Images: The Kayapo Appropriation of Video', *Anthropology Today* 8(6): 5–16.
——— 2002. 'Representation, Polyphony and the Construction of Power in a Kayapo Video', in K.B. Warren and J.E. Jackson (eds), *Indigenous Movements, Self-representation, and the State in Latin America*. Austin: University of Texas Press, pp.229–50.
——— 2006. 'Political Innovation and Inter-ethnic Alliance', *Anthropology Today* 22(5): 2–10.
Ulloa, Astrid. 1992. *Kipará: dibujo y pintura: dos formas Emberá de representar el mundo*. Bogotá: Universidad Nacional de Colombia.
Urry, J. 1990. *The Tourist Gaze: Leisure and Travel in Contemporary Society*. London: Sage.
Velásquez Runk, J. 2009. 'Social and River Networks for the Trees: Wounaan's Riverine Rhizomic Cosmos and Arboreal Conservation', *American Anthropologist* 111(4): 456–67.
Wade, P. 2000. *Music, Race, and Nation: Música Tropical in Colombia*. Chicago: University of Chicago Press.
Wassén, H. 1935. 'Notes on Southern Groups of Chocó Indians in Colombia', *Ethnologiska Studier* 1: 35–182.
Williams, C.A. 2005. *Between Resistance and Adaptation: Indigenous Peoples and the Colonisation of the Choco 1510–1753*. Liverpool: Liverpool University Press.
Wulff, E. 2001. 'Dance, Anthropology of', in N. Smelser and P. Baltes (eds), *International Encyclopaedia of the Social and Behavioural Sciences*. Amsterdam: Elsevier, pp.3209–12.

PART III

Dance, Identity and the Nation

Chapter 7

Moving Shadows of Casamance: Performance and Regionalism in Senegal

Hélène Neveu Kringelbach

Stuck at the end of the Cape Verde Peninsula, its sprawling neighbourhoods built tightly with concrete houses, Dakar, the capital of Senegal, feels like a place in transit. People and buildings alike seem to be in perpetual movement. But there is one form of movement that begins in the late afternoon, as the sound of drumming ripples through the city: it is the movement of dance troupes rehearsing in cultural centres,[1] schoolyards, on the flat roofs of houses and on the beach. Dancing or drumming with a troupe is a hugely popular activity, and in 2002 veteran theatre leader Mademba Diop estimated that there were at least 300 dance troupes in Senegal at any given moment.[2] Most groups are located in Dakar as well as in the coastal tourist resorts and in the Casamance, the verdant region south of the Gambia. With an average size of fifteen to twenty members per troupe, several thousand people are performing or have done so at some point in their lives.

Several genres of performance exist side by side, and sometimes overlap. There are contemporary dance companies as well as popular dance, hiphop or Bollywood dance groups. But for historical reasons which I outline below, the most popular genre is the one locally called *ballets traditionnels*. I call this genre 'neo-traditional' so as to reflect the nature of what is essentially a modern phenomenon, albeit one that is concerned with local histories. As Peter Mark has suggested, what distinguishes these artistic dances from the practices which inspired them is that they are divorced from 'local social and political structures and with the religious ritual that undergirded precolonial society' (Mark 1994: 570). In these 'ballets', dance, music and theatre are mixed in flamboyant recreations of local culture. Neo-traditional performance also overlaps with the music videos that constitute the main marketing tool of the Senegalese music industry.

By virtue of its history, the genre is also caught up in national and regional political agendas. In this chapter I suggest that dance and musical performance offer privileged insights into the making of political subjectivities 'from below'. To do this,

I focus on the Dakarois troupes which identify themselves with the Casamance. A linguistically, culturally and religiously diverse region, the Casamance has known an armed separatist conflict since 1990, but the idea of an independent Casamance dates back to the colonial period (Lambert 1998). It is widely regarded, therefore, as the most important threat to the integrity of Senegal, a nation drawn up from colonial boundaries. Jola speakers are the most numerous in the Lower Casamance, but other parts of the region are shared more equally between Jola, Mandinka and Fulani speakers as well as smaller groups like the Manjaco and Balanta. All groups straddle the borders of neighbouring countries as well: the Gambia, Guinea Bissau and Guinea. The Casamance is therefore one of the regions where colonial boundaries have been most acutely felt.

Drawing on fieldwork carried out in Dakar between 2002 and 2011, I attempt to explore the political significance of neo-traditional performance in Senegal. More specifically, I examine the ways in which an art form that was codified for purposes of nation building was appropriated by minority groups, particularly by Jola speakers from the Lower Casamance. The first Casamançais troupes were established by associations of migrants in Dakar in the 1950s. Their to-and-fro movement between Dakar and the Casamance contributed to the articulation of a regional cultural consciousness, and in this sense the troupes have been entangled in Casamance separatism from the outset.

Dance and the Performance of Ethnicity

This chapter builds on the idea that dance is a particularly effective form of 'cultural performance' (Parkin, Caplan and Fisher 1996). The notion of 'cultural performance' was inspired by Abner Cohen's idea of a dialectical relationship between power and symbolism. In his work on Hausa ethnicity in Ibadan, Cohen (1969) argued that the Hausa had massively converted to the Tijaaniyya brotherhood in order to preserve the moral unity that was essential to the survival of their economic interests in long-distance trade. He later extended this work to performance, particularly in his diachronic study of the Notting Hill Carnival (Cohen 1993), in which he argued that the artistic and the political could not be separated from each other. Parkin elaborated on Cohen's ideas, pointing to the 'metaphorical capacity for cultural performance to say things sideways' as that which wins people's adherence in a much stronger way than propositional arguments do (Parkin 1996: xxxiii). This metaphorical quality means that performance is capable of encapsulating a multiplicity of messages. When performance is made to embody national or regional identities, this is particularly salient because it is flexible enough to accommodate changes in those identities. For example, as I suggest later, the fact that Casamançais associations in Dakar express their distinctiveness through dance is not necessarily because people from the region dance more or better than others, but because this enables them to celebrate their distinctiveness while including elements of the dominant Wolof culture without having to openly acknowledge this.

Is there, then, anything about dance that distinguishes it from other forms of performance? In Senegambia, performance usually includes elements from music, dance, theatre and praise oratory, and whether there is a clear semantic distinction between them depends on the context. In Wolof, the word *sabar* is an overarching term for a genre which includes a participatory type of event, a repertoire of rhythms, a dancing style and an ensemble of drums. But dance is almost always central to performance, and participants talk about the dance itself as something that has the power to make one lose control of oneself. I suggest that this is because dance is intensely pleasurable to performers and audiences alike. The pleasurable dimension of dance is evident in the chapters by Skinner, Lüdtke and Theodossopoulos in this volume, and I have written elsewhere about emotionality in Senegalese women's dances (Neveu Kringelbach 2007). From my own experience as both a participant and an observer, I became convinced that dancing generates a particularly intense version of what Parkin (1985), referring to performance more generally, calls the 'moving together' of reason, emotion and the body.

A similar point is made by Askew (2002) in her study of musical performance and nation building in Tanzania. She argues that nation building only happens when nationalist ideologies are reappropriated 'from below', and that musical performance is one of the most important means Tanzanians have used to explore and imagine nationhood. Her study echoes Cohen's work when she reflects on the malleability of performance: 'the very tenuousness of performance, its susceptibility to modification, unrehearsed action, unanticipated response, and the contingencies of everyday life – renders it a powerful social force' (Askew 2002: 5). She also refers to the idea that music works because it is pleasurable: 'Musical performance, as one easily identifiable and highly emotive element of cultural practice ... constituted an integral component in Tanzania's cultural policy from its inception' (Askew 2002: 13–14). Her study is remarkable in the way in which it uses music and dance to draw out the complexity of nation building. In Senegal too, dance was mobilized to help create a colonial, and later national culture.

From Colonial School Theatre to Parisian Cabaret

Although Senegambia has rich performing traditions by virtue of the existence of hereditary categories of specialist performers, the *griots*, it was the promotion of theatre in the colonial school system that set modern theatre in motion. At the centre of this was the Ecole Normale William Ponty,[3] set up by the French authorities in Gorée in 1915 to train indigenous schoolteachers and colonial administrators. It was moved to Sébikotane, east of Dakar, in 1938, and students from all over French West Africa were sent to be trained there.

In 1935 the new director, Charles Béart, introduced 'school theatre' to the Ponty curriculum. The students were asked to write plays with the explicit aim of illustrating their 'native' traditions. The idea was to encourage them to preserve a connection with local cultures and with rural life in particular (Béart 1937). While these students epitomized the successful *évolués*,[4] there was indeed a fear that they might lose touch with the populations they would have to teach or administer on behalf of the French. The Ponty plays were a landmark in the emergence of modern theatre in West Africa (see Jezequel 1999), but they also betrayed the ambiguity of the colonial regime: whilst being controlled and sometimes censured by the French staff (Mbaye 2004), they also provided the students with opportunities to express anti-colonial sentiments by staging the lives of heroes of anti-colonial resistance. *Bigolo*, for example, was written and staged by Ponty student Assane Seck (Foucher 2002), who later became a prominent Senegalese politician. After being demobilized from the French army at the end of the Second World War, Seck studied in Paris where he re-staged *Bigolo* with a troupe of African students (Senghor 2004).

The Ponty plays were interspersed with musical interludes and short choreographic pieces perceived as innocuous folklore by the colonial administration. But one student, Guinean poet Fodéba Keita, was to transform this youth theatre into live national 'heritage'. After leaving Ponty, he went back to Guinea to teach but soon made his way to Paris, where he became part of the flamboyant cohort of Francophone students around Léopold Sédar Senghor, Alioune Diop and the emerging Negritude movement. Assane Seck, poet David Diop, actor Maurice Sonar Senghor (Léopold's nephew), actress Annette Mbaye d'Erneville, dancer-actors Féral Benga and Habib Benglia also gravitated around the movement and discussed ways of embodying Negritude ideas on stage. It was there that Keita set up his first dance troupe, *Les Ballets Africains de Fodéba Keita*. The Ballets Africains toured Western and Central Europe, performed at the Théâtre de l'Etoile in 1953 and the Théâtre des Champs Elysées (Sonar Senghor 2004), the most prestigious Parisian venues at the time, and toured major American cities. The repertoire featured dances from across West Africa with 'special emphasis on the Mandinka folklore of Guinea and Casamance' (Kaba 1976: 202). But the Ballets Africains also had a distinctly Parisian flavour. When reviewing their opening show in New York, dance critic John Martin remarked that although the dancing and drumming were unmistakably 'ethnic', the flamboyant ladies' costumes were 'indubitably authentic as well as being Folies Bergères' (Martin 1959).

Following Guinea's independence in 1958, the group was renamed Ballets Africains de la République de Guinée and toured the world as the nation's 'cultural ambassadors'. Keita was appointed Interior Minister in Sékou Touré's first government, and although Touré later turned against him,[5] Guinea's early cultural policy was Keita's creation. Despite the growing rivalry between Sékou Touré and Léopold Sédar Senghor over political leadership in the region, the artists in their entourage knew each other well from the Parisian years. Maurice Sonar Senghor had collaborated on Keita's first shows in Paris, and there was therefore direct continuity between the Ballets Africains and the creation of the National Ballet of Senegal in 1961.

A Nationalist Project

In Senegal, as in other newly independent African states in the 1960s, governing elites needed to gather very diverse populations around the idea of the nation. In order to construct a stable working state, they needed people to feel a sense of belonging and 'imagine' the new political entity they were now part of (Anderson 1983). One of the major projects to that effect was the creation of the National

Theatre, which consisted of the National Ballet, the National Drama Troupe and the Traditional Instrumental Ensemble. The Daniel Sorano Theatre, a modern building opened in 1965 in the heart of Dakar's administrative centre, would later house the three troupes. Sonar Senghor, who had returned to Senegal in the twilight years of the colonial regime, was appointed director. By then the Ballets Africains had already performed in Dakar twice, in 1956 and 1957, and the future President Senghor had been sufficiently impressed to write a long commentary on the second show.[6] In the rivalry between Sédar Senghor and Touré, the Senegalese National Ballet was designed to outshine the Ballets Africains.

Officially, the repertoire attempted to celebrate the diversity of the nation. But there was an implicit hierarchy between different ethnicities on the one hand, and between the urban and the rural on the other. Following the Ballets Africains, many of the dances were inspired by ceremonial practices from the Casamance, where new performers were recruited each year.[7] There was also an emphasis on rural life, and Wolof culture and urban life were hardly represented, as if there was no need to do so since it was assumed that they formed the core of the nation. But there was a double objective to be achieved with those at the 'margins': they had to be co-opted into the nationalist project, and they had to be imagined by Wolof speakers as forming part of the nation. But the creation of the National Theatre was the project of a group of literati steeped in French, especially Parisian, culture. Eriksen reminds us that 'the growth of bourgeois elite culture' is one of the characteristics of the development of European nationalisms (Eriksen 1993: 101). The same happened in Senegal, where initially at least, the construction of the Sorano Theatre was an attempt by the Senghor regime to develop a taste for theatre among the urban elite. Paying to sit on cushioned seats in an imposing air-conditioned room to watch performances was evidently not a form of entertainment that was designed for the masses. This was a space in which the elite could gather, elegantly dressed in suits and evening gowns, and in one gesture show off their taste for the high arts as well as their commitment to President Senghor's nationalist project. During the two decades that followed independence this seemed to work.

The resonance of this project with ordinary citizens is more difficult to assess. Sonar Senghor (2004) writes at length about the National Theatre's efforts to popularize its work by putting on performances in large workplaces and in Senegalese towns outside the capital, but his insistence on the effort required betrays the distance there was, at least initially, between the National Ballet and ordinary audiences. The Ballet did, however, foster the performing arts as an attractive profession for youths with the right skills. One did not need to be articulate in French to become a dancer or a musician, and therefore recruitment was not restricted to the educated elite. On the contrary, the traditional association between public performance and griot status in many parts of Senegambia meant that few dancers and musicians came from educated, middle class families.[8] Musicians and singers in particular came from griot families or from ethnic groups with no caste-like stratification such as the Jola. This was not always the case for the dancers, some of whom were recruited during Sonar Senghor's travels through the country. For them, in addition to the pleasure of dancing, the troupe represented an exceptional opportunity to travel and acquire the highly desirable status of a *fonctionnaire*, a civil servant.[9] Indeed, national audiences only represented one side of the nation-building project. The other raison d'être of the National Ballet was to project President Senghor's political and intellectual power onto the world stage. To achieve this, the troupe was sent to perform around the world. The United States, in particular, remained Senegal's National Ballet's main destination until the late 1990s. Showcasing the cultural wealth of the Senegal-Guinea-Mali region was also President Senghor's way of establishing himself as a key African leader, a role for which he competed with the likes of Sékou Touré in Guinea, Kwame Nkrumah in Ghana and Julius Nyerere in Tanzania. By contrast with their more openly political agendas, Senghor sought to impose his leadership in the idiom in which he had already established his legitimacy: the arts.

In official discourse, the work of the National Ballet was part of a project of revival and preservation of regional traditions. In practice, however, this was never a simple transposition of 'traditional' dance practices onto the stage. For one thing, those practices had never been static. For another, the choreography was the collaborative result of Sonar Senghor's theatrical ideas and the dances and movement styles his performers had grown up with. But this was not a work of historical recovery comparable to the invention of *Bharata Natyam* in India in the nineteenth and twentieth centuries (see Meduri 2005). Throughout the 1960s and 1970s Senegalese neo-traditional performance became increasingly codified, but it also became more popular as it was taken up by hundreds of people in youth theatre troupes and in the professional groups set up by former members of the National Ballet.

Southern Resonance and Local Appropriation

Askew (2002) argues that there is a gap in the literature on nationalism concerning the way in which nationalist projects become reappropriated 'from below'. She reminds us that nation building is a mutual process of engagement between the state and its citizens. The way in which neo-traditional dance was taken up differently in various parts of Senegal is a good example of this process. For reasons I shall now outline, it was eventually in the Casamance and among Casamançais migrants in Dakar that neo-traditional dance found the strongest resonance.

The massive migration that took place from the Casamance to Dakar (especially from the Lower Casamance) in the 1960s and 1970s (see Lambert 2002; Foucher 2002), which followed a long history of seasonal mobility in Senegal's southern region, played a crucial role in this. Although census figures do not give a complete picture of the phenomenon, they are indicative of a rise. The 1955 census reported 5,338 migrants from the Lower Casamance settled in Dakar; by 1961, the number had already doubled to 10,350. By the next census of 1988, the reported number of permanent migrants from the Ziguinchor region (approximately corresponding to the Lower Casamance) had jumped to 52,886 (Foucher 2002: 41–44), out of a national population of 6.91 million at the time (ANSD 2010). As Casamançais migrants established hometown associations stretching across Dakar and the Casamance, they also set up theatre troupes, both for recreation and as a way of maintaining a degree of distinctiveness from Wolof culture. In the 1960s already, the state newspaper *Dakar-Matin* regularly featured reviews of the shows presented by these troupes. This fed back into the Casamance, where popular theatre was already well established thanks to the introduction of school theatre in the 1940s.[10] One of the main dance troupes I have followed is a good example of this feedback process. Set up in Dakar in 1972 by migrants from Thionk Essyl in the Lower Casamance, *Bakalama*, which is the Jola name of the tree that produces fruits from which calabashes are made,[11] was initially set up as a theatre troupe to 'keep the youths from Thionk Essyl occupied', give them a space in which to have fun among themselves, and 'prevent them from turning to drugs and banditry' in the face of growing difficulty in finding employment (see fig. 7.1).[12] Hamer (1981), who did research in Thionk Essyl in 1978, found that 15 per cent of the population were engaged in seasonal migration and that 18 per cent were permanent migrants, with almost half of these settled in Dakar (cited in Foucher 2002: 50–51). Most of the women worked as house employees, which is consistent with informants saying that the first generation of women dancers worked as maids during the day and came to rehearsals in the evening.

Since 2005, Bakalama has organized a small annual dance festival in Thionk Essyl during which the troupe not only performs but also holds training workshops, thus contributing to the feedback process. The festival is a moment of interaction highly valued by the troupe, whose members have told me how moved they had been to see ordinary women join in the dances during performances inspired by fertility rituals.

Figure 7.1 Bakalama women dancers performing in Dakar, April 2003.

After migration, the second factor in the emergence of these troupes was school theatre. Some of the troupes set up in Dakar were staging plays written by Casamançais literati, such as Saliou Sambou, a prominent Jola politician who was later to become the governor of Dakar. He wrote texts for Bakalama in the 1970s, some of which the troupe are still performing today, to his great pride. The fact that the plays staged in the Casamance included choreographed 'traditional' dances meant that young people learnt dances from each other, thereby bypassing earlier, longer trajectories of apprenticeship with their elders (Foucher 2002: 113). As a result of this, a double feedback process was taking place: on the one hand, the National Ballet and other troupes found it easiest to recruit performers from the Casamance because many were already familiar with 'traditional' choreography and modern theatre techniques. On the other hand, to-and-fro movement between Dakar and the Casamance meant that more troupes were being set up throughout the region, particularly in the rural Lower Casamance. It also happened that Germaine Acogny, the future leader of the pan-African Mudra Afrique dance school in Dakar, was posted as a sports teacher to a secondary school in Ziguinchor in the late 1960s, and it was there that she first taught dance.[13] She says it is there that she first learned some of the regional dances, and often refers to the influence of the Casamance in her work.

Like the Ponty plays, the Casamançais creations were meant to be both entertaining and educational, and included long choreographic sequences. There were also plays with an overt political message, such as Béla's explicitly anti-colonial *Death of Amilcar Cabral*.[14] But texts presented a problem: if performed in Jola they remained obscure to most Dakar audiences, and if performed in French they appeared elitist. As a result of this conundrum, many troupes gradually abandoned the textual elements to focus on dance. This way, the most distinctive Casamançais elements – the movement style, specific drums such as the *bougarabou* ensemble, accessories, rhythms and dress – could be kept without audiences feeling excluded. This also points to the emotive qualities of dance discussed earlier, as this type of performance found more resonance with audiences than the textual elements. The problem of language and the local audiences' taste for total spectacle, rather than just the textual, comes into focus in Sonar Senghor's memoirs. During one of the National Theatre's first tours of Senegal in the 1970s, he remembers the reaction of a spectator who complained loudly, in Wolof, that the first part of the show was a comedy in French: "'Hey! You! When will you stop your grotesque squeaking? Nobody understands a thing. You are making fun of us. Come on, start the show!'" (Senghor 2004: 167). Sonar Senghor suggests that this reflected the animosity of the audience towards spectacle that was too textual, too static and not in the least bit participatory. This had been, of course, the choice of a man used to the Parisian stage and the bourgeois veneer of the Dakar's theatres. Casamançais troupes, by contrast, were becoming equally comfortable in Dakar and in the rural Casamance thanks to their versatility. They were also helped by the state-led creation of an image of the Casamance as a bastion of traditionalism in the 1970s. The objective was to promote tourism in the region, and indeed some of the regional troupes found work in the hotels of Ziguinchor, Cap Skirring and even the Gambia. But this also fostered a self-consciousness and an interest in local performing traditions; in the 1980s Peter Mark (1994) noted that although the *semaine culturelle* in Mlomp and Thionk Essyl was designed to attract tourists, audiences were mostly local.

At present there are dozens of neo-traditional troupes in Dakar and its sprawling suburbs. Significant proportions of them perform dances from the Casamance, from which come the majority of performers. Their names are meant to evoke the cultural distinctiveness of the region by referring to places (*Les Tambours du Fouladou*, 'the drums of the Fouladou') or Casamançais cultural practices such as initiation (*Forêt Sacrée*, 'sacred grove'). In a discourse that seems modelled on that of the separatist movement, ethnicity is downplayed for the benefit of a broader Casamançais identity,[15] even when the group is an offshoot of a hometown association: dances from the various parts of the region are often included in the repertoire, thereby creating an illusion of regional unity. What comes across in these troupes is that Casamançais culture is the Wolof's 'other'.

Another important way in which they distinguish themselves is by consistently using the idiom of kinship in everyday relations. Many performers describe their troupe as 'a big family', and indeed it happens often that people marry within their dance troupe. Siblings, cousins and childhood friends are constantly encouraged to join, and the relatedness that is shaped by everyday dance interaction is constantly emphasized in conversations with outsiders.

In the case of Jola troupes, the egalitarian ethos that is widely regarded as a marker of Jola identity in Senegal is consciously cultivated. In a nation dominated by the highly stratified Wolof ethos, this is a mark of distinction which has been used both by the separatist movement and by the Senegalese state to explain Jola 'cultural difference',[16] and the performers are conscious of this. Although there is a hierarchy between performers on the basis of experience, within the same 'generation of experience' the strong egalitarian ethos is often reinforced by a childhood spent in the same neighbourhood. The core of Bakalama's founders, for example, lived in Fass, and a large number of its members have been to school together. In this example, the egalitarian ethos is put into practice via weekly meetings at the rehearsal space. Chairs are set up in a circle and meetings are conducted in Wolof to allow everyone to participate since not all performers are fluent Jola speakers, or even Jola. The latest performances are discussed to see how they can be improved, and new projects or problems are brought forward. Women's voices are equal to those of men, and seniority in the troupe is more meaningful than gender. A share of the income is set aside to pay younger apprentices while they are being trained and do not perform on a regular basis. Members who fall ill are sent to consult traditional practitioners in the Casamance, and the group takes care of some of their expenses. The group may even intervene in family conflicts on behalf of junior members. In other words, it is not only the people's attachment to Thionk Essyl and Jola identity that holds the troupe together, nor is it simply a matter of money. What matters, at least equally, is the troupe's capacity to act as a surrogate family, in particular by creating an atmosphere of togetherness and protecting those in need of care. If such practices are necessary to retain members and maintain continuity in the repertoire, they also fit perfectly with the culturalist agenda. Discourse and practice reinforce each other in a constant feedback loop, and this is nowhere as visible as in what happens on stage.

Stylized Jola Rituals

One of the main concerns of Senegal's National Ballet in its early days was to reclaim precolonial history. This was a widespread project throughout the continent and, as Askew (2002) reminds us, ministries of culture in newly independent African states were often put in charge of promoting versions of precolonial history that would fit well with the need to unify heterogeneous regions into nations. In French West Africa, the *évolués*, the literati educated in the colonial education system, set out to write histories of the precolonial past and of the rural present, often merging the two to create an impression of continuity. Inspirational sources ranged from their own experiences to regional storytelling traditions with plenty to offer, and included European plays and folk tales learned in French schools. These stories remain the backbone of the neo-traditional genre today, albeit with a gradual transformation to reflect more contemporary themes. There are also troupes that do not perform actual stories but rather a repertoire of dances and rhythms, which bring life to the weddings of the wealthy, major sports events, political rallies and official ceremonies.

Casamançais troupes in Dakar distinguish themselves through their emphasis on regional practices. Regional life – as it is imagined for the stage – draws on real life, but it also works by obliterating the elements that do not fit within the discourse of cultural distinctiveness. Jola troupes make a point of singing in Jola and occasionally in some of the other languages of Casamance but rarely ever in Wolof – despite the fact that some have introduced Wolof *sabar* rhythms into their repertoire. These songs often celebrate the historical feats of known Jola figures or comment on life in the rice fields. Life is always portrayed as rural, and rituals such as the Jola initiation, the *bukut*, are favoured over Christian or Muslim rituals. During a four-week training workshop I attended in Dakar in October 2002, one of the dances taught to the young performers was presented as that of the *kambaj*, or Jola initiates. We learned Jola songs, including one in honour of Ansumana Diatta, a Muslim cleric chosen by the French as canton chief in the Djougouttes in the early twentieth century (Mark 1976: 117–18, cited in Foucher 2002: 91). The training, led by an older Jola master, was followed by sessions in Wolof during which two drummers gave their account of the *bukut* process they had gone through. Naturally they did not reveal what took place during their three-week seclusion in the forest, but they circulated photos of themselves in full initiates' dress and handed out printed versions of their own accounts of the ceremony.

In a similarly selective way, work in the rice fields features often in choreography, but not peanut cultivation, despite the fact that peanut farming spread through the region in the 1920s and 1930s following the collapse of the rubber trade (Mark 1977). Remarkably, the Casamançais conflict is also conspicuously absent. Several performers told me that this was deliberate because one could never be sure which side people were on. It also matters that in order to perform abroad, all troupes need the support of the Senegalese authorities. It is needed for local events too since the state owns the main performance spaces, technical equipment and the buses needed to carry people around the country. One manager told me that over the years he had spent hours in the corridors of the Ministry of Culture courting various officials and making his troupe valued for their professionalism and peaceful approach. As a result the troupe is often called upon to perform at official events, not only in the Casamance but also in Dakar and elsewhere in Senegal. It was even selected as one of the troupes representing Senegal at the thirtieth anniversary of the Libyan Revolution in 1999, and at the second Pan-African Cultural Festival in Algiers in 2009.

One of the flagship pieces Bakalama often performs both at home and abroad is *Kañaalen*, which illustrates the ways in which elements from various sources are combined to create the illusion of a bounded, timeless Jola culture. In the Casamance, *kañaalen* is a sorority of women who have undergone a long ritual process after failing to become pregnant, undergoing several abortions or losing young children. The decision to send a woman off to become an *añaalena*, an initiate, is taken by the village's female expert in protective rituals, the *ati eluñey* (Fassin 1987). For three to five years, the initiate is sent away to live in an adopted village. Her 'seclusion' there begins with a forest ceremony led by women in a procreative age from her village of origin. Following this, she is left to stay with an ordinary family in her new village where the ritual process involves daily humiliation by other women. Initiates are highly visible in village life as they must dress like fools and perform acts of buffoonery that would be completely inappropriate otherwise (Fassin 1987; Mark 1994). After resuming a normal life in her husband's village, an initiate continues to be expected to act as a buffoon during public ceremonies, and for those who do give birth subsequently, further sessions are required to maintain the efficacy of the ritual protection. *Kañaalen* sororities have been formed in Dakar and other Senegalese cities where simplified versions of the ritual have been devised to accommodate urban life.

Bakalama's piece, which I first watched in 2003 in a 45-minute-long version, is inspired by these sororities. It features a succession of tableaux with male and female dancers performing separate choreographies led by drummers and a lead singer-dancer who plays the role of the *añaalena*. After a rhythmic opening played on Casamançais drums, the piece begins with a synchronized dance by six to eight men. They sing in Jola, each holding a fake *kajendo*, a tool used for wet rice cultivation. The dance suggests the rhythmic movement of this type of work, with ample forward-throwing gestures which have little to do with actual rice-farming techniques. They wear a sleeveless half-length tunic fastened at the sides with straps and matching loose trousers of printed cotton cloth. At the end of the sequence, women's voices rise from the back of the stage. The men stop, look at each other in surprise and run away from the women now entering the stage wearing half-length, shiny batik-printed *boubous* (loose robes with wide sleeves) and long matching wrap-around skirts. They sing in Jola and step in rhythm, doing small and perfectly coordinated footwork, using both hands to hold the raffia baskets filled with rice plants they are carrying on their heads. Then, they simultaneously lower the baskets to the ground and start simulating the gestures involved in re-planting rice, still singing and stepping in rhythm, bodies bent over the ground.

The next scene introduces the main characters, a young man and a young woman. They fall in love, and their wedding stretches over a succession of tableaux featuring recognizable practices from the Casamance, but not exclusively Jola. One of the women following the bride carries the suitcase she will bring with her when she joins her husband's home. The 'suitcase' ritual is reported in the Wolof literature (see Diop 1985), and I have seen it performed at weddings in Dakar. The bride arrives surrounded by her kinswomen, her head completely covered by a richly embroidered cloth. But her happiness does not last: in the following tableaux, she is rejected by her husband because she has not yet become pregnant. She is scorned by everyone in the village, and once alone she prays, in French, for fertility. We understand from her monologue that her co-wife has children. The village women are seen gossiping and harassing her husband. Two of them ostensibly court him while the childless woman goes on to visit *kañaalen* priestesses in the forest. She submits herself to the ritual which is portrayed as a succession of joyful virtuoso dances. At this point, loud cries of enthusiasm rise from the audience. At long last she is healed, and the piece ends up with the whole village marvelling at the sight of her newborn baby.

Undoubtedly, *Kañaalen* is in many ways faithful to its claim of Jola-ness, particularly in the songs and the material culture of the piece. In some performances the skirts are made of the indigo-dyed cloth identical to the type every Jola woman had to possess from the 1930s onwards to be properly dressed during important ceremonies (Foucher 2002: 72–73). Despite their stylized design, the men's costumes bear a striking resemblance to military uniforms: loose red-and-blue trousers with a small raffia skirt on top for some, epaulettes and tall red, fringed hats. One is strongly reminded of the uniforms of the *gardes de cercle* colonial police. So, while the dances bear no traces of violence, the costumes reinforce the perception of the Jola as a warrior society.

Similarly, the calabash the main character takes with her into the forest carries the fringe of hanging beads characteristic of the decorated calabash carried by an *añaalena*. In some scenes the women clap small wooden sticks against each other in a polyrhythmic beat characteristic of the Lower Casamance. The movement style is emblematic of Jola dances: both legs alternate in a rapid and powerful stomp, feet flat, with the knees bent and the body leaning forward at a 45-degree angle. The arms are held away from the body and, in contrast with the Wolof *sabar*, they are never higher than the shoulders. The energy emanating from this movement appears directed towards the ground, as opposed to the aerial style of the *sabar*. However, whereas in Casamance these dances are often performed for hours at a time, on stage they are shortened and choreographed to avoid being too repetitive. Common to the neo-traditional genre throughout Senegal is the way in which rhythms are accelerated to impress local audiences with the virtuosity of the performers. Velocity embodies youth, strength and skill, and is highly valued by performers as a mark of distinction from non-professionals. But in the case of Casamançais troupes, the movement style, rhythms and velocity are fairly close to real-life events, such as weddings and initiation ceremonies. As a result, non-professional audiences often join in with great pleasure during non-choreographed sessions designed to be participatory.

At a different level, backstage the troupe maintains its engagement with Thionk Essyl, but in a different way from the previous generation. Whereas the parents transferred most of the troupe's profits back to Thionk Essyl for various development projects, this income is now needed by the performers, their families and for the upkeep of the company. A share is given towards education projects and the central mosque in Thionk Essyl, an important gesture in a troupe in which most members define themselves as practising Muslims.

The Shadows of Mutual Engagement

Aside from the consciously displayed Jola elements, however, these troupes quietly engage with Wolof culture and the symbols of the Senegalese nation. This is in marked contrast with what Peter Mark observed in Thionk Essyl in the late 1980s, and is probably due, in part, to the fact that this was a different generation of performers. Whereas members of the older generation were migrants, the current generation grew up in Dakar. One of the most visually striking aspects is the use of the Senegalese flag in outfits and drums (see fig. 7.2). Bakalama's MySpace webpage now features photos of the performers on tour in Spain, carrying a Senegalese flag

Figure 7.2 Bakalama musicians performing in Dakar, April 2003.

with them.[17] This is in part due to the influence of football as Casamançais youths in Dakar are often keen supporters of their national team. Furthermore, a significant number of performers have been football players at some point and, for them, the flag is a symbol of success in football before being a symbol of the nation.

The introduction of Wolof rhythms and popular dances is another aspect of this flag-waving practice. A few years ago, Bakalama developed a Wolof *sabar* programme when a Haalpulaar drummer trained in various styles joined the group. This enabled the group to widen the range of events it was able to perform at. One of the Jola women dancers has even made a solid reputation for herself as a *sabar* teacher, and she has taught as far afield as the United States. Closer to home, the leader of a Jola troupe in Pikine, a suburb of Dakar, told me that he had let his young performers introduce Wolof popular dances into their shows so that the youths would have something familiar to relate to. This mixing does not happen by accident. Rather, it is the ability to modulate the balance of Jola and national elements depending on the audience and the location which has ensured the success of troupes like Bakalama both at home and abroad. But there is more to this mixing of elements than mere artistic strategy: it also points to and facilitates a degree of integration of younger generations of Casamançais people in Wolof-dominated urban culture. Within this negotiated space, attachment to Jola and wider Casamançais identity, and to a locality of origin, remains essential as a cultural resource which can be drawn upon, especially in the context of a drawn-out conflict in which Jola identity is being constantly redefined.

There is, finally, a less visible transformation that is taking place: transnational migration and the development of an African dance scene in Europe, in which Senegambian performers are heavily implicated. In Bakalama's case, a growing number of touring opportunities have resulted in a high turnover of performers, with half of the troupe settling for longer periods in various European countries. The previous generation travelled to Japan and France in the 1970s and 1980s, but they came back because they had family commitments and secure jobs as civil servants. For the current generation, however, travel or migration is often a necessary step towards securing a decent living. Women performers are now as mobile as the men, and they increasingly travel on their own, sometimes with the support of male family members. Although Senegalese performers are generally very mobile, the mobility of women on their own seems to be more significant in Jola troupes than in others. This exhibits a striking continuity with the way in which the circular migration of young women became generalized in Lower Casamance from the 1950s onwards, a phenomenon which has been described extensively in the literature on the region (see Hamer 1981; Linares 1992; Lambert 1999; Foucher 2002). Like the men who had left earlier, the women maintain links with their former troupe, often contributing financially to its activities and even regrouping for common performances in Europe.

In the various countries in which they reside, the more successful performers teach African dance or West African drumming to European aficionados in dance studios, community centres and, increasingly, in schools and summer camps. So, teaching and performing dances and rhythms from all over Senegal is another way in which Casamance performers use the resources of the wider nation. While abroad, the performers plug themselves into existing networks of Senegalese artists and local chapters of the Senegalese Muslim brotherhoods. Casamançais performers, therefore, at once use and contribute to the transnational resources of the wider nation. This mutual engagement shows a degree of accommodation between the Casamance and the Wolof-speaking mainstream which does not always appear in Casamançais separatist discourse.

The Power of Dance and Musical Performance over Discourse

It is no coincidence that dance and musical performance are so often mobilized to help shape local, ethnic and national identities. This is because they are flexible enough to quickly accommodate inevitable changes in the content of these identities. What better forum to display Jola and broader Casamançais identities than the urban dance troupes that have become so popular with local audiences? Casamançais troupes in Dakar have gradually acquired the capacity to embody culturalist, localist and nationalist agendas depending on the context of the performance simply by modulating elements in dances, rhythms, instruments, songs and material culture.

Ironically, it was the Senegalese state that made all this possible. Casamançais migrants in Dakar have skilfully appropriated the very traditionalist discourse that the state had used to maintain the southern region in a position of inferiority in the national imaginary. These migrants knew the discourse as many were civil servants themselves. One may even ask whether this was a conscious strategy or whether this reappropriation happened because they had absorbed state discourse so well? Foucher's (2002) work on the Casamançais literati would support the latter option. This reappropriation was put into practice in the conscious recreation of folklore for the stage, thus representing Casamançais cultures as old (thereby justifying claims of autochthony), noble, tolerant and egalitarian – in other words, the nation's golden repositories of 'culture'. This is significant in a country in which 'culture' had been almost exclusively associated with the *Quatre Communes*, the four centres of old French presence in northern Senegal (Dakar, Gorée, Rufisque and Saint-Louis).

With time, and the renewal of generations, however, the culturalist agenda is discreetly giving way to more pragmatic agendas. The role of neo-traditional performance in shaping a regional identity remains strong but, whereas it used to be central alongside the recreational dimension, it is now enmeshed with the need to earn a decent living. This livelihood/profession/professional practice requires travelling and maintaining networks abroad in order to gain access to global artistic and educational circuits. The previous generation had a different outlook upon their practice as they held fairly secure jobs as civil servants. The young adults of today, by contrast, cannot afford to simply 'do' politics or recreation. The secure jobs their elders held are no longer available and, with the previous generation now retired, whole families are relying on the ability of younger artists to negotiate lucrative opportunities for themselves. These can take different forms, from four-star hotels and regional dance festivals to schools, summer camps, universities and even businesses in Europe and elsewhere. Dance, it would seem, succeeded in promoting a form of national culture, but one much more fragmented and unpredictable than Senghor and his nephew ever envisaged.

Notes

1. Dakar and the other major Senegalese cities have a network of state-owned 'cultural centres' modelled on the former colonial *centres culturels* aimed at promoting French language and culture. Most were built between the 1950s and 1970s.
2. See 'Réflexions sur la danse au Sénégal: la danse traditionnelle comme moteur de création', *Le Soleil*, 10 October 2002, p.x.
3. I am grateful to Vincent Foucher for drawing my attention to the importance of the William Ponty plays in the genealogy of Senegalese theatre.
4. The term *évolués* designated African individuals who were literate, educated in the French system, wore European clothes and displayed conspicuously modern lifestyles.
5. Touré had Keita executed at Camp Boiro, a military jail, in 1969.
6. The commentary appeared in *L'Unité Africaine*, 5 August 1959. This was the magazine of the Senegalese Socialist Party, published from 1959 to 1984. It is reproduced in Senghor (2004: 64–67).
7. Interview with Bouly Sonko, National Ballet director, Dakar, January 2004.
8. In Wolof, Haalpulaar and Mandinka society, griots, or praise singers, belong to the hereditary men-of-skill categories in the traditional status ranking. Griot is a French term for traditional performer or praise singer that cuts across ethnic boundaries, hence its use here. Men-of-skill (artisans and griots) generally have an ambiguous status in these societies, but they are also powerful in significant ways. For a discussion of the association between performing skills and griot status in Senegambia, see, e.g., Irvine (1989), Wright (1989) and Panzacchi (1994).
9. Interviews with former National Ballet dancers, Dakar, January 2004 and January 2009.
10. Foucher writes on the spread of school theatre in rural Lower Casamance: 'School theatre progressively became a defining feature of educated elites throughout West Africa: in every city which hosted a sufficiently large number of educated men, theatrical groups were set up. In Lower Casamance, because of mass schooling, theatre was to have a particularly strong impact … During the 1950s and 1960s, most villages of lower Casamance had their own theatrical companies, which performed during the summer holidays' (Foucher 2002: 111).
11. Some of the troupe members explained that this was a tree with far-reaching roots, and that the name Bakalama was therefore meant to symbolize a strong attachment to their place of origin (Thionk Essyl) in spite of migration. This is, however, a contested version of the name's significance. Saliou Sambou told me that the name had initially referred in a joking way to one of the troupe's first musicians, who used to carry a small calabash with him.
12. Interview with four Bakalama members, Dakar, June 2007.
13. See the film *Mudra Afrique*, dir. A. Waksman (1980), 56 min.
14. See 'La "Mort d'Amilcar Cabral" par la troupe Béla', *Le Soleil*, 17 February 1977, p.3.
15. On the framing of the separatist discourse as regionalist rather than ethnic, see Faye (1994) and Lambert (1998).
16. Foucher (2002) shows how the culturalist argument, which emphasizes the distinctiveness of Jola culture, has been appropriated by both sides of the conflict.

17. See http://www.myspace.com/bakalama. Retrieved 1st September 2009.

References

Anderson, B. 1983. *Imagined Communities: Reflections on the Origin and Spread of Nationalism*. London: Verso.
ANSD. 2010. 'Données démographiques et sociales', *Agence Nationale de la Statistique et de la Démographie*. Retrieved 1st October 2010 from : http://www.ansd.sn/publications_demographiques.html
Askew, K. 2002. *Performing the Nation: Swahili Music and Cultural Politics in Tanzania*. Chicago: University of Chicago Press.
Béart, C. 1937.'Le théâtre indigène et la culture franco-africaine', *L'Education Africaine*, special issue, xx: 3–14.
Cohen, A. 1969. *Custom and Politics in Urban Africa: A Study of Hausa Migrants in Yoruba Towns*. London: Routledge and Kegan Paul.
——— 1993. *Masquerade Politics*. Oxford: Berg.
Diop, A.-B. 1985. *La famille wolof*. Paris: Karthala.
Eriksen, T.H. 1993. *Ethnicity and Nationalism*. London: Pluto.
Fassin, D. 1987. 'Rituels villageois, rituels urbains: la reproduction sociale chez les femmes joola du Sénégal', *L'Homme* 27(4): 54–75.
Faye, O. 1994 'L'instrumentalisation de l'histoire et de l'ethnicité dans le discours séparatiste en Basse Casamance', *Afrika Spectrum* 29(1): 65–77.
Foucher, V. 2002. 'Cheated Pilgrims: Education, Migration and the Birth of Casamançais Nationalism (Senegal)', Ph.D. dissertation. London: School of Oriental and African Studies.
Hamer, A. 1981. 'Diola Women and Migration: A Case Study', in L.C. Phillips (ed.), *The Uprooted of Western Sahel*. New York: Praeger, pp.183–203.
Irvine, J.T. 1989. 'When Talk Isn't Cheap: Language and Political Economy', *American Ethnologist* 16(2): 248–67.
Jezequel, J.-H. 1999. 'Le "théâtre des instituteurs" en Afrique Occidentale française (1930–1950): pratique socio-culturelle et vecteur de cristallisation de nouvelles identités urbaines', in O. Goerg (ed.), *Fêtes urbaines en Afrique: espaces, identités et pouvoirs*, Paris: Karthala, pp.181–200.
Kaba, L. 1976 'The Cultural Revolution, Artistic Creativity, and Freedom of Expression in Guinea', *Journal of Modern African Studies* 14(2): 201–18.
Lambert, M.C. 1998. 'Violence and the War of Words: Ethnicity vs. Nationalism in the Casamance', *Africa* 68(4): 585–602.
——— 1999. 'Have Jola Women Found a Way to Resist Patriarchy with Commodities?', *Political and Legal Anthropology Review* 22(1): 85–93.
——— 2002. *Longing for Exile: Migration and the Making of a Translocal Community in Senegal, West Africa*. Portsmouth, NH: Heinemann.
Linares, O. 1992. *Power, Prayer, and Production: The Jola of Casamance, Senegal*. Cambridge: Cambridge University Press.
Mark, P. 1976. 'Economic and Religious Change among the Diola of Boulouf (Casamance), 1890–1940: Trade, Cash Cropping and Islam in Southwestern Senegal', Ph.D. dissertation. New Haven, CT: Yale University.

―――― 1977. 'The Rubber and Palm Produce Trades and the Islamization of the Diola of Boulouf (Casamance, 1890–1920)', *Bulletin de l'Institut Français d'Afrique Noire* 39B(2): 341–61.

―――― 1994. 'Art, Ritual and Folklore: Dance and Cultural Identity among the Peoples of the Casamance', *Cahiers d'Etudes Africaines* 136: 563–84.

Martin, J. 1959. 'Dance: "Ballets Africains" – Keita Fodeba Company Demonstrates Liveliness in Opening at Martin Beck', *New York Times*, 17 February, p.28.

Mbaye, A. 2004. 'L'autre théâtre historique de l'époque coloniale: le 'Chaka' de Senghor', *Ethiopiques* 72, retrieved 2nd February 2005 from: http://www.refer.sn/ethiopiques/article.php3?id_article=84

Meduri, A. (ed.) 2005 *Rukmini Devi Arundale (1904–1986): A Visionary Architect of Indian Culture and the Performing Arts*. New Delhi: Motilal Banarsidass.

Neveu Kringelbach, H. 2007. 'Cool Play: Emotionality in Dance as a Resource in Senegalese Urban Women's Associations', in H. Wulff (ed.), *The Emotions: A Cultural Reader*. Oxford: Berg, pp.251–72.

Panzacchi, C. 1994. 'The Livelihood of Traditional Griots in Modern Senegal', *Africa* 64(2): 190–210.

Parkin, D. 1985. 'Reason, Emotion and the Embodiment of Power', in J. Overing (ed.), *Reason and Morality*. London: Tavistock, pp.134–49.

―――― 1996. 'The Power of the Bizarre', in D. Parkin, L. Caplan and H. Fisher (eds), *The Politics of Cultural Performance*. Oxford: Berghahn, pp.xv–xl.

Parkin, D., L. Caplan and H. Fisher (eds). 1996. *The Politics of Cultural Performance*. Oxford: Berghahn.

Senghor, M.S. 2004. *Souvenirs de théâtres d'Afrique et d'Outre-Afrique*. Paris: L'Harmattan.

Wright, B. 1989. 'The Power of Articulation', in W. Arens and I. Karp (eds), *Creativity of Power: Cosmology and Action in African Societies*. Washington: Smithsonian Institution Press, pp.39–57.

Chapter 8

Ballet Folklórico Mexicano: Choreographing National Identity in a Transnational Context
Olga Nájera-Ramírez

Since its emergence in the late 1950s, *ballet folklórico* has become an enormously popular dance form that is widely practised throughout Mexico and the United States, and performed throughout the world. Although *folklórico* dance continues to be a vibrant transnational expressive medium through which Mexican communities on both sides of the US–Mexico border create and pass on a strong sense of group aesthetics and identity, serious scholarship on this dance genre is a relatively recent development. Some twenty-five years ago, when I published an article on the social and political dimensions of *folklórico* dance (Nájera-Ramírez 1989), material on the subject was scarce indeed. Over the past two decades, however, several important works have been published in Spanish that provide a lot more insight into the complex history of this dance form in Mexico (Dallal 1986, 2008; Tortajada Quiróz 1995, 2000; Parga 2004). To date, there is little published on the practice and significance of *folklórico* dance in the United States (but see Nájera-Ramírez, Cantú and Romero 2009).

The purpose of this essay is to provide an overview of the emergence and development of the Mexican *folklórico* dance genre in Mexico and in the United States. I will show that this dance form emerged in large part as a response to the romantic nationalist sentiments that motivated artists, intellectuals and politicians to search for ways of presenting and promoting new visions of Mexican national identity during the post-revolutionary period. As a state sanctioned expression of *lo mexicano* or 'Mexicanness' through which the diversity of Mexican culture or *mexicanidades* was displayed to audiences everywhere, *folklórico* dance became a discursive construct that enabled disparate ethnic and regional communities to envision themselves (and each other) as legitimate members of the Mexican nation. Entangled in issues of authenticity, commercialization and legitimacy, *ballet folklórico* offers an important site for examining the multifaceted and often contradictory forces at play in the transnational development of this expressive form. Therefore, I will also explore the politics of identity as played out in this vibrant and widespread transnational cultural expression. Finally, I will demonstrate that despite these complications and contradictions, *ballet folklórico* has become extremely influential in shaping the cultural imaginary of Mexican national identity at home and abroad.

Definitions

I begin by defining and elaborating upon two terms that are central to this essay: cultural imaginary and *folklórico* dance. I use the term 'cultural imaginary' to refer to the full range of cultural productions by which cultural identities are constructed, disseminated and experienced.[1] Following Américo Paredes, whose scholarship on Mexican expressive culture demonstrated a nuanced understanding of the complexities of national and cultural identities,[2] I show that interrogating the means through which a community imagines itself as part of a nation provides insight into the politics of identity and representation, particularly in the context of globalization, in which people, cultures and goods circulate beyond the geopolitical borders that define a nation-state. Specifically, I argue that *folklórico* dance, like other Mexican transnational expressive forms, 'simultaneously challenges and strengthens pre-existing conceptions of national and cultural identities' (Nájera-Ramírez 2001: 168). Attesting to the power of the imaginary, even Mexican-Americans who have never been to Mexico frequently come to identify as Mexican through their participation in and enactment of Mexican *folklórico* dance. However, within the realm of *folklórico* dance, Mexican-Americans perform almost exclusively as bearers of tradition, not as legitimate active producers of culture who contribute to and thus expand what it means to be Mexican. This raises the question regarding how Mexicans living in the United States fit within the Mexican national imaginary. I will return to this point in the latter part of the chapter.

With respect to *folklórico* dance, I stress that although it is often glossed over as 'Mexican folk or regional dance,' Mexican *folklórico* dance is more accurately defined as a stylized and choreographed dance form developed for theatrical stage presentation that is based on, or otherwise informed by, regional folk dances and traditions of Mexico. More specifically, *folklórico* dance presentations consist of various *cuadros* (suites) that represent different cultural regions of Mexico through movement, music, costumes and sometimes stage backdrops or scenery.[3] The *zapateados* (footwork that consists of intricate stomps, heel and toe patterns) are characteristic of most dances although the specific type of *zapateado* varies from region to region. Another common feature is that these are courtship dances in which the dancers often imitate the movement of animals (horses, iguanas, vultures) found in the local environment. To better illustrate, let me briefly describe the *jarocho* region.[4]

Originating in the southern coastal plain of the state of Veracruz, the expression *son jarocho* refers to a music and dance genre forged from hybridized African, Indigenous, and European traditions. Characterized by a polyrhythmic foundation and improvised lyrics, *son jarocho* is played by a *conjunto jarocho* (*jarocho* ensemble) that typically includes harp, *requinto* (a melodic guitar-like instrument) and a *jarana* (a small, eight-stringed, five course guitar-like instrument that provides the rhythmic foundation). Sometimes a *pandero* (tambourine) and *quijada* (the jawbone of a donkey) are used for percussion. Often performed on a *tarima* (wooden platform), the syncopated, percussive footwork that is reminiscent of, but not identical to, flamenco dance steps, complete the ensemble.

The humid tropical climate and the cultural roots are expressed in the costumes, dance movements and stage scenery. Women wear white lacy skirts and blouses, a black embroidered apron, a solid brightly coloured *rebozo* (shawl), and a pair of white hard-heeled shoes. A large *tocado* (head piece) consisting of bright tropical flowers and a *peineta* (decorative hair comb) and a lacy fan complete the costume. Men wear a white *guayabera* (embroidered button-down shirt with big pockets and pleats down the front) over white trousers, a *paliacate* (kerchief), a palm-fibre hat and a pair of white boots (see fig. 8.1). To accentuate the footwork, the dancers' shoes have nails hammered into the toe and heel of the sole (fig. 8.2). Women's skirt movements are graceful and flowing, reminiscent of gentle ocean waves. Dance movements may also imitate local animals. For example, *La Iguana* features men imitating the slithering jumps and gyrations of an iguana that attacks the women. Frequently, the tropical backdrop will include palm trees and ocean scenery.

In Mexico, *folklórico* dance as defined above is currently referred to more precisely as *danza folklórica escénica* (theatrical folk dance). But in the US, this dance form is most commonly referred to simply as *folklórico* dance. In the course of a *folklórico* presentation in a theatre, dance troupes will present six or more regions of Mexico thus providing audiences with a riveting variety of regional cultures. In any combination, *folklórico* dances work to capture and display the richness of *lo mexicano*, or 'Mexicanness'.[5]

Figure 8.1 Grupo Folklórico de la Universidad de Guadalajara, circa 1965.

Figure 8.2 Arce Manjares family performing in Guadalajara, circa 1960s

Forging a National Identity: The Search for *Lo Mexicano*

Although Mexico gained independence in 1821, the first hundred years of independence was tumultuous to say the least. Rural–urban divisions as well as political instability exacerbated Mexico's lack of economic, racial and social integration. Indeed, fifty distinct leaders ruled the nation before Porfirio Díaz assumed the presidency in 1876 (Cockcroft 1983: 62). His thirty-five years of tyrannical rule, referred to as the *Porfiriato*, brought remarkable material prosperity to Mexico but Díaz's reign proved an economic and social disaster for the common citizen who did not share in the benefits of his campaign to modernize Mexico. By all accounts, Diaz's repressive regime shunned the masses and their culture (Cockcroft 1983; Sherman and Meyer 1979). Influenced by positivist intellectuals, referred to as the *científicos*, Díaz espoused a racist ideology that viewed indigenous people and working-class mestizos as obstacles to Mexico's development, while European people, trends and artistic expressions were regarded as the standards of modernity and progress. By the end of the nineteenth century, at the height of the *Porfiriato*, emulating French culture signalled a 'true measure of aristocratic success' (Sherman and Meyer 1979: 473).

At the turn of the twentieth century, Mexico experienced a social revolution that toppled the Díaz regime and promised a new beginning for the country. The Mexican Revolution of 1910 ignited a romantic nationalist movement that inspired artists, intellectuals and government agencies to look to their native culture as the basis for the development of a new Mexican national identity. Muralists, musicians, architects and writers sought to create a national style that highlighted the peasantry and indigenous population as the source of an authentic Mexican identity (Knight 1990). This explosive interest in *lo mexicano* positioned traditional and regional dances as ideal ways to acknowledge the cultural diversity within the Mexican nation while simultaneously providing evidence for its unique character as a nation (Nájera-Ramírez 1989). It was in this context that indigenous and regional folk dance assumed national importance.[6]

Several government agencies and institutions participated in early efforts to collect, preserve and disseminate dance. The Secretaría de Educación Pública (SEP) sponsored numerous endeavours involving Mexican traditional dance. The Misiones Culturales (Cultural Missions), for example, whose stated goal was to create a united national society (Saenz 1927; Sánchez 1936), assumed the task of collecting folk dances throughout the nation. The idea was to document these vernacular expressions before they disappeared and to disseminate them through the state school system as a way of preserving them. It was thus that *folklórico* dance, however decontextualized and simplified, became an integral part of the elementary school experience. The Cultural Missions programme also sponsored various dance festivals in order to promote an interest in indigenous and traditional dance (Tortajada Quiróz 2000: 16).

During the early 1930s, SEP established the first national dance school, the Escuela Nacional de Danza, under the auspices of the Departmento de Bellas Artes (Department of Fine Arts).[7] In 1932, under the directorship of revolutionary artists

Carlos Mérida and Carlos Orozco Romero, the school developed a specific focus on Mexican dance. While the Escuela Nacional offered classes in various genres of dance, the principal goal was to provide students with the foundational skills and knowledge to create 'a totally Mexican dance form' (*una danza netamente mexicana*) (Dallal 1986: 84). Members of the faculty engaged in researching vernacular dance forms, producing choreographies for festivals sponsored by the school, and, of course, developing and teaching the curriculum (Tortajada Quiróz 2000: 18). The Escuela Nacional de Danza offered two courses on Mexican dance titled *Ritmos mexicanos* (Mexican rhythms) and *Bailes mexicanos* (Mexican dances), taught by sisters Gloria and Nellie Campobello respectively. Trained in classical ballet, they sought to choreograph classical ballets based on Mexican nationalist themes. Indeed, by 1931 the Campobello sisters created a suite inspired by the Mexican revolution entitled *Ballet Simbólico 30–30* that received widespread acclaim (Dallal 1986: 83; Tortajada Quiróz 2000: 18). In 1940, they published a book, *Ritmos Indígenos*, based on their research into Mexican vernacular dance. The Campobello sisters eventually established the dance company, Ballet de la Ciudad de México, which focused exclusively on injecting Mexican themes into classical ballet, but by 1947 the dance troupe had dissolved (Cerón 2005).

Beginning in 1940, there began a Mexican modern-dance movement (*movimiento mexicano de danza moderna*) that lasted through to 1959 (Dallal 1986). The Mexican modern-dance movement spawned many talented dancers, choreographers, directors and researchers who worked collaboratively with other nationally oriented artists such as Carlos Chávez, Miguel Covarrubias and Blas Galindo. Curiously, however, two North American dancers and choreographers, Anna Sokolow and Waldeen Falkenstein, the latter better known simply as Waldeen, spearheaded the modern dance movement in Mexico (Dallal 1986: 105). Carlos Mérida, director of the Escuela Nacional de Danza, invited Anna Sokolow to present a series of performances at the Palacio de Bellas Artes in Mexico City. Although Sokolow, who had trained with Martha Graham, had previously performed in Mexico on several occasions, this time she stayed in Mexico and founded the Grupo Mexicano de Danzas Clásicas y Modernas made up of students from the Escuela Nacional. In 1940 Sokolow worked with the Ballet de Bellas Artes and subsequently established a modern dance group called La Paloma Azul (the Blue Dove) dedicated to the development of dance pieces based on Mexican themes and images. While Sokolow's company lasted only one season, she is nonetheless credited with establishing the foundations of an indigenous Mexican modern-dance movement.[8]

In 1939, SEP invited Waldeen, trained in classical ballet and modern dance, to direct the Ballet de Bellas Artes. Like Sokolow, Waldeen selected a group of dancers enrolled in the Escuela Nacional de Danza to perform her choreographies. According to dance critic Alberto Dallal (1986: 92), Waldeen was among the first choreographers to develop modern dance based on Mexican dances. Her dance suite *La Coronela*, for example, which debuted on 23 November 1940, alluded to the oppressed conditions of the *pueblo* (the common people) and featured Silvestre

Revueltas's nationalist symphonic music and Jose Guadalupe Posada's engravings (*grabados*). Both Waldeen and Sokolow contributed significantly to the development of nationally inspired theatrical dance in Mexico and mentored many aspiring dancers.

The establishment in 1947 of the Academia de Danza Mexicana by nationalist music composer Carlos Chávez, director of the newly inaugurated Instituto Nacional de Bellas Artes, proved to be another significant development in Mexican dance. Directed by Guillermina Bravo and Ana Mérida, the academy offered classes in classical ballet, regional and modern dance. Founding members of the Academia de Danza included Josefina Lavalle, Marcelo Torreblanca and Amalia Hernández, each of whom made important contributions to *folklórico* dance (Dallal 1986: 109, 120).

Josefina Lavalle, a student of the Escuela Nacional de Danza and a former member of Waldeen's Ballet de Bellas Artes, developed numerous choreographies, wrote several important books on Mexican dance, and ultimately founded the Fondo Nacional para el Desarrollo de la Danza Popular Mexicana (FONADAN), a national research institute devoted to the research and collection of traditional indigenous dance.

Torreblanca and Hernández are of particular interest because they exemplify polar extremes of the approach to *folklórico* that continue to be hotly debated to this day. As I have noted elsewhere, a critical and often controversial issue lies in determining how much individual creativity may be applied to original dance forms without totally distorting them (Nájera-Ramírez 1989: 22). Marcelo Torreblanca, an ardent supporter of vernacular dance and a former teacher with the Misiones Culturales programme, offered classes in Mexican folkdance at the Academia de Danza. Miguel Vélez, one of Mexico's leading *folklórico* dance authorities, and a former student of the Academia de Danza, describes Torreblanca as follows:

> Torreblanca is a dance purist; he is a man who does not permit one to create a choreography. He insisted that we dance exactly the way that indigenous people, the natives of each place, danced, something that was not possible. A folkloric dance company is created for Bellas Artes with students from the Academy and the director is Torreblanca. Unfortunately, he does not have a vision of making a spectacle for a general public. He makes a very limited spectacle, the students have to learn long routines, in which each number lasts five or six minutes and the public does not accept it.[9]

Torreblanca's *folklórico* group, undoubtedly one of the first official *folklórico* dance troupes in Mexico, never achieved national acclaim. Nonetheless, Torreblanca devoted his life to documenting the indigenous and traditional dances of Mexico and remains an important figure in the development of *folklórico* dance in Mexico for instituting a 'purist' approach to folklore that persists today (Heredia Casanova 2002). If nothing else, his approach emphasized the importance of conducting ethnographic investigation.

In contrast to Torreblanca's conservative approach to folklore, Amalia Hernández utilized Mexican folkloric materials as the foundations for developing a theatrical dance spectacle. Best known for establishing and directing the Ballet Folklórico de México, Mexico's premiere *folklórico* dance group, Hernández started her career with Danza Moderna Mexicana, and trained in classical ballet, modern and Mexican regional dance. In 1952, she performed with Ballet Moderno de México, directed by Waldeen, and when the director left Mexico the following year Hernández became the new director of the company. It was here that Hernández began incorporating Mexican folk dances into her own dance productions. Despite criticism for integrating folk dances into modern dance, Hernández continued her work and founded the Ballet de Mexico to make presentations for television. Her group performed a range of dance genres ranging from classical ballet to African dance.

By 1959, Amalia Hernández became more focused on *folklórico* dance. With Felipe Segura as artistic director, Hernández and her dance troupe, the Ballet Folklórico de Mexico, participated in the Festival of the Americas in Chicago where they achieved great success (Dallal 1986: 479–80). Upon their return, Hernández's dance troupe, under the auspices of the Departmento de Bellas Artes, initiated weekly performances at the Palacio de Bellas Artes as a major tourist attraction. At this point, Segura resigned from the company devoting his attention to the Ballet Concierto Mexicano. During the presidency of Adolfo Lopez Mateos, the Instituto Nacional de Bellas Artes selected Hernández's group as the official cultural ambassador of Mexico. Although she attained great success, Hernández also received much criticism. As Mexican dance scholar Guillermina Galarza notes:

> Ms Hernández's work was of course extremely valuable. Many times it has been said that she was the best cultural representative that Mexico had for a long time. But her cultural representations often excluded the cultural essence because she took some of their regional characteristics, she enriched herself by consulting with the best informants and the best dancers of a region. But then she would transform the movement, the costumes and the sequences such that the informants were disillusioned in her results. Often they commented, 'I did not share all that work just so she could destroy it'.[10]

Despite such criticism, Hernández's Ballet Folklórico de Mexico became the most influential dance troupe in disseminating, and thus setting the standard for, *folklórico* dance, particularly during the 1960s and 1970s. At that time, the Ballet Folklórico de Mexico performed for domestic as well as foreign audiences. Hernández's troupe performed on a Mexican television programme once a week, featured three performances a week at the Palacio de Bellas Artes in Mexico City, and travelled throughout the world as the official representative of Mexico.

The Early Years of *Folklórico* Dance: A Case Study

The status of *folklórico* dance outside the Mexican capital deserves attention because it illustrates the multiple ways in which *folklórico* dance was disseminated, cultivated and performed. It is important to bear in mind that to this very day, regional dance continues to be practised as a vernacular form at local festivities and religious ceremonies. Moreover, as noted earlier, by the 1930s and 1940s, folk dance performances formed an integral part of the elementary-school experience throughout the country as a way of promoting ideas of nationhood. In addition, however, dance enthusiasts throughout Mexico took up performances of folk dances long before the establishment of institutionalized *folklórico* dance groups for theatrical presentation. Prior to the 1940s and 1950s, folk dances were typically performed as part of larger events, such as the welcoming of a foreign dignitary, the inauguration of a politician or another cultural performance, such as the *charreada* (Mexican rodeo). Rene Arce, director of the Grupo Folklórico Ciudad de Guadalajara, reports that his father often performed for such special occasions. He describes the situation as follows:

> My father, Dr Raul Arce Manjarres, lived in Guadalajara as a young child and as an adolescent. He studied at the Teacher's College and in the School of Medicine. At that time, there were no formal *folklórico* groups; they were not organized as such. Back then, Dr Francisco Sánchez Flores would call together a group of dance enthusiasts to perform for a specific event. They got together to practice and decide which songs they would dance, what costume they would wear. Everyone possessed their own costume. They'd decide if they would wear sandals, boots, peasant trousers, or if they would wear the *caporal* suit. And that is how they would dance.[11]

Francisco Sánchez Flores became an important pioneer of Mexican dance in Guadalajara. In fact, according to Rafael Zamarripa: 'The most important figure of traditional Mexican dance in Western Mexico is Dr Francisco Sánchez Flores. He is the father, he was the director of the Department of Education, he was a painter and he developed the choreographies that gave the Mexican state of Jalisco its identity such as *La Culebra*, *El Caballito* and *El Jarabe Largo Ranchero*, among others'.[12] Zamarripa also reports that Sánchez Flores had two dance partners, Elisa Jacobo Nieto, who became better known as Chiquina Palafox, and Maria del Refugio Garcia Brambila, best known as Miss Cuca, both of whom contributed significantly to the development of dance in Guadalajara. Speaking of Miss Cuca, Zamarripa recalls: 'Ms Cuca was a teacher of physical education and had many jobs in that capacity. At the Beatriz Hernández Boarding School, she had a marvellous group of girls that she trained in dance and they won all the national competitions. Those girls from the Beatriz Hernández School in Guadalajara were champions. No one could beat them!'.[13] The boarding schools at which Miss Cuca taught participated in national cultural sports meetings at which people represented the folklore of their home state. Importantly, each group presented a research report that became the first dance records published as *memorias* (reports) on regional dance.[14] In addition, Miss Cuca taught at various schools and organized a dance group at the Escuela Normal (Teacher's College) that became the official state representative. Despite being designated as the representative of the state of Jalisco in regional dance, Zamarripa notes:

> Ms Cuca did not have a dance academy. We practised the seven or eight traditional songs on the patio of her house. And we only danced those. We danced at fairs and at events as a part of a larger event; we were not the main attraction. We were not a ballet, we were just a group who performed six or seven songs and that's all.[15]

It was not until Hernández's Ballet Folklórico de Mexico won first prize in a folkdance competition in Paris that folkloric dance companies became more formalized and institutionalized throughout Mexico. Zamarripa reports that in 1964, under the charge of la Señora Clementina Otero de Barrios, the Instituto Nacional de Bellas Artes announced a national dance competition. Although most groups had no formal training, the response was enormous. He notes: 'the directors of the university-based folkloric groups became quite enthused and began preparing. We prepared and practised so much that the competition gained an incredible importance'.[16] The country was divided into four geographical areas and each group participated in their respective area. A national competition, held in Mexico City, brought together the groups that had won the event in their region. This competition continued for about four years, establishing certain groups as the new 'pioneers' of *folklórico* dance. He recalls:

> Among that group was Professor Miguel Vélez, from Yucatan, Carlos Acereto, and a wonderful teacher from Monterrey. Andrade is from Monterrey. From Tamualipas, Franco and from Chihuahua, Antonio Rubio. From Durango, Santos Salas. From San Luis Potosí, Antonio Amendarez, and from Nayarit, Jaime Buentello. So those were the groups that survived. And they did so with such strength that no one has been able to destroy them despite the fact that the government has changed little by little. Those were the pioneers of Mexican *folklórico* dance from 1964 to the present.[17]

Today, *folklórico* groups have multiplied significantly not only in Mexico but throughout the United States as well.

Folklórico Dance in the United States

Prior to the 1960s, *folklórico* dance in the United States existed in three contexts: first, as part of the variety shows performed at *carpas* or travelling tent shows; second, at community events and celebrations wherever there was a significant

Mexican population; and third, occasionally in the public schools as part of physical education activities (Nájera-Ramírez 1989). However, the practice of *folklórico* dance in the US truly blossomed during the late 1960s and 1970s as part of the Chicano civil rights movement. This movement was a political and social response to the many adverse conditions and social injustice to which people of Mexican ancestry living in the US were subject. Like the romantic nationalist movement in Mexico during the post-revolutionary period, Chicanos turned to Mexican expressive cultural forms as sources of knowledge and inspiration. During the height of the movement, Chicanos utilized *folklórico* dance presentations as an important counter-discourse of resistance against Anglo domination, cultural erasure and the demeaning portrayal of Mexicans. *Folklórico* dance proved ideal as a way for Chicanos to publicly display the beauty and diversity of their Mexican heritage and to help dispel negative stereotypes of Mexicans.

Sincerely interested in recuperating and validating their Mexican history and heritage through dance, Chicanos invited master dance teachers from Mexico to come to the US to teach at dance workshops. In addition to teaching footwork, skirt work and choreography, the *maestros* (teachers) often provided lectures on music, costume and regional culture so that students would better understand the historical, cultural and social significance of the Mexican people and the traditions that these dances represented.

In principle, inviting *maestros* from Mexico was an excellent way for Chicanos to ensure that *folklórico* dancers in the US had access to valuable information that was not available in print, particularly since the scholarship on *folklórico* dance was extremely limited at the time. However, as noted earlier, Mexican dance instructors differed in terms of their ideological approach to *folklórico* dance: some espoused the more conservative approach established by Torreblanca, which focused on documenting and preserving old traditional dances; while others adhered to the spectacular approach spearheaded by Amalia Hernández that relied heavily on her own artistic creativity and imagination. These ideological differences among the *maestros* complicated, but did not eliminate, the idea of using *folklórico* dance as a valid source of historical and cultural information. Moreover, Mexican *folklórico* dance instruction in the US has focused almost exclusively on learning material from Mexican *maestros* but typically does not provide instruction on how to conduct research, how to develop choreography or how to produce *folklórico* shows. This may help explain why, unlike other expressive forms that were cultivated during the Chicano civil rights movement, *folklórico* dance did not represent the Chicano experience. That is to say, a typical *folklórico* performance will feature dances from Jalisco, Nayarit and Baja California, but they generally will not feature the *quebradita, el paso duranguense* or any other dances that have been produced and/or are associated with Mexicans in the US (*mexicanos en los Estados Unidos*). Russell Rodríguez (2009) has poignantly asked: Why is it that the *folklórico* dance form rarely includes representations of the Chicano experience? As he astutely notes, in other expressive forms, such as murals and theatre, Chicanos developed a recognizable

Chicano art form that gives expression to their experiences as Chicanos; that is, as Mexicans living in the United States.

A good example of an expressive form that gives expression to the Chicano experience is *orquesta tejana* (a musical form among the Texas-Mexican population) or *la onda chicana* (the Chicano sound) popularized during the Chicano civil rights movement by bands such as Little Joe y la Familia. This band recorded many classic *rancheras* (a country-style song) and composed a lot of original songs (such as 'Díganle'), but they did so in a very distinctive style that Mexicans on both sides of the border could easily identify as Chicano (hence the term *onda chicana*). The distinctive features of the style include lyrics sung in English and Spanish, and the classic blend of traditional *ranchera*, polka rhythms and big-band instruments (trumpet, saxophone, trombone) that are reminiscent of the sounds of James Brown, Tower of Power and *mariachi* music. As ethnomusicologist Manuel Peña explains:

> In many ways, the successful consolidation of so many distinct styles reflected the nationalistic spirit of the Chicano Power Movement that swept through the [American] Southwest in the late 1960s. Imbued with this spirit, Chicanos tried to sweep aside internal class and regional differences and to present a unified Chicano cultural front. This powerfully unifying impulse affected musical culture, and orquesta responded with vigour. It moved rapidly towards a synthesis of all the disparate elements that had been wanting to coalesce during the formative years – ranchero versus *jaitón* [high class], Mexican/Latin versus American, conjunto versus orquesta and simple versus sophisticated. In the new orquestas all of these were apt to be combined – within the same piece! (Peña 2004)

Only rarely has the Chicano experience been presented in *folklórico* dance. Indeed, I can only think of a few examples. The primary example is the dance suite presented in Luis Valdez's play *Zoot Suit* (1979), and subsequently in the 1981 film version of the play.[18] Inspired by the dances he saw in the play, Frank Trujillo, choreographer for the National Chicano Dance Theater in Denver, Colorado, conducted research within his own family to produce an original *Zoot Suite*-style dance suite for his company, one which did not borrow movements from the play. Juan Rios, former dancer of National Chicano Dance Theatre, explains:

> It was a company that wanted to create material, performances that talked about the Chicano experience as well as the Mexicano experience. So they wanted to keep the beauty of the Mexicano, the soul of Mexican culture through the dance, but at the same time move forward with some new ideas, you know? We worked on a piece about the Zoot Suite era, something about the farm workers, and then there was a contemporary piece about the urban Chicano and Chicana. We were experimenting and it was an amazing experience.[19]

Several *folklórico* dance companies in the US integrated the dance suite from *Zoot Suit* into their repertoire during the early 1980s, but as far as I know dance groups in Mexico never did so.

Another example of a *folklórico* suite specifically created to reflect the Mexican experience in the US involved Roen Salinas. In 1994, whilst director of the Guadalupe Dance Company in San Antonio, Texas, Salinas invited one of Mexico's most distinguished choreographers, Rafael Zamarripa, to help him develop a dance suite that reflected the experiences of Tejanos, Mexican inhabitants of Texas. I believe that a major reason for selecting Zamarripa is that he considers dance first and foremost as a form of communication. His concern is not simply to preserve dances from the past as antiquarians or traditionalists do, but rather to use dance as way to say something about Mexico and Mexicans. Therefore he does not limit himself to reproducing dances from the past. Instead, he creatively choreographs dances to represent a cultural environment or regional social experience. For example, he developed a piece titled *Salineros* based on the work that salt miners did in Colima. Aware that salt miners were marginalized in the history of Mexico, Zamarripa decided to develop a dance through which he could tell the world about their lives and experiences. Impressed with the ways in which the workers used their bodies to perform their daily tasks in the salt mines, Zamarripa decided to work side by side with them to embody their actions. Based on his experience among the workers and in the community, Zamarripa developed his choreography to convey their experiences to a larger audience.

Similarly, when Zamarripa developed the dance suite for the Rio Bravo Company, he worked to capture various aspects of Tejano history and culture through dance. The result was *Rio Bravo*, a dance production that consisted of four parts: 'El Principio', indigenous Tejano roots; 'El Viejo Mercado', the cultural life of a market square in 1800; 'Nostalgia', vibrant social life influenced by Czech, German and Polish music and dances; and 'San Antonio Hoy', inspired by the contemporary country-and-western nightclub line-dance scene. It bears mentioning, however, that Zamarripa has never featured the *Rio Bravo* suite in his company's repertoire nor, to my knowledge, has any other *folklórico* group in the United States or Mexico.

More recently, Zamarripa has been developing a new suite based on contemporary cultural experiences in Comala, Colima. Impressed by the social ambience in the restaurants surrounding the plaza where *mariachis* (a folk ensemble featuring various guitar-like instruments, violins and trumpets), *conjuntos norteños* (northern ensembles featuring the accordion) and other musicians stroll amongst the customers offering to play songs for locals enjoying regional delicacies (*antojitos*) as they socialize with one another, Zamarripa decided to capture this scene through dance. As he explained:

> In Comala people gather every day at noon to drink beer, punch, soft drinks or tequila. I find that people go there to enjoy the food, to drink but also to leave evidence that they are alive, that they have returned from the United States in these fancy trucks and that they have a lot of

money, that they wear chains, and that they are alive. People want to been seen in circulation – they feel the need for attention, to put themselves on display. And when I observe this behaviour, I feel like expressing that experience through dance ... So I go and study how people behave. I'm very interested in getting inspired by what I observe. For me, I feel the need to express that through dance so that others will learn about this experience.[20]

I visited Zamarripa a year later and asked him for an update on this new suite. Regrettably, he told me that he ended up omitting the transnational migrants who returned to their hometown of Comala flaunting their new material goods such as fancy trucks, new clothes and gold jewellery because he felt that he portrayed them in an extremely stereotypical manner. Nonetheless, Zamarripa's approach to *folklórico* dance has sparked off an idea among some Chicanos of a need to produce *folklórico* dances that reflect Chicano life and experience in the US. As one local dancer notes:

I see *ballet folklórico* in the United States personally, as part of an expression of us here in the United States. We have our roots in Mexico, our descendents are from Mexico, but I think that ... seeing the way the *maestro* Zamarripa creates things in Mexico, it's real important, so that the young people here take what we brought here and create something for ourselves. To give it our own flavour and to give it its own life.[21]

Conclusion

This chapter demonstrates that, for many Mexicans, *folklórico* dance served as an important artistic expression that was mobilized to instil a sense of community among Mexicans on both sides of the US–Mexico border. During the post-revolutionary period, vernacular and indigenous dance forms were used by the state as part of the nation-building project to symbolically establish social cohesion within Mexico. By portraying the diversity of cultures that constitute the Mexican nation, *folklórico* dance performances presented throughout the world subsequently proved quite useful in attracting tourism to Mexico. In the 1960s, Chicanos enthusiastically took up *folklórico* practice to assert their pride in their Mexican heritage and to affirm their connection to Mexicans in Mexico. However, Chicanos have not fully participated in developing *folklórico* dance. While Mexicans in Mexico seem to embrace Chicanos as part of the larger Mexican community, it appears that cultural expressive forms informed by the social experience of living in the US are not considered legitimate or authentic forms of Mexican culture. Such a view reinforces the prevailing notion that Mexicans in the US are somehow not 'real' or 'full' Mexicans. It also highlights the fact that as regional dance became increasingly institutionalized and 'theatricalized' the connection between stage presentation and the living reality it was supposed to represent became less apparent. Moreover, the staged version of regional dances became the standard by which the regions were defined and resulted in the 'museumification', or fixing or freezing, of culture.

Folklórico dance remains a key site through which exclusion and inclusion in the Mexican nation is produced and disseminated, but clearly the extent to which Chicanos achieve 'representation' will be up to them. Today *folklórico* dance is a vibrant and growing transnational cultural practice that reinforces pre-existing conceptions of national boundaries but simultaneously expands the notion of cultural identities as extending beyond national borders.

Notes

1. For more discussion of these concepts, see Saldívar (2006).
2. For an excellent discussion of Paredes's theoretical contributions, see Saldívar (2006).
3. Describing dance in words is a basic challenge that scholars have consistently encountered. As Drid Williams (2008: 153) notes, 'and then they danced' is wholly inadequate for dealing with dance in scholarly writings. One way to address this challenge is to employ other means of disseminating information on dance. My documentary film, *Danza Escénica: El Sello Artístico de Rafael Zamarripa* (2010) represents my attempt at explaining what *folklórico* dance is and to highlight the process involved in producing *folklórico* dance. For more information on the documentary, see http://www.olganajera.com.
4. For a full discussion of jarocho dance and music, see Sheehy (1979).
5. *Lo mexicano* literally means 'things Mexican' but refers to cultural expressions of the common folk.
6. At the same time, other forms of vernacular culture, such as agricultural and medicinal practices, were perceived as backward (Nájera-Ramírez 1989).
7. According to Dallal (1986: 82–85) this school changed names several times. Originally founded as the Escuela de Plástica Dinámica, under the directorship of Russian dancer Hypolito Zybine in 1929, the name changed to Escuela de Danza in 1930 when the school was officially inaugurated. In 1932 the school became known as the Escuela Nacional de Danza.
8. On Sokolow's work in Mexico, see the information on the Jewish Women's Archive website: www.jwa.org/exhibits/wov/sokolow/mexico.html, retrieved 9 March 2007.
9. Interview with Miguel Vélez, May 2006. Sadly, Miguel died in June 2010.
10. Interview with Guillermina Galarza, 18 January 2005.
11. Interview with Rene Arce, 19 January 2005.
12. Interview with Rafael Zamarripa, 17 March 2004.
13. Interview with Rafael Zamarripa, 17 March 2004.
14. Interview with Guillermina Galarza, 18 January 2005.
15. Interview with Rafael Zamarripa, 17 March 2004.
16. Interview with Rafael Zamarripa, 18 March 2004.
17. Interview with Rafael Zamarripa, 18 March 2004.
18. For the film, see *Zoot Suit*, dir. Luis Valdez (1981), 103 min.
19. Interview with Juan Rios, August 2006.
20. Interview with Rafael Zamarripa, 19 March 2004.
21. Interview with Rick Mendoza, 19 March 2005.

References

Cerón, I. 2005. 'La raiz del movimiento nacionalismo e identitdad en la danza moderna mexicana', *Correo del Maestro* no.112. Retrieved 5 June 2006 from: http: //www.correodelmaestro.com/anteriores/2005/septiembre/2artistas112.htm.

Cockcroft, J.D. 1983. *Mexico: Class Formation, Capital Accumulation, and the State*. New York: Monthly Review Press.

Cohen, J. 2006. 'Waldeen and the Americas: The Dance Has Many Faces'. Retrieved 5 May 2006 from: http: //www.uhmc.sunysb.edu/surgery/waldeen.html.

Dallal, A. 1986. *La Danza en México*. Mexico City: Universidad Autónoma de Mexico.

———— 2008. *El Ballet Folklórico de la Universidad de Colima*. Mexico City: Universidad de Colima.

Heredia Casanova, M. 2002. *El Legado del Maestro Marcelo Torreblanca*. Guadalajara, Mexico: Universidad Autónoma de Guadalajara.

Knight, A. 1990. 'Racism, Revolution and the Indigenismo: Mexico, 1910-1940', in Richard Graham (ed.), *The Idea of Race in Latin America, 1870-1940*. Austin: University of Texas Press, pp.71–113.

Knight, A. 1994. 'Popular Culture and the Revolutionary State in Mexico, 1910–1940', *Hispanic American Historical Review* 74(3): 393–444.

Meyer, M. and W. Sherman. 1979. *The Course of Mexican History*. New York: Oxford University Press.

Nájera-Ramírez, O. 1989. 'Social and Political Dimensions of Folklórico Dance: The Binational Dialectic of Residual and Emergent Culture', *Western Folklore* 48: 15–32.

———— 2001. 'Haciendo Patria: La Charreada and the Formation of a Transnational Identity', in C. Velez-Ibanez and A. Sampaio (eds), *Transforming Latino Communities: Politics, Processes, and Culture*. Lanham, MD: Rowman and Littlefield, pp.167–80.

Nájera-Ramírez, O., N. Cantú and B. Romero (eds). 2009. *Dancing Across Borders*. Champaign: University of Illinois Press.

Parga, V. 2004. *Cuerpo Vestido en Nación: Danza Folkórica y Nacionalismo Mexicano (1921–1939)*. Mexico City: Consejo Nacional para la Cultura y las Artes-Fondo Nacional para la Cultura y las Artes

Peña, M. 2004. "Orquesta Tejana: The Formative Years." *University of Texas Libraries*. Retrieved 10 March 2012 from: http://www.lib.utexas.edu/benson/border/arhoolie2/orquesta.html.

Rodríguez, R. 2009. 'Folklórico in the United States: Cultural Preservation and Disillusion', in O. Nájera-Ramírez, N. Cantu and B. Romero (eds), *Dancing Across Borders: Danzas y Bailes Mexicanos*. Champaign: University of Illinois Press, pp.335–58.

Saenz, M. 1927. 'Nuestras Escuelas Rurales'. *Mexican Folkways* 3(1): 44–52.

Saldívar, R. 2006. *The Borderlands of Culture: Américo Paredes and the Transnational Imaginary*. Durham, NC: Duke University Press.

Sanchez, G. 1936. *Mexico: A Revolution by Education*. New York: The Viking Press.

Sheehy, D.E. 1979. 'The Son Jarocho: The History, Style, and Repertoire of a Changing Mexican Musical Tradition'. Ph.D. dissertation, University of California, Los Angeles.

Tortajada Quiróz, M. 1995. *Danza y poder*. Mexico, DF: Instituto Nacional de Bellas Artes. Centro Nacional de Investigación, Documentación, e Información de la Danza José Limón, 1995.

———— 2000. *La Danza Escénica de la Revolución Mexicana, Nacionalista y Vigorosa*. Mexico City: Instituto Nacional de Estudios Históricos de la Revolución Mexicana.

Williams, D. 2008 'The Sorrow of the Dance Analysts', *Visual Anthropology* 21: 151–55.

Chapter 9

Dance, Youth and Changing Gender Identities in Korea

Séverine Carrausse

This chapter explores anthropological ways of looking at dance as a social practice and as a means of discovering and demonstrating the body as a socio-cultural construction. I examine the historical background of Korean folk dance and dance movement, and explore the relations between socio-cultural change and youth identities in contemporary Korean society.

Looking at South Korean youth cultural activities, particularly a sport dance circle at the Seoul National University campus, I attempt to understand how socio-cultural change has influenced individuals, especially young people, in terms of their conceptions of identity and relationships with others.[1] I argue that Korean youth dancing embodies changes in their self-defined identities in ways that challenge traditional Korean ideas about the self, socially acceptable ways of displaying the body, and gender relations.

Beyond its aesthetic expression, dance reveals itself as a powerful site for the construction of social identities and the mediation of social relations. In a pragmatic way, dance involves the problem of the relationship between individual and society, and connections between individuals. Pierre Bourdieu (1987) asserted that there was a way of learning and of understanding with the body that was situated below consciousness, in a 'pre-reflexive' way that could not be verbalized. For him, processes of bodily incorporation depend on an assimilation of the properties of social relationships where gestures, behaviour, manners of speaking, thinking and acting are 'caught' by socialized individuals. Based widely on mechanisms of identification and imitation implemented through action (by 'making' things) and/or by watching others act, incorporation can be explained as the bodily and sensory appropriation of gestures and cognitive behaviour which are then enacted in specific social contexts. At the same time, individuals differentiate themselves from others through practices such as everyday interactions, social activities, hobbies, clothing and artistic performances. Dance, then, takes on various dimensions: it expresses abstract ideas and specific elements, and also enables individuals to enter into non-verbal and verbal communication with others (Hanna 1988; Washabaugh 1998).

I focus then on the conventionalized social and bodily practices of various dance events, both within traditional Korean dance and within sport dance, which have different cultural histories. By watching bodies move, I infer patterns of form and interaction which are distinctive in both genres and moments of performance. This study was carried out in parallel with research into socialization processes involving university students in South Korea, Portugal and France (Carrausse 2010). While I was in Seoul (February 2002 to July 2003), I joined both a university student circle involved in sport dance and a Korean Pongsan mask dance class at the National Centre for Korean Traditional Performing Arts (국립민속국악원). My aim was to understand how university students dealt with their cultural background, and how much the way they socialized in this environment was a combination of conventionalized social and bodily practices on the one hand, and new patterns of interaction legitimating a greater proximity of bodies on the other hand. By presenting key aspects of each one, I attempt to draw a contrast between a traditional Korean dance and the sport dance events performed and enjoyed by the youth. As the university students deal with the practice of Western dances and their own background of Confucian-inspired morality, their (re)presentation of themselves shapes their individual and social identities.

Traditional Dance Performance in Korea

Traditional Korean dances give us insight into Korean culture. They are widespread at both aristocratic and commoner levels and consist of court dances as well as a variety of folk and religious dances. Buddhism, Confucianism and Shamanism have all contributed to the development of these dances. As a result, traditional Korean dances are an expression of a metaphysical philosophy which Koreans have long believed in: the human body is considered a universe in itself, and humanity's ideal existence lies in its perfect harmony with heaven and earth (Park 1983). Traditional dances are a delicate combination of inner spirit and revelation.

There is a great emphasis placed upon natural movement. Motion in the upper body is stressed, following the tempo of breathing rather than the heartbeat. The most notable features of Korean dance, particularly court dances, include the creation of a feeling of suspension with the feet and an ongoing quality of energy, which contrast with the sense of heaviness suggested by the curving lines of bodies wrapped in traditional clothing. Although Korea is no longer a monarchy, court dances are still performed in a theatrical setting where they both entertain and remind people of the heritage of the past.

Dancers use their shoulders, arms, wrists, hands and heels, and there is a consistent alternation between upward and downward movement initiated by the alternative bending and extending of the knees. Folk dances from the countryside are livelier than the more formal and peaceful court dances. We can easily imagine the energy that spreads out from such popular rituals, in direct relation to the agricultural cycle and the cosmic entities that also give life to religious dances or rituals such as shamanic ones.² In the past Korean dances embodied a wide range of feelings, supported by music. The highly stylized court dances require discipline and elegance in order to express the aestheticism of the inner spirit; these are accompanied by the music of the ruling class, an elegant musical style with a slow beat that produces a solemn yet magnificent ambience. Folk dances – and especially mask dances (*talchum*, 탈춤) – show spontaneity, humour, freedom and satire. These are the dances and the music of the commoners.³

Court dances were called *jeongjae* (정재), meaning 'showing talent to a superior', and were used to entertain the royal family as well as court functionaries and foreign diplomats.⁴ Dancers were for the most part *kisaeng* (기생), female professional entertainers.⁵ During a court performance, each movement is solemn and graceful without outward extravagance. This should be understood in the light of Confucianism's value of respect in human relationships, such as filial devotion. Even though dancers are accompanied by splendid stage settings and costumes, their movements are never dramatic, but always serene and self-composed. Nowadays Korean traditional dance and music are being revived as they are perceived to sustain Korean national identity and culture. This is considered especially important as the country has undergone troubled periods in its modern history, with frequent wars and episodes of foreign control. The best artists are recognized as 'national living treasures', responsible for the transmission of their art to selected talented students. Through such connections, dance and music may be traced back through several generations of masters.

Costume

Korean traditional dress is called *hanbok* (한복), an abbreviation of the term *hanguk boksik* ('Korean attire'), and in Korean culture traditional costume is still a strong indicator of national identity and values.⁶ The costume covers the whole body, hanging comfortably. The design of the *hanbok* has changed over time according to the economic and political context of the period.⁷ Forms, fabrics, colours and designs in *hanbok* provided an indication of social status, circumstance and even age.⁸ The upper classes wore *hanbok* of closely woven ramie cloth or other high-grade lightweight materials in warm weather, and *hanbok* of plain and patterned silks the rest of the year. Law and resources limited commoners to wearing cotton at best, as well as white everyday clothes (supposed to represent purity, chastity and integrity), though for special occasions they wore dull shades of pale pink, light green, grey, and charcoal.⁹ The upper classes dressed in a variety of colours, though bright colours were generally worn by children and girls and subdued colours by middle-aged men and women. The hairstyle also followed a variety of designs.

The *hanbok* is characterized by its simple lines and the fact that it has no pockets. Men's *hanbok* consists of a short jacket and roomy trousers (*baji*, 바지) bound at the ankles. This is comfortable when sitting on the floor as Koreans do. Women's *hanbok* consists of two major parts: a bolero-style jacket (*jeogori*, 저고리) and a wraparound skirt (*chima*, 치마). The *jeogori* is made up of two front panels with sleeves extending from drop shoulders, a stiff collar and two front ribbons. It has gone through many changes over the years in terms of length, refinement of the collar, and the use of long ribbons. The two ribbons played an important role, not only keeping the *jeogori* closed but also serving as an ornamental ribbon called *otgoreum* (옷고름). The colour of *otgoreum* varies according to that of the *chima* and the *jeogori*. Today's fashion designers are increasingly seeking inspiration in the *hanbok* and other older styles to create fashions adapted to modern lifestyles. *Hanbok* has been modernized with modern fabrics, cuts and colours of every hue allowing for the expression of individual taste. Still, age and special occasion determine the colour. *Hanbok* are also classified according to their purposes: everyday dress, formal dress and ceremonial dress. Ceremonial dresses are still worn on certain occasions, including a child's first birthday, for the rites of manhood, marriage, mourning and memorial services. Special dresses are made for specific political, religious or artistic representatives of Korean culture.

Women always look graceful in the *chima*, whether they are standing, sitting or walking. They also appear taller when wearing the traditional skirt, for it creates the illusion that the legs are long. The fullness of the *chima* allows the wearing of any number of undergarments, a vital advantage given Korea's cold winters, and also makes it wearable during pregnancy. For proper appearance, the *chima* should be pulled tight so that it presses the breasts flat and the slit should be just under the shoulder blade. The left side of the *chima* should be held beside the left breast when walking to keep it from flapping open and revealing petticoats. Canoe-shaped socks and shoes (rubber-made) complete the *hanbok*. Dancers make use of tight-fitting dance shoes with turned-up toes, which makes them look as if they caress the floor with their feet, curling their toes upward before placing the heel on the floor and then gently rolling the entire foot down (Van Zile 2001a). *Hanbok*, as a ritual dress, used to represent the visible manifestation of intangible Confucian virtues such as benevolence, propriety, wisdom and trust. Consequently, in addition to its role in delineating social status, *hanbok* represents conformity to Confucian codes of ritual attire (Yang 1997).

While performing, traditional dancers are dressed in such magnificent and colourful costumes. Some of them include long white or rainbow-striped sleeves which cover the dancers' hands and trail to the ground. They use a variety of sleeve-tossing techniques to give an impression of ethereal movement, as if the sleeves were intermediaries between heaven and earth. When not wearing long ribbon-like sleeves, dancers manipulate accessories (a fan, a scarf, a sword or a drum), each of which gives its name to the dance. Contact between dancers' bodies never occurs. Traditional dances emphasize the individual, even when the dance is performed by a group. Each dancer executes a solo dance, synchronized or not with the whole group, always paying attention to the others. Costumes are heavy because of their materials, and allow neither ample movement nor bodily proximity, especially the women's *hanbok*. They are designed so that dancers only exhibit the extremities of their bodies: arms, hands and head. As feet and leg movements are hidden under the *chima*, women dancers usually give an impression of airy and ghostly motion, occasionally interrupted by moments of suspension.

Through *hanbok* and dance movement, we gain insights into Korean gender relations, values and sexuality. For example, the wide pleated skirts hiding the curves of women's bodies reflect the Confucian ethic. As women were subjected to strict rules of chastity and fidelity, covering any erogenous part of the body became a way to avoid or eliminate male desire. Moreover, there are different standards of sexual morality for men and women, and women's virginity is emphasized.[10] Although the *hanbok* has no visibly erotic attributes, it is suggestive: female dancers often tease with subtly insinuated attractiveness, such as a performance with precise footsteps displaying a piece of undergarment or an ankle. Korea has developed and adopted several religions that have moulded its sexual values, family structure, concepts of love and gender roles, both in public and private spaces. However, Confucian ethics have left a long-lasting mark, one which has given rise to a specific habitus and still shapes modern Korean society.[11]

Mask Dances

Talchum (탈춤) means 'mask dance'. It is not only a dance performed by masked dancers, but also a drama played by masked characters enacting a person, a supernatural being or an animal. Very popular under the Joseon dynasty, it emerged from the ancient tradition of integrating dance, music and drama, all of which relate humans to powers larger than themselves. Despite former occasional affiliations with the court, mask dances are closely associated with villages, and there are many regional variants. Such dances embody criticism of authority and are a form of social satire. By presenting reprehensible attitudes to the public in a humourous mode, *talchum* has cathartic and moral functions. Dancers make fun of things they would not normally discuss in public (Van Zile 2001a: 180). Mask dances also concentrate themes and models which apply to varying degrees to the sport dances described below, such as being a safety valve for the community, participating in a transmission process through social interaction, creating social solidarity, expressing conflict or enhancing community cohesion.

In Korean, *tal* (탈) is one of the many words that designate 'mask'; it also means 'disaster' or 'disease'. Korean masks contain a piece of black cloth fixed to the sides to facilitate the wearing of the mask, to cover the back of the head and to imitate silky black hair. Laces are used to fasten it behind the dancer's head. The primary materials for making masks are paper, wood, leather, mud, fur and gourds. Paper and gourd masks are favoured because these are more simple to make and especially light to wear while dancing. Masks can be categorized into two kinds: religious and artistic. The religious masks are worn during shamanic rituals to expel demons and to represent invisible deities and spirits. Artistic masks are mostly used in dance and drama, but to some extent these also perform a religious function. Masks used for ritual ceremonies have slowly evolved into masks intended for artistic performances, and they vary according to their region of origin.

Most Korean masks are in one piece, but some of them contain mobile parts such as (blinking) eyes or mouths that strengthen facial expressions such as laughter or anger. The village of Hahoe near Andong in the east of the Korean peninsula has preserved both cultural and material heritage in a sort of live museum that welcomes Korean traditional craftsmen and holds mask dances. It is said that the masks of Hahoe, nine faces of which still remain, are the oldest wooden masks in Korea. They reflect the expressions and bone structure of Korean faces, the various statuses in Korean society and the main characters in satire: monks, brides, aristocrats, scholars, butchers, servants, old widows, fools, ladies. Some are wooden and made in one piece, presenting a smiling face with a wide-open or shut mouth, or angry expressions with the chin and the upper lips pressed together. Others are made of two pieces, the chin being separated and connected to the top half by laces, and function just like a human jaw, giving vocal expression to the dancer-actor. The mask that represents the fool has no chin, and legend tells how the creator of Hahoe masks died before he could complete it.

In general, the shapes of the various masks are grotesque and greatly overstated, and their colours are intense: mask-dance dramas were usually performed during the night, lit by fires. The shadows of the mask, sculpted in wood, exaggerate the drama or the comedy of the situation. If masks were less extreme in expression and colour they would fail to deliver the themes of the drama. Religious masks and those for daytime performances are much less vivid. Red, black, white, yellow and other basic colours are chosen for contrast. The colours also identify the sex and age of the characters. An old person's mask, for example, is black, a young man's is red, and the one that represents a young woman is white. In traditional Korean philosophy, colours are associated with directions and seasons, with black standing for the north and winter and red standing for the south and summer. In many of the *talchum* dance dramas, the young man always wins over the old in a symbolic gesture of summer triumphing over winter. Mask dances, therefore, are a symbol of fertility. Most of the masks depict human faces but some represent deities, and there are also masks of real and imaginary animals, such as the Bukcheong's lion dance (북청사자놀음). An interesting feature is that the masks of *yangban*, the upper class gentlemen, are almost always deformed in some way, with harelips, a lopsided mouth, a distorted nose or squint eyes – a reflection of the commoners' mockery of the privileged classes.

While in Western culture masks are understood as a means of covering one's true identity, the opposite is true in Korea: the main word for mask, *tal*, means 'the unveiling of one's true face'. It is believed that with the power of a mask, the individual is enabled to reveal their emotions. In the spirit of this philosophy, in the finale, dancer-actors used to remove their masks, showing their faces to the amazement of the audience.

The Korean mask-dance drama is usually performed outdoors. During the Koryo and Joseon dynasties it was executed on an improvised stage called a *sandae* (산대) or up on a sloping incline so that the audience below could see. A dressing room was installed to the left of the stage, and musicians were seated to the right. Dancer-actors were all males until *kisaeng*, female entertainers, joined them in the 1920s (probably because of the disappearance of the court dance under Japanese colonization) and took up the role of shamans and concubines. Lively dance accompanied by vigorous music take up the major part of the performance, with actors stopping to deliver their lines with much gesticulation and exaggerated mime. Many of the roles do not have any dialogue of their own but act in pantomime with an extraordinarily stylized form of release. Additionally, string, wind and percussion instruments get along with silence to match and emphasize one's mask role. The dance enlivens the drama and functions to round off each scene but is also performed without any regard for the progress of the plot.

The dance themes remain varied. Under the Joseon dynasty, popular themes included the nobleman who portrays life under the constraints of the ruling class, with cynical remarks about sinful monks and complaints against a corrupted society. The stories were based on a sense of rebellion felt by the common people regarding the reality of their lives. Like the folk literature of that period, it appeals to audiences by ridiculing apostate Buddhist monks, decadent noblemen and shamans. The conflict between an ugly wife and a seductive concubine was another popular theme, and remains so. But *talchum* has also changed over time, and its satirical elements have become even more pronounced. Religious and spiritual elements, on the other hand, have declined as mask dances have become a form of entertainment. Yet the dimension of social commentary remains, even though dancers have become professional.

The mask-dance drama is composed of several acts different from those in modern plays. They are a loose presentation of several episodes in a combination of styles. Because the spoken lines of the actors have been passed down the generations through an oral tradition, they are quite flexible and subject to improvisation. The dance part can be lengthened or shortened easily, so that the entire performance can take anywhere between three or four hours to a whole night. Another sign of joyful celebration, and probably the most remarkable feature of the Korean mask dance, is the enthusiastic participation of the audience. The performance usually ends with the audience joining in the dance to the music of a shrill horn, bringing it to a truly explicit life-enhancing finale (Cho 2005).

Following the popular democratic movement of the 1980s, university campuses have allowed the revival of Korean traditional performance, mask dances in particular. Youths were attracted to them because of their strong moral, religious and political character, as an instrument to support their mobilization for democracy. Since then, concerns have changed towards a search for personal fulfilment rather than the pursuit of national aims. Moreover, greater competitiveness over university entrance through national examinations has caused students and their families to focus on schooling and extra-curricular activities, forsaking leisure and sporting activities. As a result, entering university gives students a taste of freedom. For the first time in their lives they are free to choose their own recreational and social activities, and to spend their time as they wish. With the global spread of Latino and dances involving couples reaching South Korea, many students have been attracted to these kinds of dance. In the process, the dances have transformed relations between young educated women and men, reinvented a form of sensitive and emotional expression, and allowed a reconsideration of the process of socialization itself, as I will discuss below.

A University Student Circle

While pursuing my research on the Seoul National University campus, I became interested in a circle of sport dance called Fiesta. I discovered that the university students involved as social dancers exhibited a cultural and emotional identity very different to that of their peers. And so I began to investigate this matter. I attended meetings and dances, and I participated in social activities before and after dancing. I built up friendships with some of the organizers and members, and maintained communication with several members after returning to France.

This university student circle should be viewed in the light of Korean 'dancing culture'. Throughout its modern history, Korea has experienced a number of sociopolitical changes, including invasions by its larger neighbours: the demise of the kingdom as a tributary state of China, Japanese colonial rule (1910 to 1945), the liberation and division of the country (1945), military control by the United States (1945 to 1948), the Korean War (1950 to 1953), and much instability under dictatorial or corrupt regimes since then. In this context, South Koreans have come to regard education as the most formidable instrument for success under rapidly changing circumstances. Parents invest a great deal of capital in their children's education because they believe this to be the best investment in future welfare, for their children as well as for themselves. At the same time, religious traditions shaped by Confucianism, Buddhism and Christianity have left their mark on premodern and modern education in Korea (Lee 2000a). Confucianism has it that humans are perfectible through education and that only the most learned should govern the country (merit value). South Korea's rapid economic growth since the 1960s and the shift to democratization in the 1980s have all conspired to produce 'education fever' (Seth 2002). Other causal mechanisms have led to a rapid expansion of education, creating a host of problems, such as the focus on college entrance examinations, the enormous financial burden on families due to private tutoring, and the struggle to maintain equality of opportunity regarding education within the family. This zeal for education is ultimately related to employment: parents spend a large portion of their income on their children's private tuition to prepare them for college entrance examinations at prestigious universities. Furthermore, girls are encouraged to attend good universities so that they may meet an attractive marriage partner. High school students are exhorted to sacrifice all leisure activities and concentrate on scholarly achievement. Entering a respectable university is then regarded as something of a liberation. At university, student circles (*dongari*, 동아리) are opportunities to experience this freedom, whether it is for practising a favourite hobby or for meeting friends and future lovers.

In South Korea, national culture stresses collectivism, hierarchy and social harmony. Identifying three religious-philosophical systems underlying Korean thought and communication patterns, Yum (1987) asserts that Confucianism is the most important influence, especially in shaping modes of non-verbal communication and ideals of collectivism in Korean culture. South Korean students have often been involved in community events since childhood, especially through their parents' social networks; they know how important this is in preparing opportunities for education (such as collecting relevant information about education) and professional careers. It is then compelling for them to follow this process of social networking when joining a student circle at university.

The student circle Fiesta was created in December 2000 by a small group of students who had taken sport-dance classes at Seoul National University. At the time the tutor needed several couples of students to help her organize the 'old year's farewell dance party'. She asked those who had the best dance skills in her four classes to participate. The party was so successful that those students decided to continue learning and take pleasure in sport dance. They also enjoyed each other's friendship, and so fifteen of them got together to establish the circle. But running and organizing a circle was no easy feat for the founding members. They were carried forward by their own determination and passion, and the goal of a 'light in each of [their] hearts'.

In March 2001, the first freshmen joined Fiesta. The circle's activities were structured around two regular meetings each week in a large dance studio at Seoul National University. A couple of hours were dedicated to each meeting: the first hour was generally based on the learning of basic steps, while the next hour involved an opportunity to practise. After these meetings, some of the members – usually the senior ones – would meet for dinner. Those moments were very important for the members' socialization and were a key opportunity for me to conduct my research. They were occasions to listen and join in with Fiesta gossip and to find out about what was going on.

To encourage newcomers to join Fiesta, a membership training event (MT) is organized at the beginning of each semester. The MT is one of the most common events in university student culture in South Korea: it is a weekend retreat in the countryside for university students (similar to the events organized for company employees). It is an opportunity to break the ice and get to know one another through various activities: quizzes, sketches, singing, dancing, preparing meals, chatting and playing drinking games with *soju* and beer. Fundamentally, MTs are set up to bring the group closer together through a shared experience. But on an individual level, these weekend getaways can be seen as an opportunity to bond with the person one has been attracted to for some time. They are one of the few occasions for South Korean university students to socialize with members of the opposite sex.[12] This is a time for experimenting with identities and possible life partners, and so fervent Fiesta members often join other dance clubs and go dancing in popular districts of Seoul, for instance in Hong-Dae (dance clubs such as Macondo, Bonita, Sabor Latino), Itaewon (Caliente) or Apkujeong-Dong (La Salsa, Gachi). But they usually say that dancing on campus is an exceptional experience and is much more exciting. Presumably, this is because dancing with peers inside the university is much easier and reassuring for them, a chance to enjoy oneself in a safe environment.

Since Fiesta was the first social dance club at Seoul National University, it has attracted many students and has continued to grow. Forty to fifty students join the club every semester. After just one year of activity, Fiesta had become one of the most famous circles on the campus, not only in terms of membership numbers but as a group which was known for its innovations in leisure activities and sociability, proposing the practice of fashionable dances (Latin dances and various dances involving couples) and facilitating meeting opportunities of a new kind. In order to gain momentum, the former heads of Fiesta applied for official support in 2002. After a two year monitoring period, Fiesta became an official Seoul National University circle in September 2004.

The evolution of the circle in just a few years exemplifies different stages of growth. For the founders, everything was new, and the difficulty of establishing a society brought them closer together, like members of a small family. After two semesters of activities, many of them had to leave campus for various reasons, such as graduation, professional work and military service.[13] Formal sport dance was initially taught alongside salsa and swing classes, and a professor of physical education took part in Fiesta's activities as an instructor. At a later stage the most advanced students took charge of the instruction of salsa and swing, partly because of those students' ability and popularity, and partly because there was no instructor to teach formal dances professionally. As it developed over a year and a half of existence, Fiesta slowly became a different type of community. Younger members enrolled in the group, and some talented dancers joined the club and introduced new dances, such as the American eight-beat swing called 'lindy hop'. After three years of existence, Fiesta came of age. The level of the dancing had improved, the rules had become formalized, and many new faces had joined the circle. The turnover was rapid, with people usually staying on for one or two semesters. With such frequent membership 'regeneration', the circle must pay great attention to its new members. The organization therefore adapts basic courses for beginners and involves senior members in their delivery, which gives them an additional role besides leading the performances.

Salsa, jive, line and ballroom dancing are taught whenever someone is available to teach. Line dancing is very popular, maybe because it is similar to some traditional Korean dances. The dancers, one behind the other in a row or several parallel rows, execute the same movements in a synchronized manner. The choreography is usually simple and easy to remember. In general, South Korean youths use line dancing to give life to a slogan (which might be political, religious or social through campus events). The official name of Fiesta is the 'Swing and Latin Dance Club', as they mainly enjoy swing and salsa dances. Their regular meetings allow them to learn and take pleasure in dancing, as well as to practise for a big party at the end of the semester. New members are taught swing dance in the spring semester (March to June), and salsa dance in the autumn (September to December). They also learn about dance etiquette – for example, how to ask for a dance and how to treat your dance partner with respect.

For new members, organizing a party at the end of each semester is one of the most exciting objectives of Fiesta. The party serves to introduce this new dancing culture to all university students. This brings students together, in the true sense of the word 'association' or 'circle'. Even though it is a form of non-verbal communication, many people enjoy and 'understand' Fiesta social dances without knowing the language and the culture of the countries the dances came from. The 'Fiesta-ness' experienced in those dances, and especially Latin American ones, are considered exotic by South Korean students.

One of the founding members expresses this attraction: 'Fiesta offers many chances to perform. Members can [perform for] many audiences, dance in bright lighting, win a storm of applause'. Fiesta parties are divided into three sections: performances, teaching the audience the basic steps of social dance, then sharing a social dance for all. Between 2001 and 2004, Fiesta organized twelve parties, drawing over 300 students each time. Many South Koreans now see sport dance as a hobby thanks to the media (for example, through Western dance movies), and Fiesta has capitalized upon this interest to create a young dance community.

The way Fiesta members got together, through parties or after-dance meetings, was similar to other South Korean university student gatherings: each grouping had several core members and a constant flow of peripheral members. When the dance meeting was over, some dancers went home immediately, while others joined a different group. Yet others went to the university library to study. A number of dance participants would often go for dinner nearby, accustomed to the same *hof* (South Korean bar, 호프) that sponsored Fiesta's parties. They would drink beers and *soju* (소주, a rice drink), and share Korean side dishes (*anju*, 안주). From time to time they would move onto a karaoke room (*norebang*, 노래방), and then to another bar or to a restaurant for a meal. In South Korea, such leisure spaces are open all night, and people move from one place to another with great ease. Bills are paid with the money collectively pooled for such evening events by the members (5,000 to 10,000 wons, which is about 4 to 8 euros) until all has been spent.

Fiesta and Changing Identities

Membership in a circle such as Fiesta affects the identities of the participants by virtue of the dancing style as well as the organizational structure, social activities and use of space which make up associational life. The status given by the university administration is also important. The students fulfil themselves through dancing, while transforming 'traditional' cultural practices.

'We think of dancing as a poem, we write with our bodies, instead of our hands. We express our passion for life with our dance', notes one of the dancers. Passion for dancing is an essential consideration for joining Fiesta. As previously mentioned, interest in dance activities has long been a part of South Korean cultural history. Dancing in couples became trendy in the middle of the 1960s, probably due to the presence of American soldiers on the Korean peninsula and to the students who had gone to study abroad. However, at that time it was regarded as an immoral activity and as damaging to the ethical values of the nation. Consequently, social dancing in public was forbidden and had to take place in private. Social dancing gradually evolved and began to incorporate Korean rhythms and steps. It was officially recognized by the South Korean government in 1988, whilst sport dance was introduced as a sport at the Seoul Olympic Games.

Most South Korean university students do not have any experience of dancing in couples, and members of Fiesta are considered exceptional. Their passion for dancing attracts other students. One of the oldest members of Fiesta that I met during fieldwork joined the club in the first semester of graduate school. 'It was not an easy decision for me, but my desire to dance was stronger than fear', she explained. Having lived in Russia for a while, she missed the 'European way of giving thanks, greetings, expressions with skin contact', such as kissing on the cheeks or the occasional hug. In fact, the most attractive, but also the most upsetting, aspect of social dancing for these students is precisely the interaction with a partner. Skin-to-skin contact with the opposite sex and the public display of sensuality are relatively new in South Korea, but at the same time it is combined with strict social rules: there is a codified way of holding the partner's hand, another hand folding neatly around the lady's waist, or around the man's neck or shoulders. There is a codified way of letting the hand slide on the partner's body during a spin. Yet, spontaneity and improvisation enter into the contact process through the various dance figures, whether reproduced or created. All parts of the body can be seen as potential surfaces for contact between dancers. Although couples can break away and dance individually (spoken of as 'shine' in salsa), there should be contact between the man and the woman for most of the dance. Initially, many young South Koreans found this awkward: to dance with someone of the opposite sex was something new, and holding each other while making eye contact was a thrilling challenge. One of the former members confessed that for her, 'couple dance [was] the first time that two people shared the moment of perfectly caring for each other'. She continued and said that everyone who had not experienced this should know how this felt and let the experience inspire their lives. People find it important to choose the right match partner in social dancing, because, symbolically, the dances create the image of a perfect life together with a member of the opposite sex.

In South Korea physical contact between man and woman, usually referred to by the 'konglish' word *skinship*,[14] is hardly seen outside the private sphere. Fiesta therefore appears to be a sensational opportunity to make close contact with a person of the opposite sex. Fiesta thus attracts many single university students. Another very popular way of encountering members of the opposite sex is through *meeting* (미팅) and *sogaeting* (소개팅), which occasionally happens through Fiesta events. *Meeting* is an arranged date at a coffee shop or similar location for an equal number of men and women; matchmakers are usually friends and acquaintances. *Sogaeting* is another 'konglish' word (*sogae* means 'introducing') alluding to a laid-back arranged meeting set up by a mutual friend. A blind date or *seon* is more conventional because it is usually arranged by the parents and puts the emphasis on marriage. Through Fiesta, many of its members become lovers, but these relationships do not often last very long. Awareness of the emotions that may arise from dancing in couples means that some members resent seeing their lover dance with another partner. Others break up and find that they are too embarrassed to continue dancing. Love relationships and dancing in such a circle are difficult to reconcile, partly because of the cultural aspect of *skinship*, and partly because of the symbolized desire, and erotic and even sexual character, of the dances. Though it is said that between dancing partners there should be only sincere friendship and partnership, members often expect there to be more than that. They certainly remember their emotions when they first held their partners: 'the heart was beating hard', 'hands got sweaty out of nervousness'. After the initial frisson, holding hands and dancing with a partner becomes a habit and the excitement gradually disappears. A senior member once revealed to me: 'skinship became so natural in Fiesta. However, this was not so for the rest of the students outside of Fiesta. Some called Fiesta "a club for dating and coupling!" Of course, the misunderstanding faded away after a time'. Beginners are indeed known to fantasize when faced with the physical proximity of their new dance partners. But it is also the obvious break with traditional hierarchy and the strict running of circles that distinguishes Fiesta from other leisure organizations. Sporting circles in particular are heavily influenced by Korean military discipline. Fiesta, by contrast, accommodates the liberal behaviour of its members, many of whom are attracted to the end-of-semester parties despite impending university exams. Among regular members, these hours of daily social dancing create a convenient context for getting together. They undergo an almost religious conversion which is facilitated by their love of dancing, and transforms their vision of what it means to be young, of family relationships and even of their future career prospects.

Dress is also important in the fashioning of identities. Fiesta members all had their own fashion style, although there was no formal dress code. Almost none of the senior members would dress in formal social dance attire purchased in specific stores, except for formal performances. Women often wore a skirt and a knitted top, and men sported trousers and a shirt. Most of them just brought a pair of thin-soled shoes suitable for dancing. Proper dancing attire was expensive, and so the majority of the members would wait before making such an investment. Whereas the senior participants knew the importance of self-presentation and often sported a style both smart and relaxed, and very feminine for the girls, new members wore sportswear. Women tried to draw attention to themselves through conventionally feminine attributes such as youth, beauty and grace in dancing. Some indulged in the cosmetic surgery that has become so fashionable in South Korea for youths in their teens and twenties. The ideal is to acquire big eyes through double-lid surgery, a sharp and pointed noise, a small chin and mouth, and a pale complexion.[15] Men, meanwhile, want to display their general physical strength and their ability to dance. They also seek to show their economic security through the conspicuous consumption of new technologies or motorbikes for example; during dates they are expected to entertain the women.

Fiesta gave shelter to and was a friendly haven for its student members while they sought relief from an extremely competitive academic environment. In this circle they could find empathy, camaraderie and emotional comfort among people who were of similar social status: other young, educated South Koreans. There was indeed a class-based dimension to this kind of sociality, as people shared both academic and socio-cultural knowledge (institutional social capital or 'privileged information'). This latter advantage is created by an individual's location in a web of relationships.[16] Given the importance of social networks in South Korea, as mentioned earlier, these relationships have the potential to be transformed into contingent relations. In that way, Fiesta provides not only a stage on which members can perform their status, but also a space from which status can be built up.

Conclusion

This chapter draws on anthropological research on two kinds of dance that exist in parallel in South Korea: traditional dance and Western social dance. The coexistence of different modes of interaction between young men and women is embodied in the practice of both dance forms by university students. The educated youth express their desire to 'design' gender identities and relations in their own terms, incorporating both 'traditional' and 'modern' dimensions. But despite the visible transformation in gender relations that comes across in university students' social dancing, this chapter suggests that Confucian principles continue to shape interactions between individuals. Each Fiesta participant I met tried to assert their new gender identity while fitting (consciously or not) within the more conservative socio-cultural environment.

The Fiesta example also suggests that leisure practices shape subjective experiences, not only by maintaining a sense of belonging and Confucian values regarding community, but also by providing a space in which people can experiment with individual strategies. By participating in these activities, 'Fiestarians' create a collective identity and group solidarity, while at the same time developing in a very specific way their individual and gender identities as South Korean university students. Meanwhile, traditional Korean dances are still alive and refer to the history and culture of South Korea. Their revival in the 1980s on university campuses provides a basis for imagining the history of the nation.

Notes

1. The generic term 'sport dance' indicates a short and technical learning intended to be displayed around fashionable dances; in this chapter, the term is used in preference to others (ballroom dances, Latin dances, social dances, dances in couple, etc.) as it enhance the competitive character of the dance through physical performance.
2. In Korea, human life was thought to be influenced by a variety of invisible beings. Through shamanic practices that included offerings, the shaman (usually a woman – the *mudang*, 무당) begged the spirits to intercede in the destiny of the world. On Shamanism in contemporary South Korean society, see Kim (2003).
3. Korea has produced a large number of musical instruments, and a total of sixty different

kinds are preserved at the National Classical Music Institute in Seoul. Chordophones, aerophones, idiophones and membranophones are almost equally developed, thirteen to seventeen instruments for each category.

4. See Van Zile (2001b: 36) for further discussion of *jeongjae*. The first kingdom on the Korean peninsula was probably formed in 2333 BC. From 57 BC until AD 668 the three kingdoms of Koguryo, Paekche and Silla ruled the peninsula until its unification. Chinese influence resulted in the adoption of a centralized bureaucracy, and Buddhism and Confucianism were widely introduced. The Unified Silla Period, AD 668 until 935, was a golden age for Korean culture. It adopted Confucianism and blended it with the Korean monarchy; high positions in the central administration were determined by a mix of family connections and Confucian principles that assigned everyone a place in society in a hierarchical manner. The central administration was composed of high-ranking civilian and military officials selected through a national examination open to anyone, and nobility of virtue gradually came to substitute nobility of blood. During the Koryo dynasty (918 to 1392), an aristocratic government was instituted separately from the military administration. Buddhism was established as the state religion and came to have great influence in the political and administrative spheres. The Joseon dynasty (1392 to 1910), the last on the peninsula, went through various political and economic reforms, through neo-Confucianism, and the invention of *hangeul* (한글), the Korean alphabet.

5. Because their occupation was to entertain men, the *kisaeng* developed special skills through extensive training in poetry, music, arts and dance: the skills of courtesanship. Assigned as professional entertainers to the court, the upper government bureaucracy and even distant military outposts, *kisaeng* were among the few women who had free access to public events while belonging to a lower social group.

6. Since 1996, South Korea's Ministry of Culture and Tourism has encouraged the general public to wear the *hanbok*. Facilitated by Koreans' fondness for their own traditions, the campaign has promoted the creation of new *hanbok* styles that are practical for everyday use. Since Korea was originally composed of a single ethnic group, *hanbok* as a traditional dress is synonymous with national dress, and forms a highly effective expression of Korean identity.

7. The *hanbok* was probably worn very early on, but it was transformed during the Three Kingdoms period (57 BC to AD 668). Toward the end of this period, China introduced silk mandarin robes that were adopted by royalty and officials. After signing a peace treaty with the Mongol Empire, the kings of the late Koryo dynasty began to marry Mongolian women, and government officials adopted Mongolian fashion. As a result the *chima* skirt was shortened, as was the *jeogori*, which was hiked up above the waist and tied at the chest with a long, wide ribbon (instead of a belt) while the sleeves were curved slightly. During the Joseon dynasty, *jeogori* or women's *hanbok* was gradually tightened and shortened.

8. The colours used in the clothing derived from the five basic colours of Oriental cosmology: red, yellow, blue, white and black, which symbolize the five traditional elements: fire, earth, wood, metal and water.

9. *Hanbok* are made of traditional hemp or ramie cloth, muslin cotton, silk, satin and even fur, depending on weather conditions (*Encykorea*, digital edition of the *Encyclopedia of Korean Culture*, published in 2001 by the Academy of Korean Studies and DongBang Media Co.).

10. The husband is compared to the sky's force (*yang*) and the wife is depicted as the ground's suppleness (*yin*). She must, therefore, be obedient to her husband and chaste. Directly linked to patriarchy and filial piety, the education of girls was legally and socially defined

under the Joseon dynasty and was illustrated through proverbs, adages, books, and so on. These Confucian virtues remain perceived in a positive light today (Sautet 1996: 39–54).
11. As quoted by Cowan, Bourdieu has described habitus as 'systems of durable, transposable dispositions' that generate and structure 'practices and representations ... without in any way being the product of obedience to rules' (Cowan 1990: 22–23). Cowan frequently appeals to the concept of habitus (Bourdieu 1977) in order to explain the ways in which dance expresses fundamental social constructions of gender identity. Though conceived in terms of a habitus, the Confucian value-practice system does not mean that individuals are captives of this structure; it is more the system of Confucian values and relations itself that becomes the structure and instruments for the strategic practices of individuals, reproduced in constant changes and local adjustments, probably without any real consciousness of this by the actors involved. The hierarchical order in everyday social relationships is the most significant example of the long-lasting impact of Confucianism; Confucian virtues such as fervour for education (to maintain or enhance social status), hard work, emotional control and sincerity (to do what is right) are some other patterns.
12. Even today, students have few chances to be acquainted with individuals of the other gender as the South Korean school system generally separates girls and boys.
13. Because of the military instability of the Korean peninsula, South Korean able-bodied men above the age of eighteen are required to serve twenty-six months in the army (or twenty-eight months in the navy or the air force). Military service strongly affects university students in their studies and in their behaviour: after military service, men tend to become more masculine, disrespectful towards women, and enjoy womanizing. Generally speaking, though Fiesta male participants' attitude may be influenced or changed through military service, it is obvious that their manners regarding women, and an open-minded opinion concerning dancing in couples, for example, are significantly different from other South Korean men, whether before or after military service.
14. The word *skinship* (스킨십) is known as a 'konglish' word, an English-derived word or phrase which has been adopted in South Korean vernacular. *Skinship* is a term encompassing physical contact and intimate touching between close friends, such as holding hands, hugging, cuddling, kissing, and so forth.
15. The influence of the global media is a contributing factor here. Looks are important to increase the chance of being well integrated into the community, finding a good life partner, an attractive job, and so on. The relatively low price of cosmetic surgery in South Korea has made it more accessible to all social classes. It has become so ordinary that girls may get eyelid surgery as a high-school graduation present.
16. Bourdieu defines social capital as 'the aggregate of the actual or potential resources which are linked to possession of a durable network of more or less institutionalized relationships of mutual acquaintance and recognition – or in other words, to membership in a group – which provides each of its members with the backing of the collectivity-owned capital, a "credential" which entitles them to credit, in the various senses of the word' (Bourdieu 1986: 248–49).

References

Bourdieu, P. 1977. *Outline of a Theory of Practice*. Cambridge: Cambridge University Press.
_____ 1986. 'The Forms of Capital', in J.C. Richardson (ed.), *Handbook of Theory and Research for the Sociology of Education*. New York: Greenwood, pp.241–58.

_____ 1987. 'Programme pour une sociologie du sport', in *Choses dites*. Paris: Minuit, pp.203–16.

Carrausse, S. 2010. 'Les sociabilités étudiantes. Etude comparative de trois universités en Corée du Sud, France et Portugal', Ph.D. dissertation. Paris: Ecole des Hautes Etudes en Sciences Sociales.

Cho, D.I. 2005. *The Spirit of Korean Culture Roots: Korean Mask Dance*. Seoul: Ewha Woman's University.

Cowan, J.K. 1990. *Dance and the Body Politic in Northern Greece*. Princeton, NJ: Princeton University Press.

Hanna, J.L. 1988. *Dance, Sex and Gender: Signs of Identity, Dominance, Defiance, and Desire*. Chicago: University of Chicago Press.

Jeong, B.H. 1997. 'The Characteristics of Korean Traditional Dance', *Korea Journal* 37(3): 93–109.

Kim, C.H. 2003. *Korean Shamanism: The Cultural Paradox*. Aldershot: Ashgate.

Lee, J.K. 2000a. *Historic Factors Influencing Korean Higher Education*. Seoul: Jimoondang.

_____ 2000b. *Korean Higher Education: A Confucian Perspective*. Seoul: Jimoondang.

Park, S.B. 1983. *Buddhist Faith and Sudden Enlightenment*. Albany: State University of New York Press.

Sautet, S. 1996. *Les femmes ? De leur émancipation ('entretiens' avec Confucius, Platon, Aristote, Augustin, Avicenne, Thomas d'Aquin, Hume, Schopenhauer, Stuart Mill, Nietzsche)*. Paris: Lattès.

Seth, M.J. 2002. *Education Fever: Society, Politics, and the Pursuit of Schooling in South Korea*. Honolulu: University of Hawaii Press.

Van Zile, J. 2001a. 'The Many Faces of Korean Dance', in A. Dils and A.C. Albright (eds), *Moving History/Dancing Cultures: A Dance History Reader*. Middletown, CT: Wesleyan University Press, pp.178–190.

_____ 2001b. *Perspectives on Korean Dance*. Middletown, CT: Wesleyan University Press.

Washabaugh, W. (ed.). 1998. *The Passion of Music and Dance: Body, Gender and Sexuality*. Oxford: Berg.

Yang, S. 1997. *Hanbok: The Art of Korean Clothing*. New Jersey: Hollym.

Yum, J.O. 1987. 'Korean Philosophy and Communication' in D.L. Kincaid (ed.), *Communication Theory: Eastern and Western Perspectives*. San Diego, CA: Academic Press, pp.71–86.

Chapter 10

Preparation, Presentation and Power: Children's Performances in a Balinese Dance Studio

Jonathan McIntosh

In Bali the performing arts ensure that important cultural values, such as the preference for balance and harmony, are passed down from one generation to the next. Children learn about these values from a young age when they attend music and dance performances at temple ceremonies with their parents and by watching recordings of traditional performances broadcast on the Balinese television channel, Bali TV. However, children also embody these cultural values by choosing to engage in traditional arts activities of which learning to dance remains one of the most popular. Children who choose to learn to dance usually attend lessons at local dance studios (*sanggar tari*) once or twice a week. When children first attend lessons their teachers usually instruct them on how to correctly execute the movements and patterns that form the rudiments of Balinese dance technique. It is not that boys and girls do not know these basic movements; when children commence dance lessons they already possess substantial 'tacit' dance knowledge (after Polanyi 1958), intuitively embodied from their observations of live performances and from watching television. When children include such movements in their play, this acts as a kind of early rehearsal before formal instruction (McIntosh 2006). Nonetheless, children must actively learn these movements so that their bodies know, through the various sensations involved in dancing, how to perform individual actions and positions correctly as part of choreographic sequences. By focusing upon the ways in which boys and girls are prepared and presented for dance performances in a village dance studio, this chapter investigates how teachers subordinate children in the teaching and learning process. Throughout such a process the 'presumed malleability of behavior underpins the pursuit of discipline' (Dyck 2008: 13). In Bali this sense of dance discipline 'entails not only [the] technical means for exercising power over self and/or others but [is] also an essential symbolic medium for defining and articulating preferred social practices, objectives, and ways of being' (Dyck 2008: 12). As a result of this power and discipline, a child's body gradually becomes more powerful, through the acquisition of technical dance skills. This then enables a child to obey and follow the dance teacher's instructions during lessons. Despite these enhanced capabilities, however, a child's body also becomes docile (Foucault 1991) because it can be subordinated, manipulated and controlled with ease by the dance teacher.

In addition to exercising power over children during dance rehearsals, teachers subordinate children's bodies during preparations backstage before a performance when they apply make-up to children's faces and dress children in their costumes. To describe how dance teachers exercise power over children in this context, that is, immediately prior to a performance, I draw upon an approach developed by Wulff (1998a, 1998b, 2002) in her research on the culture and career of ballet dancers. Unlike many other scholars who study dance, Wulff focuses primarily on dancers, choreographers, technicians and directors off the stage rather than the performance on stage. Wulff argues that such an approach to the study of dance is important because '[b]ackstage ethnography around performance, especially the narrow liminal zone in the wings, will anchor the productions of the framed illusion on stage socially' (Wulff 1998b: 104–5). Through the use of the word 'liminal', Wulff (1998b: 116) argues that ballet performance is a form of ritual because it is a 'prescribed formal behaviour for occasions not given over to technological routine, having reference to beliefs in mystical beings or powers' (Turner 1964: 20). For Wulff, studying how dancers prepare themselves in dressing rooms or in the wings off stage, immediately before a performance, leads to a further shifting of the 'transformative qualities of rituals' (Wulff 1998b: 116). For children in Bali dance performances are a form of ritual; performances differ from rehearsals because they are occasions when children get to put on make-up, dress up in costumes and perform in front of an audience. Moreover, before the commencement of such events, delicate offerings of flowers and rice are presented to the deities of the Balinese Hindu religion so that the stage upon which the children will perform is sanctified. By focusing upon dance steps and body movements in rehearsals and the preparatory processes of make-up and costuming, this chapter also presents a 'backstage ethnography' (after Wulff 1998b) of children's dance performance. Such an approach will demonstrate how teachers subordinate and exercise power over children's bodies and detail also the main preparations that go on behind the scenes prior to a children's dance performance.

To begin, the chapter introduces the reader to a Balinese dance studio where I conducted research in 2003 and 2004. An examination of 'in-house' performances at this organization then provides a context with which to explore why these presentations are integral to children's development as dancers. Following this, the chapter explains why the usual routine of children's dance lessons changes immediately prior to a performance. In particular, the discussion focuses upon why these changes take place and how they are supposed to help children cope better with the transition from practising dances in large groups during lessons to rehearsing the actual choreography of a dance in small groups before a performance. This transition can sometimes cause problems for children and this issue is investigated by highlighting the difficulties experienced by a group of girls when they attempt to perform the complete choreography of a dance for the first time during rehearsal. To show how the undisciplined body cannot be easily manipulated, and how, as a result, the dance teacher resorts to firm measures in an attempt to exercise power over children, the chapter draws on Foucault (1991). After describing this pre-performance rehearsal process, a chronological approach to Balinese dance performance focuses upon important practical matters of make-up and costuming to demonstrate how ideas concerning presentation are forced upon children, and how adults expect them to look a particular way in performance. The ethnography presented throughout the chapter views the world of children's dance performance from within. Thus, the chapter enables the reader to get a sense of the time it takes to transform a child for a performance while reinforcing also the ways in which children learn about the importance attached to minute aspects of presentation in Balinese dance.

Sanggar Tari Mumbul Sari

The Mumbul Sari Dance Studio (Sanggar Tari Mumbul Sari) is a privately owned and operated arts organization in the village of Keramas in the south-central Balinese administrative district of Gianyar.[1] In 1993, I Wayan Suarata (b. 1969) and his wife Ni Luh Happy Pariamini (b. 1971) established the organization. Wayan and Happy both hold tertiary dance degrees from the College of the Indonesian Arts,[2] and they are highly respected as professional performers and teachers in Keramas and the surrounding area. The children who study at the *sanggar* range from four to fourteen years of age, and to attend lessons each child must pay a small tuition fee. Boys and girls are expected to attend twice-weekly rehearsals on Tuesday afternoons and Sunday mornings, with rehearsals being held at an open pavilion (*wantilan*) in the family compound owned by the dance teachers.

In Bali children learn to perform adult dances since children's traditional dances do not generally exist. At the *sanggar* boys and girls are divided into three skill levels – elementary, intermediate and advanced – depending on their ability. At each level, children rehearse in large groups and study a specific number of dances deemed suitable for their ability, experience and gender. At the elementary and intermediate levels, boys learn male dances (*tari laki-laki*) and girls learn female dances (*tari wanita*), all of which are based upon an asymmetrical basic stance known as *agem*. Generally, the male *agem* entails adopting a wide stance whereas the female *agem* requires dancers to position their feet close together. By learning dances specific to their sex, boys and girls develop a dance technique that socializes their understandings of male and female styles of dance movement. This understanding then serves as a foundation that later informs children's study of transgender dances (*tari bebancihan*) at the advanced level. For boys this involves tailoring an unrefined or strong (*keras*) dance technique in order to adopt a more refined (*alus*) performance mode, whereas girls must develop a stronger, more masculine dance style.

During lessons, boys and girls are judged on their ability to learn and execute the technical requirements of a dance in the appropriate stylistic manner. In Bali children are expected to submit themselves to instruction methods the purpose of which is to ensure that dance knowledge is successfully transmitted from teacher to student. In order to memorize the choreography of a dance, or a section of it, a student is first of all expected to imitate the movements by means of dancing behind the teacher. When this requirement is fulfilled, the teacher then starts to manoeuvre the student's body, gradually shaping the movements of the apprentice dancer to ensure that static positions and locomotive transitions are executed in the appropriate style. During this stage, the teacher often takes hold of the child – wrapping their arms around those of the learner – while dancing. Physically taking hold of the student in this manner enables the teacher to impart their style of performance into the body of the student. This teaching method is the most expedient way for teachers to exercise power over children's bodies in the *sanggar* in preparation for performance. In addition to the physical manipulation of children, dance teachers often rely upon verbal corrections[3] and the singing of melodic and rhythmical elements extracted from the musical accompaniment, which is provided by a gamelan orchestra.[4] Thus, through verbal and physical instruction, as well as the control of practice and movement, dance teachers often hold a physical power over the children at the *sanggar*.[5]

Preparing for Children's 'In-house' Dance Performances at the *Sanggar*

Every four months the children who attend the *sanggar* participate in 'in-house' performances, which are referred to as *pentas* (literally 'raised platform' or 'stage'). As part of their attendance at the *sanggar*, all children are expected to participate in these events at which they are required to perform one of the dances they have studied during the previous four to eight months. Ceremonial festivities permitting, these performances usually take place in the months of April, August and December at the *sanggar*. A *pentas* normally begins around 7 o'clock in the evening and lasts for approximately two to three hours. Children in the elementary level perform first and are then followed by those from the intermediate and advanced levels. Due to the large number of pupils enrolled at the *sanggar*, it is not possible for all children to perform over the course of a single evening. Instead, they perform over two successive evenings when an almost identical programme of dances is presented. However, unlike during their dance lessons when they practise on the floor of the dance pavilion, for a *pentas* the children perform on the concrete stage at the rear of the structure.

Officially, a *pentas* serves as a quasi examination where the dance teachers assess children on their technical and performance skills. In theory, the success of an individual's performance determines whether or not the child will progress from one level to the next. In reality, however, this is not the case since the teachers are usually too preoccupied with other matters during a performance to examine individual pupils. These matters include applying the children's make-up, dressing them in their costumes and organizing the music so that the performance flows from one dance to the next. As a result, the teachers' decisions to allow children to advance to the next dance level are primarily based upon their observations of individuals during rehearsals. Boys and girls do not have to perform all of the dances specified for study at each dance level at the *sanggar* but they usually perform a majority of this repertoire over several *pentas* before progressing to the next level. Despite this, children are expected to dance well in order to demonstrate what they have learned in the intervening period since the previous *pentas*.

At a *pentas* children perform ceremonial and secular dances, although the occasion itself is not linked primarily to a ceremonial event. In this context, children perform ceremonial dances to demonstrate dance technique. Children are normally offered the opportunity to choose which dance they would like to perform. This choice is then confirmed or refused by the teacher. Three general reasons contribute to the dance teacher's refusal to allow a child to perform the dance of their choice. Firstly, the teacher may want a child to perform a specific dance that is appropriate for their stage of learning. Secondly, children may have performed their preferred choice before, and as a result the teacher wishes them to perform a different dance. Lastly, a child's initial choice may be refused for practical reasons linked to the organization and the programming of a performance. For example, if too many children want to perform the same dance the teachers must decide which pupils will be allowed to perform it at the *pentas*. In this case, the dance teachers either offer those children whose first choice has been refused the opportunity to perform a different dance or they simply tell children what dance they will perform. Once it has been confirmed which children will perform what dance, the teachers decide upon a running order for the performance. Reflecting the children's acquisition of dance skills at the *sanggar* and their progression through the various levels of the organization, the running order for a *pentas* also highlights the extent to which children's bodies become disciplined as a result of their training.

The Learning of 'Performance' Choreography

During the two weeks that precede a *pentas*, the format of the twice-weekly dance rehearsals at the *sanggar* changes. Children still attend rehearsals but, instead of practising the entire repertoire they are currently studying, they only rehearse the dance they will perform at the *pentas*. Dances are also rehearsed in order according to the *pentas* programme. At these rehearsals, teachers exert considerably more pressure on children to perform the correct steps and movements not only in time with the musical accompaniment but also to execute them in the appropriate style. Furthermore, the teachers concentrate on correcting mistakes that may, up until that moment, not have been addressed simply due to the large size of some of the classes at the *sanggar*. The teachers correct the children by means of verbal instructions and actual bodily manipulation to fine tune flaws in their technique. The purpose of this fine tuning is to prepare the children for the performance, with special attention paid to correct body postures, hand positions and specific eye movements. The extent to which the teachers fine tune pupils' bodies depends upon the position of each child within the hierarchy of the *sanggar*, a fact that also reflects the disciplined nature of the children's bodies concerning individual skill and performance experience. This echoes Foucault's (1991) concept of the docile body – a body which can be subordinated, subjugated and controlled with ease – and illustrates how the power that teachers exercise over children is dependent upon the children's previous acquisition of dance skills.

Teachers at the *sanggar* expect children to memorize dances prior to a performance. The Balinese notion of dancing from memory reflects Blacking's idea that 'the ultimate aim of dancing is to be able to move *without* thinking, to be *danced*' (Blacking 1977: 23, original emphasis). However, before a *pentas*, children sometimes have to learn, or adapt to, new forms of choreography in order to perform. When the children rehearse in large groups on the floor of the pavilion they dance in close proximity to each other and it is not always possible for them to practise the choreography as it would be presented in performance. The use of such 'rehearsal choreography' means that for practise purposes dance choreography is often changed to suit the limitations of the rehearsal space. This is not to say that the children learn simplified versions of certain dances. Instead, the teachers sometimes change the choreography of a dance to enable them to teach more children at any one time. When children transfer their rehearsals from the floor of the pavilion to the stage in preparation for a *pentas*, the dance teachers not only expect boys and girls to adapt quickly to the performance space but also to perform dances according to their original choreographic sequences. Issues surrounding whether or not children perform the original or a slightly altered version of the choreography designated by the dance teachers are dependent on the ability and performance experience of individual children at each level. For instance, during a *pentas*, children in the elementary level perform in straight lines facing the audience. Whereas, if the same dances were to be performed by children of the intermediate or advanced level outside the *sanggar* – for example, at a village ceremony – the teachers would insist that the original choreography be employed.

Generally, the transition from rehearsing on the floor of the pavilion to dancing on the stage does not cause children any great difficulties, with the teachers only having to make minor adjustments to the children's bodies, usually concerning the spacing between the dancers on the stage. The teachers' chief concern for those at the elementary level is to ensure that they correctly enter and exit the stage. During a *pentas* held at the *sanggar*, children enter the performance space from a room behind the stage. To do this, they pass through a single doorway concealed with a split curtain (*langse*). As the children pass through the curtain and onto the stage, they have to ensure that they are in the appropriate place and that they are in time with the musical accompaniment, provided by means of a gamelan orchestra recording played on a karaoke cassette player. Similarly, when a dance is about to finish or has finished, the children must know how to file off stage in the correct manner. This sense of stage discipline is an integral part of ordinary dance lessons and something children pick up quickly in rehearsals, through the emphasis teachers place on lining up just before the rehearsal of a particular dance. Perfecting children's stage discipline is of utmost importance to the dance teachers. This can be seen in the way that the teachers become more authoritative towards boys and girls directly before a *pentas* and how there is considerably less room for error on the part of the children. This finding is similar to Foucault's notion concerning the 'ever increasing rigorous exercises' to be performed by a pupil that are associated with the 'gradual acquisition of knowledge and good behaviour' (Foucault 1991: 161). As a performance approaches, the teachers expect the children at the *sanggar* to be able to dance to the best of their abilities and to adapt quickly to any changes deemed necessary. This also demonstrates the teacher's knowledge and teaching skills, thereby validating their status in the local community, as a poor performance would reflect badly on them more generally.

However, there are times when the transition from rehearsal floor and 'rehearsal choreography' to stage and 'performance choreography' causes the children considerable difficulties. One such example occurred during preparations for a *pentas* in September 2004 when a group of girls from the elementary group, rehearsing the dance *Tari Manuk Rawa*, were unable to exit the stage correctly. This dance, usually performed by five to seven dancers, depicts the various movements of the Balinese waterbird. Towards the end of the dance, the choreography depicts the wing movements of the waterbirds as they fly into the distance. The act of flying is portrayed through the dancers' movements – they move their arms in a particular way that suggests the flapping of a bird's wings – as they gradually dance their way off stage. To achieve this effect, the dancers adopt the basic right position (*agem kanan*) and take quick steps with alternate feet on the spot. To perform the basic right position for *Tari Manuk Rawa* the left foot is placed in front of the right foot; the right arm is lifted into the air, with the back of the hand facing upwards (the angle between the chest and the underside of the upper arm being approximately 160 degrees) and the elbow of the left hand is parallel with the left shoulder; the left palm is down with the back of the hand facing the audience; the fingers of both hands are extended and held wide apart. The reverse is true for the basic left position (*agem kiri*). Positioning the arms wide apart means that a cape – when worn by the dancer in performance – takes on the appearance of a bird in flight. Thus, through the lifting and dropping of the arms, the dancer imitates the wing movements of the waterbird. To exit the stage and finish the dance correctly, the girls – aged between six and eight years old – were positioned in a line at the front of the stage. According to the original performance choreography, two of the girls, at the right of the line, then should have separated from the remaining four children and gradually danced off stage in an S-shaped line (*ombak segara*), turning to alternate sides as they went. Once the first two girls had done this, the next two girls should have done the same, leaving the final two children to exit the stage. As the three groups turned from side to side, they should have changed from basic right to basic left positions. However, these girls had only practised this dance while standing in straight lines on the floor of the pavilion. Consequently, when it came to the conclusion of the dance, they were unsure as to which direction to turn when attempting the aforementioned choreographic sequence. Moreover, adapting to the different spatial dimensions of the stage, while executing the choreography in an S-shape, added to the children's confusion. The problems became worse when, after several unsuccessful attempts to execute this sequence, Happy's patience began to wear thin. She walked onto the stage and started to shout at the girls. As she did so, she pulled them into line and forcefully manoeuvred them around the stage in the direction in which they were supposed to dance. It was extremely unusual for either Happy or Wayan to employ such forceful teaching methods. However, due to the time constraints of the rehearsal period for the forthcoming *pentas* and the inexperience of this group of girl dancers, such methods were deemed necessary on this occasion. The failure of the children to correctly interpret Happy's verbal instructions ultimately led her to reimpose a sense of discipline upon her students by pushing and pulling them into the correct choreographic positions. Although her firm treatment of the girls may on first inspection have seemed excessive to non-Balinese observers, dance training in Bali is typically a 'hands on' process and such reactions on the part of a teacher are not wholly unexpected. Happy's exasperated efforts, however, did have the desired effect. At the next rehearsal, this particular group of girls managed to remember the step sequences and successfully completed their exit from the stage.

The aforementioned example demonstrates that even with rehearsals stretching over several months, the prior experience of individuals is crucial to how children react to pre-performance situations. If children are unfamiliar with the protocols and aesthetics of 'performance' choreography, then their bodies can quickly become undisciplined and disorientated when preparing for a *pentas*. Hence, the move from the pavilion floor to the stage is integral to the disciplining of children's bodies. By learning how to perform, the bodies of the young Balinese also become 'manipulated, shaped, [and] trained' (Foucault 1991: 136). This process also ensures that boys and girls gradually learn how to respond to the visual and vocal instructions of the dance teachers. When such an approach does not have the desired affect, as was the case in the example of *Tari Manuk Rawa*, instructors sometimes employ a 'push-and-pull' teaching technique when trying to correct a number of children at the same time.

In contrast with those in the elementary and intermediate levels, children in the advanced level learn dances with full choreography despite the fact that space in rehearsals is cramped. This is possible because fewer children study at this level. Moreover, by the time boys and girls reach the advanced level they are, more or less, accustomed to the process of transferring from the rehearsal floor to the stage in preparation for a performance. The children in the advanced level further exemplify Foucault's (1991: 138) notion of the docile body because the dance teachers are able to subordinate children's practised bodies and their increased capacity with ease.

From the above description concerning the confusion caused by changing from rehearsal to performance choreography in the dance *Tari Manuk Rawa*, it is clear that the dance teachers at the *sanggar* regard children's performances to be important. For, in Bali, dance performance is integral to the learning process; it is far more than just mere confirmation of a child's capability to fulfil technical requirements. Such a process also provides children with the opportunity to gain valuable experience by performing in front of friends and family. Nevertheless, the teachers place considerable pressure on the children to perform to the best of their ability to showcase what they have learned. In this context, errors still occur, but it is better for children to make a mistake during a performance at the *sanggar* than in front of an audience in a more public venue – for example, at a temple ceremony. Mistakes by children at a *pentas* or at a temple performance are usually met with laughter from friends and family members in the audience. Such a reaction is commonplace in Bali and serves as a means of teasing and temporarily excluding individuals before reincorporating them into the group once more (see Geertz 1973: 416). Although they may also laugh at such errors, the dance teachers take mistakes a little more seriously than most audience members. During *pentas* performances, the teachers (usually Wayan, since Happy is busy helping children with their make-up and costumes) take the time to note mistakes which are then addressed in dance lessons. The process of following up mistakes in this manner generally ensures that they are unlikely to happen again.

Make-up

One reason many children look forward to a *pentas* is because the event provides them with the opportunity to dance in costume and wear make-up, both essential elements for dance, drama and (even on some occasions) music performances in Bali. Dibia and Ballinger (2004: 20) argue that since the introduction of televised productions to the island in the late 1960s, there has been a dramatic increase in the use of make-up by performers. When viewed close up, the amount of make-up performers wear may seem excessive but the boldness of the make-up ensures that a dancer's face and facial expressions can be viewed from a distance. Children who attend the *sanggar* wear full make-up when they perform at a *pentas*. Both boys and girls wear the same basic make-up, consisting of liquid foundation and face powder. First, the face and neck are prepared with a liquid foundation, the colour of which is similar to the skin tone. Face powder is then applied with a powder puff over the foundation once it has dried. Since Balinese performers make such dramatic use of the eyes in theatrical and dance performances, make-up for the eyes is most important. Arched eyebrows are drawn on and filled in with black eye pencil. The eye socket and eyelid are then decorated with yellow, pink and blue eye shadow (blue eye shadow is applied just above the eyelid, pink to the inside corner and yellow to the outside corner).[6] These colours are blended together so that one fades into the next. The eyes are widened by thick lines of black eye pencil on the edge of the upper and lower eyelid. Next, a mixture of red and pink blusher is applied with a large soft brush to the cheeks and up the cheekbones towards the temples. A curl of hair is then pencilled on both cheeks of female dancers, and boys if they are performing *kebyar* dances,[7] such as the 'Seated Dance' (*Tari Kebyar Duduk*) or 'Dance of the Bumblebees' (*Tari Oleg Tamulilingan*). Girls also have a fringe of hair pencilled onto their forehead with black eye pencil. Male dancers performing dances in an unrefined (*keras*) style have sideburns pencilled on their cheeks instead. Following this, a faint trace of white and then bronze eye shadow is rubbed down either side of the bridge of the nose. Red lipstick completes the transformation.

The dance teachers apply the children's make-up before a performance. This is a skilled task and one in which not even the children at the advanced level are proficient. The teachers apply the children's make-up to ensure that the quality of its application and the finished result meet their high standards. As can be seen in figure 10.1, where Happy is forcefully holding the head of Tomi, a boy from the advanced level at the *sanggar*, the application of make-up also physically reinforces the teachers' exercise of power over the children. Here Happy makes decisions and illustrates the 'process of power and subordination' (Wulff 1995: 11; 2006: 129) where decision making leads an individual to exercise power over another (Lukes 1974: 25). The application of make-up is yet another example of how the decisions made by the dance teachers allow them to manipulate and exercise power over children's bodies in the *sanggar*.

It takes approximately five to ten minutes to apply make-up for a child from the elementary or intermediate class. As these children generally perform group dances, the make-up does not need to be perfect but neither is it hastily or sloppily applied. However, due to the large number of children who have to be prepared before the start of the performance, little time can be allocated to this task. Children in the advanced level arrive after the start of a *pentas*. By this time, all of the younger children are ready to perform; they are dressed in their costumes with their make-up completed. It is then the turn of those from the advanced level to have their make-up applied and be dressed in their costumes. More time is allocated to the readying of these children because they perform duets and solo dances, and their costumes

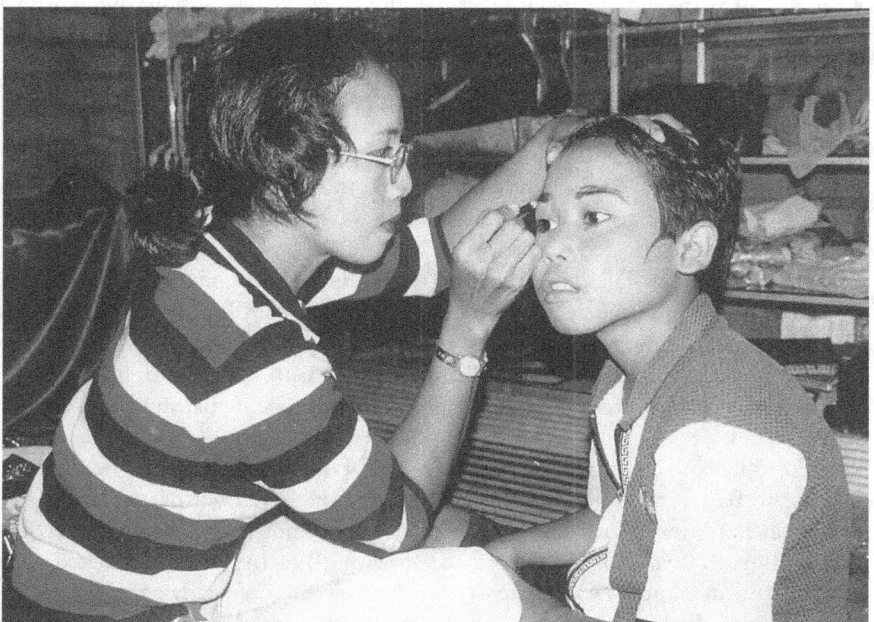

Figure 10.1 Happy applies make-up to Tomi's face prior to a pentas. *Photograph by the author.*

take longer to prepare. Even as a *pentas* begins in the pavilion, frantic preparations are often still being made in another part of the *sanggar* compound to ensure that children from the advanced level will be ready to dance at the correct moment in the programme. Children from the advanced level who are not performing often help their friends to get ready during this time. In helping their friends to get dressed in costume, the teachers' actions are reinforced and aspects integral to dance performance are reproduced through socialized activity. This process also exemplifies that although a docile body can be easily manipulated, a docile body can also manipulate others. This has to do with the protracted process of getting dressed during which time friends often intentionally place a dancer's body in certain positions. For example, this can involve the positioning of a dancer's arms above their head in order to wrap their torso in layers of fabric. Connected with this task is the squeezing of the dancer's stomach to ensure that the fabric is pulled tight and fastened in such a manner that it will not come loose in performance.

Costumes

For many inexperienced children, a *pentas* is their first opportunity to perform in front of an audience and, since Western notions of dress rehearsals do not really exist in Bali, it is also the first time they will have worn make-up and danced while wearing a costume. Despite the above examples and analyses – which seem to conform to Western notions and 'protocols' – this is a key difference between dress rehearsals in Balinese and Western contexts. In rehearsals, boys and girls are required to wear the official *sanggar* uniform: a purple tee-shirt upon which the emblem of the organization is printed; a one to two metre long piece of fabric (*kamben*) tied around the waist, and an elasticated belt (*streplus*), which is tied over the *kamben*.[8] This uniform ensures that the children gradually become accustomed to how their bodies should move in relation to specific dance costumes. Such an approach also enables children to perform in front of an audience without the need for a dress rehearsal. In a different context, that of teaching Japanese dance to students at the University of Hawaii, Kealiinohomoku (1979: 80) notes how practice uniforms worn during rehearsals 'constrict the body' and simulate the costumes worn by dancers.[9] In Bali dance teachers train children to become aware of this fact by asserting the importance of the *sanggar* dance uniform during lessons. In this way, practice uniforms are integral to the learning process because they not only serve to further discipline the body but they also ensure that children know how to move in ways that are stylistically appropriate for male, female and transgender dance genres.

Costumes also communicate important aspects of a performance to the audience because in Bali 'each dance and every character type have their particular type of dress and headdress which clues the audience into knowing who is what' (Dibia and Ballinger 2004: 20). Balinese children learn all of the codes associated with various costumes and how to relate to character roles from an early age. Like make-up, costumes allow performers to assume roles understood by audience members (Roach and Eicher 1979: 11). Both male and female dances require performers to be wrapped in many layers of costume. For female roles, a two- or two-and-a-half-metre piece of fabric (*kamben*), covered in a gold-leaf pattern (*prada*), is wrapped several times around the hips and comes to the ankles (see figure 10.2). For solo *kebyar* dances performed by males and females, including the 'Seated Dance' (*Tari Kebyar Duduk*) and the 'King of the Forest Dance' (*Tari Margapati*),[10] the *kamben* is wrapped several times around the hips and comes to the midpoint of the calves. For most female and refined (*alus*) male roles, a plain five-metre-long sash (*sabuk setagen dalam*) is tightly wrapped around the torso of the dancer. This plain sash is then covered with a gold-leaf sash (*sabuk prada*) of equal length. For unrefined (*keras*) male dances, such as the solo warrior dance *Tari Baris Tunggal*, boys wear white trousers (*celana*) with ankle coverings (*setewel*) that come halfway up the calf. Many hanging panels of fabric (*awiran*) are tied tightly around the torso with a large fabric panel (*lamak*) fastened to the dancer's chest. Underneath this is worn a blue or dark red velour shirt. A large, sometimes beaded, circular collar (*badong*) is placed around the neck with a dagger (*kris*) tucked into a belt (*setagen*) above and behind the shoulder blades. The costume for *Tari Baris Tunggal* is completed with a triangular headdress (*gelungan*) constructed from a wooden frame and decorated with shells. The shells are attached to the headdress with small springs. Thus, when a dancer moves in performance, the shells quiver and rattle as they strike against one another. This auditory element further adds to the aesthetics and tension of a performance.

Costumes can also include various accessories made from leather or plastic such as arm-bands and wristlets (*gelang kana*), decorative collars (*lumbing*) and belts (*ampok-ampok*), and a decorative length of fabric (*tutup dada*) that is passed around the chest and fastened to the top of the *sabuk prada*. Flowers (*bunga sumpang*) are also sometimes tucked behind the ears. Occasionally, real flowers are used but the use of plastic ones is commonplace. The layers of costumes that dancers wear ensure that their movements are in keeping with the style of a particular dance or genre. This is important because the way in which a costume constricts the body has implications for notions of power in Balinese society. In particular, two such notions are useful to the present discussion. Firstly, the dance teachers at the *sanggar* exercise power in relation to costumes through the action of dressing children. The teachers decide what costumes children wear, and they exercise power by means of physically wrapping costumes around children's bodies. Secondly, the costumes used in performance generally reflect Balinese society's power over dancers. For example, the tightly bound costume for *Tari Panyembrama* (see figure 10.2) reflects the role of women within a patriarchal society (see Belo 1970). In contrast, male costumes, such as the one used for *Tari Baris Tunggal*, allow for forms of gross movement, possibly reflecting the hegemony of men over women in Bali.

By manipulating children's bodies within the confines of the *sanggar*, dance teachers hope to ensure that boys and girls perform in a manner that is comparable to their own professional standards. However, this power also extends beyond the physical confines of the organization and is evident in children's bodily discipline when they perform in and outside the confines of the *sanggar*. Children's performances outside the organization most often fulfil acts of ceremonial devotion (*ngayah*) in the Balinese Hindu religion and are part of ceremonial activities that are an important part of village life (see McIntosh n.d.). At these events, children's bodies reflect the discipline to which they have been subjected, and by performing to the best of one's ability, children also have the opportunity to pay homage to their teachers. The

Figure 10.2 Costume for the female welcome dance, Tari Panyembrama. *Photograph by the author.*

showing of respect and reverence is indicative of the teacher–student relationship within the Balinese context, where tutelage by a highly regarded teacher not only legitimizes a student's position in a particular pedagogical lineage but also serves to elevate or reaffirm the standing of the teacher within a village or district. Such recognition is critical to the reputation of an individual teacher and can ultimately influence whether or not they will be invited to perform or teach in other villages nearby or further afield. In Keramas, Happy and Wayan maintain their position as renowned teachers by successfully training children to perform within the *sanggar*, a process that provides children with the technical skills and necessary experience to perform at both ceremonial and secular events.

The body discipline acquired by children, as a result of their training, also follows them outside the sanggar. This can be observed in the way children carry themselves and how they watch, discuss and comment upon the practice of other dancers. Such behaviour, as Wulff (1998a) points out in her study of the career and culture of ballet dancers, is not particular to dancers in Bali. However, what is particular to child dancers in the Balinese context is how such a process enables older children to differentiate between the quality of a dancer's technique and the style of their performance. Consequently, children in the advanced level of the *sanggar* are able to vocalize the boundary of what is socially acceptable in relation to traditional dance performance. Older children then apply this knowledge to their learning of dances not taught to them by their teachers at the *sanggar*.[11] This most often occurs as a result of watching dance performances broadcast on the Balinese television channel, Bali TV, or from viewing Balinese dance video compact discs (VCDs) and digital video discs (DVDs). Thus by possessing such instinctive mnemonic practices, children from the advanced level of the *sanggar*, more than those who study at the elementary and intermediate levels, reinforce traditional dance and social boundaries through 'the capacity to reproduce a certain performance' (Connerton 1989: 22).

Conclusion

This chapter has examined how, in the process of preparing and presenting children for performance in a Balinese village dance studio, teachers exercise power over children's bodies. The time immediately before a performance can be a fraught period for children and dance teachers alike. In performance, children must perform dances from memory and sometimes have to adjust quickly to new forms of choreography. These new forms of choreography are often different from those rehearsed by children during their twice-weekly dance lessons, and teachers have to exercise power over children to ensure that they will dance to the best of their ability and, more importantly, perform without mistakes. In order to refine children's positions and technique, the teachers employ teaching methods that are heavily reliant upon bodily manipulation and kinaesthetic transfers, and particular attention is paid to minute details of performance at all levels. Sometimes teachers use severe instruction methods, including shouting and handling boys and girls in a somewhat rough manner, to speed up the children's learning of performance choreography or to imprint movements or positions into pupils' bodies. This imprinting, especially by means of kinaesthetic transference, ensures that the children's bodies become disciplined and their teachers can easily manipulate them. Such an approach reinforces Foucault's (1991) notion of body discipline where a skilled body can better be manipulated than an unskilled body, and illustrates the power exercised by the dance teachers over children.

By examining children's dance performances in a Balinese dance studio, this chapter not only extends the work of anthropologists who have focused upon notions of power and discipline in relation to their research (see Fardon 1985; Gledhill 1994), but it also contributes to the ways in which 'ethnographers may strive to specify how, by whom, and to what effect cultural modes of discipline may be evoked, negotiated and enacted' (Dyck 2008: 12). In Bali learning to perform is an important part of the dance learning process. Furthermore, as a result of the 'backstage ethnography' (Wulff 1998b: 104) presented here, it should be obvious that the preparation and presentation of children before a performance is a serious business, one where adults pay due attention and care to ensure that boys and girls look professional and that they are able to dance to the best of their ability. By disciplining children's bodies and exercising power over children's performances, dance teachers also serve to promote the reputation of their organization. Of course, teachers stand to benefit financially if, as a result of these performances, more children choose to attend dance lessons. However, in Keramas, such an increase in the number of students would proffer little financial reward due to the small monthly fee children pay to attend lessons. Instead, the primary focus for the teachers is to maintain their status in the village through the successful training of young dancers and, by developing in their students an elevated sense of bodily discipline, to enable children to become active participants in the wider community through dance.

Notes

1. In the remainder of the chapter I will refer to Sanggar Tari Mumbul Sari simply as the *sanggar* as this was how the dance teachers and the children referred to the organization.
2. In 2003 the College of the Indonesian Arts in Denpasar, the capital city of Bali, was re-named the Indonesian Institute of the Arts.
3. Traditionally, there would have been little or no verbal communication between the teacher and a student (Ballinger 1985). During my research, however, the dance teachers employed verbal instructions frequently to correct students during lessons. Such changes are due to the influence of Western dance-teaching techniques, particularly from ballet, employed at what is now the Indonesian Institute of the Arts, Denpasar.
4. A gamelan orchestra is an ensemble, synonymous with the Indonesian islands of Java and Bali, consisting of metallophones, gongs and drums. During lessons and performances at the *sanggar*, cassette tape recordings of gamelan music accompany children's dance lessons and performances.
5. For accounts relating to the teaching and learning practices in other Balinese music and dance studios see Hough (2000), Kellar (2000) and Downing (2008).
6. Dibia and Ballinger (2004: 20) contend that the use of bright colours for eye make-up in the Balinese performing arts is a modern development stemming from the introduction of television. Traditionally, such vivid colours would not have been used.

7. *Kebyar* is an onomatopoeic term for 'to explode' or 'to burst open like a flower'. The term denotes a style of Balinese music and dance that evolved circa 1915, and also refers to a particular instrumental ensemble (*gamelan gong kebyar*) (see Tenzer 2000).
8. Other *sanggar* also require children to wear a rehearsal uniform. Generally, these uniforms are similar to the ones worn by children in Keramas. However, individual *sanggar* have their own tee-shirts which vary in colour and design; these tee-shirts are important markers of identification and *sanggar* membership.
9. Similarly, in their introduction to the Balinese performing arts, Dibia and Ballinger (2004: 20–21) discuss the various ways in which costumes shape and confine a dancer's body in performance.
10. *Tari Margapati* is a transgender dance (*tari bebancihan*), usually but not always performed by a female performer, that depicts the movements of a lion.
11. See McIntosh (2010) for an examination of the ways in which Balinese children and teenagers combine traditional dance aesthetics and performance techniques with local, national and global popular-music dance forms.

References

Ballinger, R. 1985. 'Dance in Bali: The Passing on of a Tradition', *CORD Dance Research Annual* 15(2): 172–83.
Belo, J. 1970. 'A Study of a Balinese Family', in J. Belo (ed.), *Traditional Balinese Culture*. New York: Columbia University Press, pp.350–70.
Blacking, J. 1977. 'Towards an Anthropology of the Body', in J. Blacking (ed.), *The Anthropology of the Body*. London: Academic Press, pp.1–28.
Connerton, P. 1989. *How Societies Remember*. Cambridge: Cambridge University Press.
Dibia, I.W., and R. Ballinger. 2004. *Balinese Dance, Drama and Music: A Guide to the Performing Arts of Bali*. Singapore: Periplus Editions.
Downing, S.L. 2008. 'Ajuna's Angels: Girls Learning Gamelan Music in Bali', Ph.D. dissertation. Santa Barbara: University of California.
Dyck, N. 2008. 'Anthropological Perspectives on Discipline: An Introduction to the Issues', in N. Dyck (ed.), *Exploring Regimes of Discipline: The Dynamics of Restraint*. Oxford: Berghahn, pp.1–22.
Fardon, R. (ed.). 1985. *Power and Knowledge: Anthropological and Sociological Approaches*. Edinburgh: Scottish Academic Press.
Foucault, M. 1991. *Discipline and Punish: The Birth of the Prison*, trans. A.M. Sheridan. London: Penguin.
Geertz, C. 1973. *The Interpretation of Cultures*. New York: Basic Books.
Gledhill, J. 1994. *Power and its Disguises: Anthropological Perspectives on Politics*. London: Pluto.
Hough, B.W. 2000. 'The College of Indonesian Arts, Denpasar: Nation, State and the Performing Arts in Bali', Ph.D. dissertation. Melbourne: Monash University.
Kealiinohomoku, J.W. 1979. 'You Dance What You Wear, and You Wear Your Cultural Values', in J.M. Cordwell and R.A. Schwarz (eds), *The Fabrics of Culture: The Anthropology of Clothing and Adornment*. The Hague: Mouton, pp.77–83.
Kellar, N. 2000. 'The Politics of Performance: Gender Identity in Arja and Other Contemporary Balinese Theatre Forms', Ph.D. dissertation. Melbourne: Monash University.
Lukes, S. 1974. *Power: A Radical View*. Houndmills: Macmillan.

McIntosh, J. 2006. 'How Playing, Singing and Dancing Shape the Ethnographer: Research with Children in a Village Dance Studio in Bali, Indonesia', *Anthropology Matters* 8(2). Retrieved 20 March 2011 from: http://www.anthropologymatters.com/journal/2006-2/index.htm.

———— 2010. 'Dancing to a Disco Beat? Children, Teenagers and the Localizing of Popular Music in Bali, Indonesia', *Asian Music* 41(1): 1–35.

———— n.d. 'Gendering Emotional Connections in a Balinese Landscape: Exploring Children's Roles in a *Barong* Performance', in F. Magowan and L. Wrazen (eds), *Performing Gender, Place and Emotion*. Rochester, NY: University of Rochester Press.

Polanyi, M. 1958. *Personal Knowledge: Towards a Post-critical Philosophy*. London: Routledge and Kegan Paul.

Roach, M.E., and J.B. Eicher. 1979. 'The Language of Personal Adornment', in J.M. Cordwell and R.A. Schwarz (eds), *The Fabrics of Culture: The Anthropology of Clothing and Adornment*. The Hague: Mouton, pp.7–21.

Tenzer, M. 2000. *Gamelan Gong Kebyar: The Art of Twentieth-century Balinese Music*. Chicago: University of Chicago Press.

Turner, V. 1964. 'Symbols in Ndembu Ritual', in M. Gluckman (ed.), *Closed Systems and Open Minds: The Limits of Naïvety in Social Anthropology*. Edinburgh: Oliver and Boyd, pp.20–51.

Wulff, H. 1995. 'Introducing Youth Culture in Its Own Right: The State of the Art and New Possibilities', in V. Amit-Talai and H. Wulff (eds), *Youth Cultures: A Cross-cultural Perspective*. London: Routledge, pp.1–18.

———— 1998a. *Ballet Across Borders: Career and Culture in the World of Dancers*. Oxford: Berg.

———— 1998b. 'Perspectives Towards Ballet Performance: Exploring, Repairing and Maintaining Frames', in F. Hughes-Freeland (ed.), *Ritual, Performance, Media*. London: Routledge, pp.104–20.

———— 2002. 'Aesthetics at the Ballet: Looking at "National" Style, Body and Clothing in the London Ballet World', in N. Rapport (ed.), *British Subjects: An Anthropology of Britain*. Oxford: Berg, pp.67–83.

———— 2006. 'Experiencing the Ballet Body: Pleasure, Pain and Power', in S. Reily (ed.), *The Musical Human: Rethinking John Blacking's Ethnomusicology in the Twenty-first Century*. Aldershot: Ashgate, pp.125–41.

Epilogue

Making Culture through Dance

Caroline Potter

The title of this volume highlights the exasperating yet poetic fluidity of both 'dance' and 'culture'. Both are unstable analytical constructs, reflecting collective lived experiences that are constantly in flux. As the editors point out, both dance and culture become in their doing. That culture is co-constructed through intersubjective engagement is given. But culture cannot be confined to a list of things that can be objectified; it is instead the metaphorical cooking stock, the communal medium of exchange in which we as social beings simmer that renders our world mutually comprehensible. That medium is continually replenished and infused with fresh flavours through our social acts, of which speaking and the exchange of material goods are but two examples.

There is a tendency to talk about dance as a form of 'embodied culture', implying that a culture which is 'out there' in the form of ideas (conveyed through language) and the physical environment is somehow translated 'in here' (within the body) and then represented through movement and performance. Certainly this bodily aspect of cultural reproduction is important to recognize, given the long and spurious absence of scholarly writing about the body throughout most of the twentieth century, albeit with a few notable exceptions.[1] However, 'embodied culture' reflects only one half of the mutually constitutive relationship between living bodies and society. That culture stems from bodies, rather than simply being deposited within them, has been forcefully argued by authors working within the embodiment paradigm in anthropology.[2] As highlighted by Novack (1990: 8) in her insightful ethnographic description of contact improvisation, and as collectively demonstrated by the contributors to this volume, dancing is a way of making culture – not merely reflecting it. Hughes-Freeland (this volume) emphasizes this standpoint succinctly in arguing for the consideration of dance not as 'a product or commodity which is transacted', but rather a series of social relationships 'which organise the many kinds of transactions that are found with the process of dancing across cultures'.

As an act of culture-making, dance is by definition a co-constructed process. Acts of dancing are intended to be seen, heard, smelt and felt by others. They exist only through social engagement. This may seem an obvious point, but given the tendency of many people (academic or not) to equate 'dance' with 'art' or with culture as a product, which is attributed to individual choreographers or performers and is thus devoid of much of its social history, it is a point that warrants repeating. In focusing on acts of dancing as they are co-created within today's rapid flows of people and information, the authors of this volume provide a range of empirical evidence for dancing as a particularly effective means of making and remaking culture. Observation of dancing bodies within the context of globalization and transnationalism raises fundamental questions regarding our perceptions and understandings of culture itself: Where can we empirically locate culture within fields of moving bodies? How do these acts of dancing signal to us that culture is not static but changing over time? What political agendas are enacted, which may instigate cultural shifts, when people come together to dance? And who is implicated as the 'we' and 'they' who create culture in the doing of dance? The wide-ranging and palpable ethnographic description provided within this volume goes some way towards addressing these questions, and therefore towards illuminating the relationship between (making) dance and (making) culture more broadly.

The volume is organized around three themes: globalization, tourism, and youth and national identity. The fact that each of these themes has been addressed by a plethora of anthropologists, many of whom do not focus on dance specifically, indicates the fruitful intellectual cross-fertilization that has occurred and will hopefully continue between dance scholars and social scientists (who are not, of course, always mutually exclusive groupings). As indicated by the authors, there is extensive supporting literature for each of these three themes, which therefore prove useful for framing a comparative analysis of dance in global context. But for me the volume taken as a whole prompted thinking about different (but related) scholarly debates: on cultural hegemony, on identity more broadly, and on bodily grounded sociality.

Dancing in Relation to the Dominant Order

A focus on international flows underscoring the mass engagement with ballet or jive (described by Wulff and Skinner respectively) might suggest that the spread of these dance forms, in line with other processes implicated in globalization, serve to reinforce a cultural dominance of Euro-American sensibilities and aesthetics. This 'McDonaldization of society', as it is disparagingly called, seemingly comes at the expense of movement forms that were historically developed among minority groups. This reminds us of some of the criticisms that Joann Kealiinohomoku (2001[1970]) levelled at dance scholars in her groundbreaking article, namely that in designating Euro-American ballet as 'high[est] art' and failing to recognize it as one form of 'ethnic dance' among many, writers such as Sorell were relegating all other forms of dancing to the category of 'primitive', with descriptions of frenzy and spontaneity that Kealiinohomoku argued were not supported by empirical observation of those forms within their social contexts.

However, recent developments in contemporary dance, such as the popularity of 'fusion' forms and institutional support for such forms as South Asian dances within the UK, for example, challenge the assumption of increasing cultural homogeneity. Anthropologists of dance have demonstrated that (some) historically marginalized people have found cultural traction and social recognition through performance on a national or international stage. Neveu Kringelbach's chapter in this volume is exemplary in this regard, for bringing to light the nuanced and unpredictable ways in which dancers from the southern Casamance regions of Senegal (or their second- and subsequent generation descendants in urban Dakar) have in various settings evoked Jola ethnicity, a (possibly unfounded) sense of regional cohesiveness, or Senegalese nationalism in order to further both individual and social agendas. Lüdtke similarly documents the unprecedented popularity of Salentine performance on the 'world music' stage, through which people associated with the tarantula dance have transformed their local image from backwardness and marginalization to celebration as a regional icon.

Even within a Euro-American context, ethnographic evidence suggests that dances are not imposed onto the masses by a central source of cultural dominance, but work their way upwards and outwards through a series of unpredictable improvisations undertaken by a multitude of dancing bodies. As Skinner's chapter attests, dance forms may be co-opted and redefined in an attempt to homogenize them (Cronin's Ceroc franchise, for example), but equally dancers might resist such codification by emphasizing a form's mish-mash of historical influences (such as salsa). Of course it is critical to recognize the power dynamics that influence the scale and direction of culture-making; Neveu Kringelbach's portrayal of Senghor's connection to Paris-based elites and his subsequent rise to political power renders the story of the cultural coup of troupes from Casamance all the more compelling. But in spite of the implicit or explicit efforts of those in positions of political and economic authority, the dancers portrayed within this volume do not seem to be all that 'disciplined' in the Foucauldian sense,[3] and certainly not merely the unwitting victims of an oppressive cultural machinery.

Dancing Multiple Identities

In the Introduction the editors signal that 'identity' as a singular entity has been sufficiently deconstructed by anthropologists: 'national identities always intersect with other identities shaped by gender, generation, race and class. Nowhere is this as evident as in performance' (p.15). Like 'culture', identity cannot be understood as a clearly defined and stable aspect of one's being. Instead it is a mode of social definition that may be performed in multiple ways to different audiences, and that may change within new environments or across the life course. The multiple identities through which people live may be described in terms of, but are not limited to, sociological categories such as gender, age, ethnicity, nationality and occupation. Expressions of identities serve to engender senses of collective belonging, to articulate who one is (in relation to others) as well as who one is not. The notion of identity thus has political undertones, as self-defined groups (and individuals within them) jockey for position within increasingly complex landscapes of power.

Chapters in this volume highlight the nation-state as a salient identity category that can be created, challenged and redefined through acts of dancing. The descriptive text contained within these chapters, however, implicitly critiques the very idea of 'national dance'. In line with the recognition of earlier anthropologists of the deeply rooted biases of the researcher (e.g., Leach 1966: 46), framing acts of dancing in national terms might do more to illuminate our own privileged perspective as cosmopolitan intellectuals than it does to elicit the motivations (nationalist or otherwise) of the dancers who are described.[4] While the dances might evoke notions of national identity among their mobile 'world citizen' observers, who move across and thus are keenly aware of the boundaries between nation-states, the dancers' own concerns might centre on very different aspects of their multiple identities. For example, Wulff's chapter on the uneasy relationships that exist between ballet dancers in reputed national companies on the one hand, and corporate sponsors and private donors on the other, hints at more immediate (bodily) levels of identity – those of professional occupation and social class – which may give rise to a sense of commonality irrespective of national allegiance. Evoking Bourdieu's notions of habitus (Bourdieu 1977), her analysis highlights the differing forms of capital that various participants in dance performances may seek to acquire through the encounter. For dancers it is an opportunity to build their own credibility and reputations as performers as they strive to create magical moments of transformative artistic experience. For their patrons, meanwhile, it may be much less about accessing the experience of ballet itself than the experience of being seen by and conversing with other philanthropic elites within the space of the theatre.

Theodossopoulos's work highlights the importance of community-level identity in guiding the dancing of his informants: 'when we [the Parara Puru community] do something successfully, they [the Embera of other communities] want to do it as well' (p.130). This could be interpreted, as Theodossopoulos does, as a desire among all Embera to create performances that are 'representative' of Embera-ness throughout the region. Equally, it might hint at a degree of rivalry between communities that spurs on creativity. Nájera-Ramírez documents the explicit creation and negotiation of 'Mexican' identity through *folklórico* dance, in juxtaposition to experiences within the neighbouring United States. In reality this is a transnational identity rather than a Mexican one, capturing shared feelings of distance and longing among migrants within their new context. The final two chapters of the volume, by Carrausse and McIntosh, leave me with some lingering questions on this theme: Does an anthropological preoccupation with discussing various forms of dancing in terms of national identity reflect the concerns of, as per their examples, Korean or Balinese youth in an increasingly global political economy? At what stage in the life course and to what extent do young dancers engage with nationalist discourse? Ongoing ethnographic research will be crucial for further illuminating the complexities of dancing multiple identities.

Dancing as Visceral Sociality

Dancing is certainly not the only kind of social act for culture-making; the hosting of international sporting events or the uptake and creative adaptation of 'foreign' foods spring to mind as two possibilities (among myriad others) for stirring the cultural soup. What is it, then, about various acts of dancing that compels some anthropologists to examine them as a category of their own? The contributors to this volume hint at an answer. The ephemeral nature of dancing, combined with its bodily immediacy, make it difficult to ignore in the short term. In being there, in witnessing and/or participating in the dancing, one recognizes the living, vital presence of others. Acts of dancing must be created again and again, providing great flexibility in the strength of relationships formed between participants and space for negotiating the meanings generated through each new encounter.

The reference in the Introduction to this volume to Evans-Pritchard's early description of Zande dance (Evans-Pritchard 1928) is fitting. Like this seminal article, the chapters gathered here demonstrate that the social power of dance lies in the coming together that occurs for the purpose of producing, or in response to witnessing, acts of dancing. The rhythmic, out-of-the-ordinary character of dancing calls us to take notice and engage with others who are dancing. The ambiguity of its meaning as a communicative form allows for a first encounter between people who perceive themselves to be culturally distant from one another, with at least a possibility for more meaningful and longer-term engagement. Although far from a 'universal language', acts of dancing may evoke a collective sense of bodily presence among strangers that might not be possible (at least to the same extent) through other social acts such as speaking or writing. Understanding acts of dancing in the first instance as a coming together has methodological implications. In their ongoing and future ethnographic projects, anthropologists of dance should continue to document who comes together to participate in the dancing (as creator, dancer and/or observer), what draws them (a professional obligation, a larger festival or ritual event, an advertisement, a spontaneous encounter with a live performance, and so on), and what those who attend to the dancing start to do (in sync or in parallel with others) during the encounter. In this way the living bodies of those who dance are integral to the ethnographic presentation, rather than the writing being limited to 'the dance' as an abstract but rather disembodied concept.

Authors within this volume highlight the multiple levels of bodily engagement that are possible in short-term dance encounters. Scarangella-McNenly presents the more removed perspective of the feasting tourists, who literally consume ideas of local culture while observing Coastal Salish dancers during dinner-time theatre. In contrast, the spontaneous 'disco' that Hughes-Freeland observed when a Vietnamese visiting delegation took to the stage during a choreographed performance by their Lao hosts gives the sense of a more mutual bodily synchrony, such as the 'striking' moment when the dancers crouched down together at the same point in the song (p.105). The managed social dancing between Embera performers and their international visitors described by Theodossopoulos seems to fall somewhere in between. The relative differences in levels of 'cultural distance' between dancers and members of the audience is secondary to the fact that, first and foremost, acts of dancing require a basic acknowledgement of the presence of, for example, Coastal Salish people in British Columbia, whether or not the audiences fully validate the performers' cultural claims (Scarangella-McNenly, p.84). Hughes-Freeland goes further in highlighting deeper levels of bodily engagement that can occur through longer-term 'tourist' relationships, such as ongoing exchanges between visiting dance scholars and choreographers who come from abroad to study with celebrated local teachers.

The sociality fostered through acts of dancing can be described as 'visceral'. Parkin uses this term, referring to 'both the insides of the physical body and the "inner states" of emotional expression' (Parkin 2007: 241), when discussing the palpable social energy that may be generated among crowds. For him the term also signals the connections between people that go on 'between as well as within bodies' (Parkin 2007: 241), and in using it he attempts to transcend earlier distinctions between 'the biological' and 'the social' as discreet aspects of human life. Building on Durkheim's notion of 'effervescence' (Durkheim 1957[1915]: 190), Parkin suggests that moments of 'visceral charge' (Parkin 2007: 244) – ranging from the ecstasy of religious gatherings to the violent trauma of nationalist riots – are unpredictable in their outcomes (which can have lasting personal or political ramifications) precisely because these encounters are strongly physically felt and temporarily suspend everyday patterns of relatedness. In viewing the acts of dancing described by this volume's contributors as examples of bodily grounded sociality, with the potential for producing the kind of 'visceral charge' that can interrupt the usual flow of human relations, we can begin to understand why a coming together through dance might be a particularly effective means of culture-making, and why anthropologists should continue to give it serious attention.

Concluding Remarks

The opening paragraphs of this volume's Introduction imply connections between form and place in the social production of dances. But these chapters collectively (and refreshingly) do not reproduce such reified interpretations of 'the dance' as rigid and belonging to one group or geographic area. The emphasis on transnational flows and the social production of performance (especially between dancers and their various audiences), as portrayed through ethnographic description, elucidates the contingency and flexibility of each dance form as it continually emerges in its social and historical context.

The editors work from the starting point that culture can be understood as 'the meanings and practices acquired (in various ways) in social life' (p.10), and that by focusing on acts of dancing, anthropologists will be better able to understand and comment upon culture (p.10). Certainly this is a worthy project, as the intangibility and slipperiness of 'culture' mean that we as researchers must identify its more readily perceptible manifestations (such as dancing) in order to describe and analyse what culture is. But if anything, the chapters in this volume highlight the insufficiency of defining culture as merely a catalogue of shared meanings and practices. Culture is not the dance itself; rather, it is a tacit and durable sensibility of mutual understanding, a feeling of 'simmering within the same pot' (to use the aforementioned analogy of cooking stock), that may arise through the repeated coming together of dance participants over time. Thus, the Embera of Parara Puru who practice and perform together day after day (and year upon year) have a sense of living within a common medium, in a way that a visiting tourist from a cruise ship who takes part in a one-off performance will not. But the collective responses of the dancers to the tourists, the flows and negotiations that surround the creation and enactment of dances (as documented by the volume's authors), suggest that culture as a feeling of visceral sociality exists.

A general ethnographic principle also emerges from this volume: a bodily compulsion calls each author to actively take part in the dancing. Among anthropologists interested in dance, there seems to be a collective move while in the field from the analytical distance of 'participant observation' to the sweaty, sensuous encounter of 'participant experience' (Hsu 1999: 15; Skinner 2005) – a shift that anthropologists following other topical interests might be less keen to make. Perhaps the former perspective, with which we still engage (particularly during writing up and other acts of academic representation), condemns us to remain nothing more than 'long-term tourists' as far as our informants are concerned. Participant experience, however, necessitates a heightened degree of bodily vulnerability on the part of the researcher, which might allow for more robust acts of culture-making in concert with those whom we study. In spite of the discipline's reflexive turn, anthropologists still struggle at times to adequately locate themselves within the field and recognize their research as co-constructed cultural products. Anthropologists who dance in the field, by virtue of the obviousness of their presence to both themselves and their research participants, could take the lead in continuing to develop a more embodied, reflexive way of working. The authors of this volume do not explicitly make such a call, but their work speaks for itself: dancing culture is not done merely by British ceroc-ers, professional ballet dancers, Salentine musicians at international festivals, Coastal Salish performers at the Híwus feast house, Javanese dance teachers, the Embera of Parara Puru in specially constructed dance spaces, the Casamance performing troupes of Dakar, Mexican *folklórico* dancers, South Korean youth or Balinese children. In engaging with their dances again and again, and on reflecting on that engagement in these chapters, these authors are making and remaking culture as well, on an increasingly global scale.

Notes

1. See, e.g., Mauss (1979[1934]), Merleau-Ponty (1962), Blacking (1977) and Bourdieu (1977).
2. See, e.g., the various contributions to Csordas (1994).
3. Foucault speaks of an invisible yet pervasive power that makes bodies 'docile' through subtle but unceasing monitoring, with reference to the panoptican design of prisons and other examples of the modern 'machinery of power', such as the industrial factory (Foucault 1991[1975]: 142). While these institutional forces may well be at work in the

settings described in this volume, I did not feel that they were strongly emphasized or clearly illuminated by the authors.
4. Calhoun (2008) describes inherent tensions in discourses of cosmopolitanism. On the one hand it is an ideal that emphasizes a common humanity and offers an 'ethics of globalisation' (Calhoun 2008: 429) grounded in individual rights (and therefore seemingly transcending ethnic and nationalist politics). However, its realization simultaneously requires action aimed at various 'systems and technologies', including nation-states. Calhoun argues that 'cosmopolitanism is not free-floating, not equally available to everyone, not equally empowering for everyone' (Calhoun 2008: 434) and thus can give rise to a renewed awareness and defence of national boundaries, even as elite global travellers (including academic researchers) are able to cross those boundaries more easily.

References

Blacking, J. (ed.). 1977. *The Anthropology of the Body*. London: Academic Press.
Bourdieu, P. 1977. *Outline of a Theory of Practice*, trans. R. Nice. Cambridge: Cambridge University Press.
Calhoun, C. 2008. 'Cosmopolitanism and Nationalism', *Nations and Nationalism* 14(3): 427–48.
Csordas, T.J. (ed.). 1994. *Embodiment and Experience: The Existential Ground of Culture and Self*. Cambridge: Cambridge University Press.
Durkheim, E. 1957[1915]. *The Elementary Forms of Religious Life*, trans. J.W. Swain. London: Allen and Unwin.
Evans-Pritchard, E.E. 1928. 'The Dance', *Africa* 1(4): 446–62.
Foucault, M. 1991[1975]. *Discipline and Punish: The Birth of the Prison*, trans. A. Sheridan. London: Penguin.
Hsu, E. 1999. *The Transmission of Chinese Medicine*. Cambridge: Cambridge University Press.
Kealiinohomoku, J. 2001[1970]. 'An Anthropologist Looks at Ballet as a Form of Ethnic Dance', in A. Dils and A.Cooper Albright (eds), *Moving History / Dancing Culture: A Dance History Reader*. Middletown: Wesleyan University Press, pp.33–43.
Leach, E. 1966. 'Virgin Birth', *Proceedings of the Royal Anthropological Institute of Great Britain and Ireland, 1966*, pp.39–49.
Mauss, M. 1979[1934]. 'Techniques of the Body', in *Sociology and Psychology: Essays*, trans. B. Brewster. London: Routledge and Kegan Paul, pp.95–123.
Merleau-Ponty, M. 1962. *Phenomenology of Perception*, trans. C. Smith. London: Routledge and Kegan Paul.
Novack, C. 1990. *Sharing the Dance: Contact Improvisation and American Culture*. Madison: University of Wisconsin Press.
Parkin, D. 2007. 'The Visceral in the Social: The Crowd as Paradigmatic Type', in D. Parkin and S. Ulijaszek (eds), *Holistic Anthropology: Emergence and Convergence*. Oxford: Berghahn, pp.234–54.
Skinner, J. 2005. 'Embodiment in Teaching and Learning in Anthropology', *Anthropology in Action* 12(2): v–ix.

Notes on Contributors

Séverine Carrausse holds a doctorate in sociology from the Ecole des Hautes Etudes en Sciences Sociales, Paris. Her primary research interest is in higher education systems and student sociability, with a focus on youth education and lifestyle in South Korea, France and Portugal. Her other research interests include proximity and interaction in social space, border areas, social and educational violence and inequality, inheritance and urban–rural development.

Felicia Hughes-Freeland is a Research Associate at the Centre for Southeast Asian Studies, SOAS, London University. She was previously a Reader in Social Anthropology at the University of Swansea. She has researched dance in Indonesia for thirty years. She has published widely on performance, ritual, media, gender and anthropological theory. She is the author of *Embodied Communities: Dance Traditions and Change in Java* (2008) and editor of *Ritual, Performance, Media* (1998) and *Recasting Ritual* (1998). She trained in documentary film-making at the National Film and Television School, and two of her ethnographic films, *The Dancer and the Dance* (1988) and *Tayuban: Dancing the Spirit in Java* (1996) are distributed by the Royal Anthropological Institute. Her current research is a comparative study of performance, heritage and ownership in South-east Asia.

Karen Lüdtke received her D.Phil. in Social Anthropology from the University of Oxford. She has published on her research on performance arts and well-being in the Salento, Southern Italy, in edited volumes and is the author of *Dances with Spiders: Crisis, Celebrity and Celebration in Southern Italy* (2009)/Italian translation *Balla coi ragni. La tarantola tra crisi e celebrazioni* (2011).

Jonathan McIntosh is Assistant Professor of Ethnomusicology at the School of Music, The University of Western Australia. His work is focused on the practice and performance of dance, music and song among children in Bali, Indonesia. He has published articles on Balinese music and dance, music pedagogy, applied ethnomusicology and the Indonesian diaspora in Western Australia in journals such as *Anthropology in Action*, *Anthropology Matters*, *Asian Music* and *Asia Pacific Journal of Anthropology*.

Olga Nájera-Ramírez is Professor of Anthropology at the University of California, Santa Cruz. As an anthropologist specializing in folklore, she has concentrated on documenting and critically examining expressive culture among Mexicans in both Mexico and the United States. She is author of *La Fiesta de los Tastoanes: Critical Perspectives in a Mexican Festival Performance* (1997), and also produced the award-winning video, *La Charreada: Rodeo a la Mexicana* (1997). She is co-editor of a number of volumes, including *Chicana Traditions: Continuity and Change* (2002), *Chicana Feminisms: A Critical Reader* (2003) and *Dancing Across Borders: Danzas y Bailes Mexicanos* (2009). She recently completed a bilingual documentary that traces the transnational development of Mexican *folklórico* dance through the experiences and artistic productions of the internationally acclaimed choreographer Rafael Zamarripa, titled *Danza Folklórica Escénica: El Sello Artístico de Rafael Zamarripa* (2010).

Hélène Neveu Kringelbach was a Lecturer in Anthropology and African Studies at the University of Oxford (2006-2011). Currently a researcher at the African Studies Centre in Oxford, she is working on a Leverhulme-funded research project on Euro-Senegalese families. Her previous research focused on dance troupes and self-fashioning in urban Senegal, the subject of a forthcoming monograph with Berghahn Books. Her a longer-term research interests include performance and popular culture in Senegal and in the diaspora, Casamançais dance troupes, contemporary dance in Africa, and transnational families across Europe and Africa.

Caroline Potter is Lecturer in Anthropology at the University of Oxford. Her previous research into dance involved full-time professional dance training at The Place in London, and her current work explores processes of embodiment and ongoing debates about body–mind dualism, with specific interests in dance and obesity. She is deputy director of the interdisciplinary Unit for Biocultural Variation and Obesity (www.oxfordobesity.org), which includes a working group of researchers and professional artists exploring medical and lay perceptions of 'the energized body'.

Linda Scarangella-McNenly obtained her Ph.D. in Anthropology from McMaster University, Canada. She later completed her Postdoctoral Fellowship at the Institute for Comparative Studies in Literature, Art, and Culture (ICSLAC), Carleton University, Canada. She has published in the area of tourism and native performances in the Wild West and is currently writing and researching Kahnawake (Mohawk) historical experiences with regard to exhibitions and other performance spaces. Her general research and teaching interests include the First Nations of Canada, identity and indigeneity, representation, performance and visual culture, the anthropology of tourism, narrative and oral history, and ethnohistory.

Jonathan Skinner is Senior Lecturer in Social Anthropology in the School of History and Anthropology, Queen's University Belfast. His current research interests are in social dance communities, salsa, ballroom and jive in particular. He is author of *Before the Volcano: Reverberations of Identity on Montserrat* (2004), co-editor of *Managing Island Life* (2006) and *Great Expectations: Imagination and Anticipation in Tourism* (2011), and a former editor of the journal *Anthropology in Action* (2001–2007).

Dimitrios Theodossopoulos is a Reader at the University of Kent. His earlier work examined people–wildlife conflicts and indigenous perceptions of the environment in Greece. He is currently working on ethnic stereotypes, indigeneity, authenticity and the politics of cultural representation in Panama and South-east Europe. He is the author of *Troubles with Turtles: Cultural Understandings of the Environment on a Greek Island* (2003); he is also editor of *When Greeks Think about Turks: The View from Anthropology* (2006) and co-editor of *United in Discontent: Local Responses to Cosmopolitanism and Globalization* (2009) and *Great Expectations: Imagination and Anticipation in Tourism* (2011).

Helena Wulff is Professor in the Department of Social Anthropology, Stockholm University. Her current research focuses on cultural form and expressive forms of culture from a transnational perspective. Studies of the transnational world of dance and social memory through dance have generated questions in relation to place, mobility and emotions, and visual culture. Her most recent research concerns writing and contemporary Irish literature as cultural process and form. She is the author of *Ballet across Borders: Career and Culture in the World of Dancers* (1998) and *Dancing at the Crossroads: Memory and Mobility in Ireland* (2009); she is also the editor of *The Emotions: A Cultural Reader* (2007) and co-editor of *Ethnographic Practice in the Present* (2010). Between 2006 and 2010 she was editor-in-chief (with Dorle Dracklé) of *Social Anthropology/Anthropologie Sociale*, the journal of the European Association of Social Anthropologists (EASA).

Index

Adams, Kathleen, 78, 81, 86, 91, 93
aesthetics, 12, 19, 88, 91, 161, 201, 205, 212
Africa, 7, 9, 20, 34–6, 38, 145–6, 152, 158, 220
  East Africa, 9, 95
  South Africa, 9
  West Africa, 9, 20, 22, 34–5, 38, 145–6, 152, 158–9
African-Americans, 31, 33, 35
Apolito, Paolo, 65, 67
Appadurai, Arjun, 35–6, 38, 43
Argentina, 15
audience, 2, 10–11, 12, 17, 31, 33–4, 36–7, 46, 49–50, 52–4, 56–8, 61, 63, 82, 86, 88, 93–4, 94n8, 100–101, 104, 109, 111–12, 116, 121–23, 125, 130–31, 133–4, 145, 147–8, 150, 154–7, 161, 163, 168, 173, 182–3, 187, 195, 199, 200, 202, 204, 213, 216
authentic, 11, 16–8, 40, 62, 79–80, 86, 91–3, 95n18, 107, 122, 135, 146, 165, 174
  authenticity, 14, 16–18, 61, 63, 68, 77–8, 90–93, 121–2, 134–5, 136n2, 161
  staged authenticity, 92–3

Bakalama, 149–51, 153, 155–6, 158nn11–12, 159n17
Bali, 19, 103, 110, 117, 123, 194–7, 199, 201–8

ballet, 5–6, 10, 13–16, 18, 20n8, 46, 48–57, 58n1, 114, 116, 146–8, 150, 152, 158n7, 158n9, 161–3, 165–71, 173–5, 195, 207, 208n3, 212, 214, 217
ballet folklórico, 18, 161–3, 168, 170, 174
Banes, Sally, 7, 20n4
Becker, Howard, 54
Blacking, John, 7, 199, 217, 218n1
Boas, Franz, 4, 6, 95n13
body, 1–2, 5, 7–8, 11–14, 17, 20n7, 21–5, 31, 33, 42–4, 59, 66–7, 73, 78–9, 105, 122, 138–9, 145, 154, 17–19, 181, 188, 193, 195–9, 201, 204–5, 207–8, 209n9, 210–11, 216, 218, 220
  discipline, 196, 199, 207–8
  see also embodiment
Bourdieu, Pierre, 12, 49, 56, 177, 192n11, 192n16, 214, 217n1, 218
Brandon, James, 110–12, 114, 116
Browning, Barbara, 11
Brumann, Christoph, 10
Bruner, Edward, 17, 78, 80–81, 90–92, 108, 122, 135
Buckland, Theresa, 101

Calloway, Cab, 29, 31, 34, 43n1
capoeira, 3, 11
Casamance, 18, 143–4, 146–54, 156–8, 213, 217

Casanova, Martha Heredia, 167
Ceroc, 15, 30, 39, 41–3, 44n6, 102, 213
Chakravorty, Pallabi, 78–9, 88
Chicano civil rights, 18, 171–2
choreography, 5, 13, 18, 51, 53, 110, 111, 114, 121, 126, 148, 150, 152, 167, 171, 173, 186, 196–201, 207
  performance choreography, 200–1, 207
Choreometrics, 9, 17
Cohen, Abner, 144–5
colonialism, 1, 78, 94
commoditization, 14, 15, 16, 17, 30, 63, 116
community, 4, 13, 15, 17, 52, 70, 83–6, 89, 106, 108, 121–8, 130–33, 137, 156, 162, 170, 173–4, 181, 185–7, 190, 192, 200, 208, 214
Conklin, Beth, 122, 134
CORD (Congress for Research on Dance), 6, 20n3
cosmopolitanism, 17, 218n4
costume, 16, 17, 19, 35, 53, 71n11, 85, 104, 110, 116, 146, 154, 162–3, 168–9, 171, 179–80, 195, 197, 202, 203, 204–5, 209n9Cowan, Jane, 8, 192n11
creative, 2, 30, 38, 43, 48, 101, 113, 117, 135, 215
  creativity, 9, 38, 64, 88, 90, 167, 171, 214
Cuba, 20n8, 22, 38, 102, 117
culture, 1–3, 7–15, 17–19, 35–6, 48, 50, 54, 63, 68–9, 77–83, 85, 89–93, 94n1, 100–1, 103, 106, 109, 112–13, 117, 121–3, 126, 129–36, 143–5, 147, 149, 151–8, 161–2, 165, 171–4, 175n4, 178–80, 182, 184–5, 187, 190–91, 195, 207, 211–13, 215–17
  cultural capital, 16, 55, 57
  cultural production, 77, 81–2, 93
  cultural representation, 17, 122–3, 135, 221

cultural revival, 89, 91
cultural tourism, 16, 78, 80, 82, 86, 124–5, 132

Dallal, Alberto, 161, 166–8, 175n7
dance import, 39
dance learning, 103, 208
Daniel, Yvonne, 8, 101, 122, 125, 128, 135
De Martino, Ernesto, 60, 64–5, 68, 70n3, 71n5
Del Giudice, Luisa, 69
Desmond, Jane, 6, 12, 78, 102–3, 115, 117, 135
Di Lecce, Georgio, 60, 70n5
diffusion, 14–15, 30, 34–9
Dunham, Katherine, 5
Durante, Daniele, 61
Durkheim, Emile, 216
Dyck, Noel, 194–5, 208

East Asia, 17, 100–1, 103–5, 107, 109, 111, 113, 115–17, 119, 219
  Southeast Asia, 17, 100–1, 104, 113, 116
Emberá, 17, 214–15, 217
embodiment, 11, 78, 83, 102, 117, 211
  disembodied, 15, 215
  embodied ethnography, 5
  embodied tourism, 100
  see also body
energy, 10, 12, 19, 48, 67, 105, 154, 178, 216
Erenberg, Lewis, 30, 31, 34, 36, 42
ethnicity, 5, 8, 104, 144, 151, 213
ethnochoreology, 6
ethnology, 6
ethnomusicology, 6
eurocentric, 3, 8
Evans-Pritchard, Edward, 4–5, 78, 215

Farnell, Brenda, 2, 5–6, 8, 12
festivals, 56, 100, 105, 109–10, 115–16, 126, 128, 157, 165–6, 217

folk dance, 18, 117, 163, 165, 169, 177
folklore, 7, 146, 157, 167–9, 220
folklórico, *see* Ballet folklórico
Foucault, Michel, 79, 80–81, 94n6, 195–6, 200–1, 217n3
Foucher, Vincent, 146, 148–50, 152, 154, 156, 158n10, 158n16
franchise, 30, 39, 41–3, 213
functionalism, 4

Gbere buda, 4, 5
Geertz, Clifford, 202
Gell, Alfred, 3
gender, 7–8, 12, 15, 69, 151, 177, 181, 190, 192, 196, 213, 219
gesture, 9, 36, 63, 67, 70n5, 71n5, 94n3, 117, 130, 132, 147, 153–5, 177, 182
Giddens, Anthony, 35, 43
Gisaro, 12, 108
globalization, 13, 15–16, 30, 33, 35–9, 41, 43, 46, 57, 62, 64, 68–70, 70n8, 70n13, 134, 162, 212
Goodman, Benny, 31, 33–4, 39, 43n2
Gore, Georgina, 3, 7
Gottschild, Brenda, 7, 33
Graburn, Nelson, 122
Grau, Andrée, 6–7, 19n1, 122, 136

habitus, 3, 12, 13, 181, 192, 214
 hexis, 12
Hanna, Judith, 2, 5, 6–7, 12, 19, 54, 178
Hannerz, Ulf, 10, 35–6, 38, 101–2
heritage, 13, 18, 100, 107, 110, 116–17, 146, 171, 174, 178, 182, 219
hometown association, 149, 151
Howe, J., 134, 137n10
hybrid, 15, 30, 41, 112–13, 116

identification, 1, 69–70, 132, 136, 177, 209n8
identity, 1, 8, 11–12, 14–16, 18, 30, 35, 61–70, 71n7, 78, 82–3, 102, 105, 132–3, 135–6, 151, 156–7, 161–2, 165, 169, 177, 179, 182, 184, 190, 191n6, 192, 212–14
improvisation, 10, 53, 90, 127, 129, 135, 183, 188, 211
indigenous, 11, 15, 17, 66, 77–82, 86, 88, 93–4, 122–3, 125, 128–30, 132–7, 145, 162, 165–7, 173–4
Indonesia, 17, 93, 100, 103–4, 106, 107, 110, 113, 114, 115, 116, 117

Jackson, Michael, 8, 20n6
James, Wendy, 3, 8–9
Java, 15, 106, 109–12, 114–16, 208
jazz, 31, 33, 37
jive, 12, 13, 15, 19, 29, 30–31, 35–7, 39–43, 102, 186, 212, 221
 modern jive, 15, 39–41
Jola, 18, 144, 147, 149, 150–57, 158n16, 213

Kaeppler, Adrienne, 8, 19n1
Kalela dance, 5
 see Mitchell
Kealiinohomoku, Joann, 6–7, 23, 204, 209, 212
Kenya, 3, 17
kinaesthetic, 102, 207–8
Knight, Alan, 165
Kole, Subir, 78–9, 82, 90
Korea, 19, 177–8, 181–5, 187–9, 190nn2–3, 191–3, 219
kulturkreis, 7, 9
Kuranko, 8

Lambert, Michael, 144, 148, 156, 158n15
Langer, Suzanne, 13
Laos, 17, 103–6, 116
Latin, 11, 13, 37–8, 42, 102, 117, 172, 186, 190
 Latin America, 20
lindy hop, 29–30, 32–3, 36, 186
Lomax, 9

Maalouf, Amin, 68–9
Maasai, 17
Maccannell, Dean, 63, 77–9, 90, 93
make-up, 19, 50, 195–7, 202–4, 208n6
Malinowski, Bronislaw, 4
Manchester School, 5
Maquet, Jacques, 58
marijuana, 29
Marion, Jonathan, 12–13
Mark, Peter, 143, 152–3, 155
market, 16–17, 33, 41–2, 46, 49, 51, 53–8, 61, 89, 103, 173
marketing, 15–16, 49–56, 62, 85
Mason, Kaley, 80, 87–8, 92
masquerade, 8
Mauss, Marcel, 2, 12, 217n1
McIntosh, Jonathan, 11, 16, 18–19, 194, 209n11, 214
meaning, 1, 2, 8–9, 11, 13, 16–17, 29, 65, 68, 70, 77, 79, 83–4, 86–90, 92–3, 95n19, 135, 215
Mexico, 18, 161–3, 165–71, 173–4, 175n8
  Mexican revolution, 18, 165–6
migration, 8, 14–15, 43, 62, 114, 123, 125, 148–50, 156, 158n11
  migrants, 9, 13, 15, 144, 148–9, 155, 157, 174, 214
Mitchell, Jonathan, 5
modernity, 9, 14, 43n4, 116, 134, 136n2, 165
motion, 11, 13, 71n6, 85, 145, 178, 180
movement, 2–13, 15, 18–19, 29, 31, 43, 61, 111, 123, 126–8, 135, 143–4, 146, 148, 150–51, 153–5, 162, 165–6, 168, 171–2, 177–81, 183, 196–7, 205, 211–12
multiculturalism, 111
Murray, Arthur, 33, 42–3

Nahachewsky, Andriy, 122, 123
nation, 11, 14–16, 18, 38, 40, 48, 83, 89, 134, 136n2, 144–8, 151, 155–7, 161–2, 165, 174–5, 188, 190

nationalism, 8, 147–8, 213
native, 17, 41, 48, 77–9, 81–3, 87, 89, 91–4, 95n18, 102, 145, 165, 220
neo-traditional, 18, 143–4, 148, 151, 152, 154, 157
Ness, Sally Ann, 8, 11, 135
Neveu Kringelbach, Hélène, 13–14, 18, 145, 213
New York, 7, 16, 29–35, 37–8, 43, 48, 50, 52–56, 61, 65, 146
Nigeria, 1, 7, 34
Nocera, Maurizio, 61
non-dance, 3, 8, 42
Novack, Cynthia, 6, 10–11, 211
Nureyev, Rudolf, 51, 53–4, 57

Ostrower, Francie, 55, 57
ownership, 17, 86, 90

Panama, 15, 17, 121–4, 126, 128, 131–2, 136n4, 137n12
Paredes, Américo, 162, 175n2
Parkin, David, 144, 145, 216
participant, 5, 12, 66, 70n5, 78, 89, 101, 103–4, 107, 109, 111, 115, 145, 187, 189–90, 192n13, 208, 214–15, 217
  participant observation, 94n5, 217
  participant-observer, 103

pentas, 197–204
Pietrobruno, Sheenagh, 13
Pizza, Gianni, 67
pizzica, 16, 60–68, 70n2, 70n5, 71n12
play, 3, 15–16, 31, 37, 61, 63, 66, 172, 194
postcolonial, 1, 11, 14, 78, 106, 112, 115
postmodern, 6, 10, 65
power, 3, 6, 19, 35, 49, 62, 65–9, 78–81, 83, 88, 91, 94n10, 115, 127, 144–5, 148, 157, 162, 172, 182, 195–7, 199, 203, 205, 207–8, 213–15, 217

practice, 3–7, 9–13, 15–16, 34–5, 38, 42, 50, 84, 102–3, 112, 116–17, 121–2, 125–6, 131, 135–6, 145, 148, 151–2, 156–7, 161, 169, 171, 174–5, 177–8, 186, 190, 192, 197, 204, 207, 217
proxemics, 7

Quiróz, Margarita, 161, 165–6

Radcliffe-Brown, Alfred, 4
Reed, Susan, 14, 19n1, 78, 121
resistance, 11, 30, 81, 146, 171
revitalization, 60, 70n4, 78
revival, 70n4, 83, 88–91, 100, 117, 133, 148, 183, 190
Robertson, Roland, 37–8, 57
Rodríguez, Russell, 171
Royce, Anya, 6, 19, 121
rumba, 13–14, 17, 20n8, 37, 126–30, 133, 135
  see Cuba

Sachs, Curt, 7, 20n5
Saldívar, Ramón, 175nn1–2
Salento, 16, 60–65, 66, 68, 70n2, 70n11, 70n13, 71
Salish, 16, 77–93, 94n4, 94n7, 95n12, 215–17
  Salish feasthouse, 77, 78
salsa, 11–13, 15, 19, 30, 37–9, 41–2, 102, 185–6, 188, 213
samba, 11
sanggar tari, 19, 194, 196, 208n1
Savigliano, Marta, 1–2, 8, 82
Scarangella, Linda, 79, 90–91, 95nn14–15
Schechner, Richard, 111–12, 115
Schieffelin, Edward, 12, 108
Second World War, 39, 42, 60, 146
segregated, 31
semasiology, 6, 8
Senegal, 18, 143–8, 150–51, 153–5, 157, 213

Senghor, Léopold Sédar, 18, 146–8, 158
Seth, Michael, 184
sexuality, 3, 8, 13, 181
Sheehy, Daniel, 175
sinulog, 11
Skinner, Jonathan, 11, 13, 15, 29, 42, 78, 92, 102, 122, 145, 212, 217
skinship, 188–9, 192
socialization, 4, 178, 184–5
Sonar Senghor, Maurice, 146–8, 150, 158n6
South America, 137
South Korea, 19, 178, 183–5, 187–93, 219
  South Koreans, 184, 187–8, 190
Spencer, Paul, 9, 19, 121
staged authenticity, 77, 92–3
stylestyle, 3, 9–10, 13–15, 19, 30–31, 33, 37–8, 40–43, 44n5, 48, 53, 67, 85, 88, 105, 107, 111–12, 114, 117, 128–9, 135, 145, 148, 150, 154–6, 165, 172, 179–80, 183, 187, 189, 191n6, 196–8, 202, 205, 207, 209n7
swing, 13, 15, 29–31, 33–7, 39–40, 42–3, 186
swingers, 34

tango, 1, 12, 15, 102
Tanzania, 14, 145, 148
tarantism, 16, 60–61, 64–5, 69–70
tarantula, 61, 68
Taylor, Julie, 5, 15
technology, 34, 37
theatre, 17–18, 34, 44, 49, 53, 55–7, 61, 82, 111, 114, 141, 145–50, 158n3, 163, 171, 214–15
Thionk Essyl, 149, 151, 155, 158n12
Thomas, Helen, 8, 9
tourism, 15–17, 61–3, 77–93, 101–5, 107, 109, 111–17, 121–5, 130–36, 137n9, 137n13, 138, 150, 174, 191, 212
  tourist gaze, 78–80, 83, 88, 93, 102, 116

tradition, 5, 10, 14, 56, 85, 90–92, 100, 105, 112, 115, 121–4, 126–7, 129, 133–4, 136, 137n10, 162, 181, 183
translocal, 12, 13
transnational, 11–13, 15–16, 18–19, 46, 48, 51, 53–4, 56–7, 110, 114–15, 156–7, 161–2, 174–5, 214, 216, 220
transport, 34, 123
Turner, Victor, 195, 210

urbanization, 15, 33
Urry, John, 63, 79–80, 100, 102, 124

Van Zile, Judy, 180–81, 191n4
Venda, 7, 9
visceral sociality, 215, 217
visibility, 104, 121–2, 131, 133–4

Wade, Peter, 2, 128
well-being, 65, 70, 117
Williams, Drid, 8, 19, 123, 175–6
witnessing, 78, 83–4, 87–8, 93–4, 215
Wulff, Helena, 2–3, 5, 8, 13–16, 19, 46, 50, 53, 56, 114, 121, 123, 195, 203, 207–8, 212

www.ingramcontent.com/pod-product-compliance
Lightning Source LLC
Chambersburg PA
CBHW072152100526
44589CB00015B/2191